PENGUIN BOOKS

THE ASSAULT ON INTELLIGENCE

Michael Hayden is a retired United States Air Force four-star general and former Director of the National Security Agency, Principal Deputy Director of National Intelligence, and Director of the Central Intelligence Agency. He is currently a principal at the Chertoff Group, a security consultancy founded by former Homeland Security Secretary Michael Chertoff. Hayden also serves as a Distinguished Visiting Professor at George Mason University's Schar School of Policy and Government and is the founder of the Hayden Center for Intelligence, Policy, and International Security there. He is the author of the *New York Times* bestseller *Playing to the Edge.*

The ASSAULT on INTELLIGENCE

American National Security in an Age of Lies

MICHAEL V. HAYDEN

PENGUIN BOOKS

PENGUIN BOOKS
An imprint of Penguin Random House LLC
penguinrandomhouse.com

First published in the United States of America by Penguin Press,
an imprint of Penguin Random House LLC, 2018
Published in Penguin Books 2019

ISBN 9780525558583 (hardcover)
ISBN 9780525558606 (paperback)
ISBN 9780525558590 (ebook)

Printed in the United States of America
1 3 5 7 9 10 8 6 4 2

DESIGNED BY AMANDA DEWEY

This work does not constitute an official release of U.S. Government
information. All statements of fact, opinion, or analysis expressed are
those of the author and do not reflect the official positions or views of the
U.S. Government. Nothing in the contents should be construed as asserting or
implying U.S. Government authentication of information endorsement of the
author's views. This material has been reviewed solely for classification.

*To the men and women of American intelligence
who strive to be worthy of the Republic they serve
and whose truth telling is now needed,
not just to protect us from foreign enemies,
but to save us from ourselves*

CONTENTS

The ASSAULT on INTELLIGENCE

ONE

WHY THIS? WHY NOW?

Two months into the Trump administration, Jim Comey, the head of the Federal Bureau of Investigation, and Admiral Mike Rogers, the director of the National Security Agency, were asked in an open congressional hearing if the president they were serving was misleading the nation with his claims that they or their British friends had wiretapped him while he was president-elect.

They said that he was.

It was a remarkable moment. That question doesn't get asked very often in open parliamentary session in a democracy, let alone get answered—to say nothing of being answered in that way. It made me proud to have been associated with an intelligence community that felt free to do that.

But that was not the end of the matter, at least as far as the White House was concerned. The administration stuck to its alternate version—Obama wiretapped me—even after the FBI and

NSA chiefs had confirmed that objective reality was clearly otherwise.

That had an effect on me, too. It reminded me of when I walked through the streets of war-ravaged Sarajevo as head of intelligence for American forces in Europe. It was 1994 and we were there to provide intelligence to badly stretched UN forces that were trying to police a nonexistent cease-fire among the warring Serb, Croat, and Muslim factions.

Former national security adviser Brent Scowcroft, who as a junior officer had been the assistant air attaché at the U.S. embassy in Belgrade, once told me there were no Boy Scouts in the Balkans. Enduring labels of good and bad were less useful as predictors of behavior than more transient measures of who was strong and who was weak. Still, Sarajevo had been a beautiful city, home to the Winter Olympics a scant ten years earlier. The fast-flowing Miljacka River cut through the center of town, with hills rising abruptly on either side. Sprinkled among Austrian-era government buildings were minarets, steeples, and onion domes.

But now I could also see artillery pointing down from those wooded hills and witness the destructive product of their work in the streets below. I wondered what manner of man could pull the lanyard to fire on his former neighbors, or shoot at unarmed civilians lined up for scarce water at a shuttered brewery.

What struck me most, though, as I walked about the city was not how much Sarajevans were different from the rest of us, but how much they weren't. This had obviously been a cultured, tolerant, even vibrant city. The veneer of civilization, I sadly concluded then, was quite thin—perhaps a natural thought for an intelligence officer, whose profession consistently trends pessimistic, whose work is consumed by threats and dangers, and who routinely travels to some of the world's darkest, most troubled places.

Later I learned that intelligence officers were not so alone in their dark thoughts. Robin Wright, the American chronicler of the Middle East's woes, told me that Israel's Shimon Peres once despairingly lamented to her, "We're so primitive. We're so very primitive."

Over the years it became clear to me that the structures, processes, and attitudes that protect us from Thomas Hobbes's world of "solitary, poor, nasty, brutish, and short" lives are not naturally occurring things. They are inherently fragile and demand careful tending if they are to survive.

That brought me to the idea of this book, which is not that civil war or societal collapse is necessarily imminent or inevitable here in America, but that the structures, processes, and attitudes we rely on to prevent those kinds of occurrences are under stress, and that many of the premises on which we have based our governance, policy, and security are now challenged, eroded, or simply gone.

Deeply involved in this is the question of truth. It was no accident that the *Oxford English Dictionary*'s word of the year in 2016 was "post-truth," a condition where objective facts are less influential in shaping public opinion than appeals to emotion and personal belief. Liberal British academic and philosopher A. C. Grayling characterized the emerging post-truth world to me as "over-valuing opinion and preference at the expense of proof and data." Oxford Dictionaries president Casper Grathwohl predicted that the term could become "one of the defining words of our time."[1]

Grayling is a scholar of the Enlightenment, and he concedes

that this new dynamic challenges the mode of thought dominant in the West since that era, a mode that until recently valued experience and expertise, the centrality of fact, humility in the face of complexity, the need for study, and a respect for ideas.

At its best, the craft of intelligence, at least as practiced in the Western liberal tradition, pursues these Enlightenment values. Intelligence gathers, evaluates, and analyzes information and then disseminates its conclusions for use, study, or refutation. So the erosion of Enlightenment values would certainly devalue or even threaten the practice of good intelligence. For me that was reason enough to guard against it.

But intelligence may have responsibilities here beyond self-preservation. It may share a broader duty with other truth tellers—scholars, journalists, scientists, to name a few—to preserve the commitment and ability of our society to base important decisions on our best judgment of what constitutes objective reality.

There are fundamental changes—really fundamental changes—afoot in the world and in this country. This book is about those global and domestic developments and the role that American intelligence plays in identifying and responding to them. Today's strains on *all* truth tellers compel me to write about the relevance and sustainability of the work of *my* truth tellers—the modern intelligence enterprise. That enterprise—which I have defended as essential not just to American safety, but to American liberty—now seems at odds with important elements of American life. And the stress points are no longer the traditional issues of how intelligence *acquires* information: debates about surveillance, interrogations, privacy, secrecy, oversight, and the like. The new issues have to do with how intelligence *uses* information, or, more accurately, how intelligence and other fact-based analysis will fare in a world in which even a sophisticated society like our own is trending toward decision making anchored on a priori, near-instinctive narratives—decision making based on that which can be made popular or widely held rather than on that which is objectively true.

And here intelligence is in the bunker with some unlikely mates: journalism, scholarship, the courts, law enforcement, and science. Many of these have been critics of aspects of intelligence in the past, but not so much now. Most practitioners of these other vocations now seem to recognize that intelligence professionals, like themselves, are evidence-based and pursue truth—ultimately their only safe haven—even if methodologies differ and even if *all* of us fall short of our ideals. Collectively these disciplines seem to recognize that it is not a coincidence that as a group they experience frequent and intense friction points with team Trump.

My personal lens, of course, is intelligence, and so the specifics that follow are anchored there, but the themes they represent are more universal and some of this narrative reflects an attempt to more fully appreciate current and historical commentary about our society and about who we are and who we want to be. My readings and especially my conversations have been fascinating, allowing me to test my own concepts, explore new ones, and in general be impressed by the seriousness of many American and international observers.

Of course, I have spent time talking with members of the intelligence and policy communities. Admittedly it was easier to gain access to those no longer in government, and that has required me to appreciate and synthesize (and occasionally discount) some observations and judgments accordingly.

It should also be clear that I am no longer in government, so this in no way pretends to be a continuation of the memoir of my work there, the views of an internal eyewitness, so to speak. But I do remain a concerned *external* witness, so this should be seen as an application of my experience to current events as revealed by public accounts and available documents, enriched by conversations I have had with old and new friends.

There are some very good people out there, people with long and distinguished careers spent in the service of discovering and reporting objective reality, who now find themselves in some really tough spots—tough, and a little dangerous, too. People such as James Comey, the head of the FBI, fired and publicly humiliated by the president for—according to the president—looking into the president's campaign and its alleged connections to the Russian Federation.

We're really breaking new ground when, at the six-month point of the new administration, the former head of CIA, John Brennan, and the former director of national intelligence, Jim Clapper—with more than seven decades of experience between them and a record of service for both political parties—spend a rainy afternoon in Aspen telling hundreds that they harbor deep concerns about Russian election interference, openly criticize President Trump for refusing to face that reality, and warn that "in some respects we are a government in crisis."

Indeed, although this is essentially a story about America, the Russians are never far from the main plotline—identifying, exploiting, and deepening American fissures for their own ends. That is a remarkable tale in its own right, a tale of new technologies harnessed to old purposes.

Equally remarkable is how many actions in America manifested indifference to what the Russians were doing ("I love WikiLeaks!"), or echoed Russian themes (it's a "rigged system"), or saw no issues with proffers of assistance (Trump Tower, June 9), or pushed back so long against the reality of Russian actions ("nobody really knows").

There is no effort here to build a case for or against collusion. But whatever emerges from Robert Mueller's investigation, it should not obscure the bigger story, which is still not adequately understood, and which is in a way this book's climactic case study, namely that Russia has been actively seeking to damage the fabric of American democracy, and the Trump administration's glandular aversion to even looking at this squarely, much less mounting a concerted response to it, is an appalling national security lapse.

Indeed, there is clear evidence of what I would call convergence, the convergence of a mutually reinforcing swirl of presidential tweets and statements, Russian-influenced social media, alt-right websites and talk radio, Russian press like RT, and even mainstream U.S. media like Fox News—all of whom do things for their own purposes, but all of which fits nicely with Russian purposes to sharpen and sustain divisions here.

And it continues. A quick look at articles pushed by Kremlin-oriented accounts on Twitter in early January shows that attacks on Democrats and liberals comprised more than a quarter, with discrediting Fusion GPS and the Steele dossier at 14 percent, and pushing "deep state" narratives and conspiracies constituting 13 percent. Sound familiar? When Trump speaks, the Russians amplify.

Early on in the Trump administration, never-Trumper Eliot Cohen, political scientist and historian, director of the Strategic

Studies Program at Johns Hopkins University, and formerly Condoleezza Rice's counselor at the Department of State, tweeted a note that has now become a memelike all-purpose observation of many administration actions: "This isn't normal. Its [sic] not humane, its not thought through, its not necessary, its not wise, its not decent and above all, its not American."

The accuracy and relevance of Cohen's words have not been confined to issues directly tied to the intelligence community. Last summer's tragic events in Charlottesville and the president's tone-deaf and ahistorical response come to mind.

There has been plenty of pushback against administration actions, and in the pages that follow I will often say that that is a good thing. But even that is not without dangers. Jack Goldsmith is now at Harvard Law School, but in 2003–2004 he was head of the Department of Justice's Office of Legal Counsel, where he ripped up and rewrote practically every legal opinion on which NSA and CIA were depending to underpin their most aggressive activities. Surprisingly, we became good friends. Jack doesn't like Donald Trump: he describes him as a "Frankenstein's monster of past presidents' worst attributes." But although he calls him "a norm-busting president without parallel," he also points out that institutions that have been pushing back have often defied their own norms in the process: leaks from the intelligence community; overly enthusiastic judicial opinions; new standards of negativity for the media. "The breakdown in institutions," he concludes, "mirrors the breakdown in social cohesion" that nurtured Trumpism in the first place. He identifies that as perhaps "the worst news of all for our democracy."[2]

Controversies come and go so fast in the Trump administration that it's all too easy to lose sight of the big picture, the major plotlines, the things that really matter. But even within intelligence and intelligence-related matters, I have to admit to a certain exhaustion in just trying to keep up. I have given myself the license here to choose those things that I think are particularly instructive of the larger questions. The way the president has publicly criticized and humiliated Attorney General Jeff Sessions will, for example, have deeper, broader, and longer effects on the American intelligence community than his pissy wintertime tweets comparing intelligence professionals to Nazis.

By way of a guide, the flow of the book is essentially chronological. The next chapter will be a quick attempt to describe the state of America and the intelligence community (not exactly paradise) as Donald Trump descended that escalator at Trump Tower. Following that come three chapters of the campaign (unlike any other), the transition (such as it was), and the first hundred days (chaos, often on steroids). Chapter 6 looks at the impact of the president on several core national security issues, chapter 7 explores the complex relationship between Trump, truth, and Russia, and the final chapter is my attempt to draw some conclusions—from an admittedly still evolving plot—about truth, intelligence, and America.

So there will be a lot here about Donald Trump. That's unavoidable. I have tried to be fair, although much of what I write will be judged as unfairly negative. I got that complaint in the summer of 2016 as I was engaged in a friendly debate on the *PBS NewsHour* with Kris Kobach, Kansas secretary of state and hard-liner on immigration, voter fraud, and Barack Obama's birthplace. It was, as I said, a polite session and Kris suggested that I had to get to know the quite different, personal Donald Trump. I replied that all I had to go on was the public persona, the one running for president, and if there were a different Trump in hiding, the campaign might think about rolling *him* out. There wasn't and they didn't, of course.

All that said, though, a discussion of a post-truth world, alternative facts, fact-free decision making, and outright lying eclipses any one man or administration. In other words, this is not and cannot just be about the person of the president.

President Trump says that he is not alone, but rather heads a powerful grassroots movement. I agree. He is as much effect as he is cause of the post-truth world in which we find ourselves today. A lot went into getting us here.

Indeed, in the first week of the Trump administration, the *Economist*'s prestigious Intelligence Unit's annual Democracy Index ranked the United States a "flawed democracy" in the company of states like Italy, France, Mongolia, South Korea, and Estonia and no longer a "full democracy" like Australia, Norway, Germany, and Canada. The report saw Mr. Trump not as the cause but rather the "beneficiary of the low esteem in which US voters hold their government, elected representatives and political parties." With or without Trump, the U.S. score would have slipped into the second tier. But the *Economist* added, "Populist parties and politicians are often not especially coherent and often do not have convincing answers."[3]

Will we emerge from this tested and stronger? Or will we be weaker and wounded—or even permanently altered? The founders of the Republic were disciples of the Enlightenment. The documents they left us are infused with Enlightenment values. Jefferson writes of an informed citizenry being the heart of a democracy and that when well informed the people can be trusted with their own governance. But all of that is premised on an Enlightenment vision of truth—truth based on as perfect a view of objective reality as we can muster. It is the linchpin of the whole American experiment.

What becomes of the legitimacy of that vision—the legitimacy of that experiment—in a world that has redefined or is simply indifferent to truth? And are we about to find out? That's a question whose answer goes well beyond the craft of intelligence.

TWO

WHITHER AMERICA...
AND EVERYONE ELSE?

2016

First, some important context. When he got off the escalator at Trump Tower in June 2015, Donald Trump launched his candidacy by telling us that he was very rich, Mexico was exporting rapists, everybody was ripping us off, we never had victories anymore, and although Iraq was a bad idea, we should have kept the oil.

And although he didn't quite say it then, he later added that if he did win the presidency, he would be inheriting a messy world. Messy, by the way, because of the failings of his predecessors rather than any inherent complexities. So where was the world, America, and American intelligence when Donald Trump descended that escalator and promised to disrupt things?

To begin, the world was an increasingly dangerous place, but not nearly as dangerous as the new candidate's near-apocalyptic rhetoric suggested that day.

Intelligence officers of my generation will tell you that they have actually lived in a more dangerous world. They'll remind you of stories they heard from their early mentors of the Cuban Missile Crisis and of armor standoffs at the old Checkpoint Charlie in Berlin; of going to nuclear alert themselves in 1973 when the Soviets threatened intervention as their Arab allies were collapsing; of close encounters with the Soviets along the old inner German border or at sea or in the air.

Many from the old "security services"—the electronic surveillance folks—will remind you, at the drop of a hat or a drink, of reconnaissance ships attacked in the late 1960s: thirty-four were killed in the Israeli strafing of the USS *Liberty* in 1967; the North Koreans captured eighty-three on the *Pueblo* in early 1968. Several surveillance aircraft were shot down in the 1950s and '60s, thirty-one killed in one incident alone with the North Koreans in 1969, with the Soviets shooting down other aircraft over Armenia and the Kola Peninsula late in the Eisenhower administration. Recent antics like last summer's dueling hyperbole between two emotional and inexperienced presidents (Kim Jong-un in North Korea and Donald J. Trump here) stir the memories of these veterans of a more dangerous past, but they know that we're not there—at least not yet.

But even the most hardened Cold War veteran would be quick to add that they have never seen the world more complicated than now. They'd likely raise Syria as an example and then exhaust themselves and you trying to explain the multiple layers of conflict there. Depending on how you choose to rack and stack the players, Syria is at the same time a humanitarian catastrophe, a struggle of democrats and autocrats, a sectarian and interethnic conflict, a war against terror, the latest round in an epic Sunni-Shia struggle, and a reemergence of the old East-West competition between Russia and the West.

And these veterans would also concede that things have never been more immediately interconnected. Events in one corner of the world—like terror at the Brussels airport or demonstrators being shot in Syria or missiles being tested in North Korea—create real effects in other corners with a speed and power no one has ever seen before.

All of this is so unsettling that when asked these days about global threats—the "what keeps you awake at night?" question—I usually decline to predict whose unhappy cell phone video we are going to see on that evening's news and skip over current events in favor of what I've come to call "global tectonics," fundamental shifts in the basal plates of the world's geopolitics.

One such tectonic is the rise of substate actors—groups, gangs, even individuals—who can visit the kind of destructive effects on our society that we used to associate only with malevolent state power. Cyber attacks, transnational crime, and, of course, terrorism quickly come to mind. Brent Scowcroft, one of this country's great strategic minds, called attention to this several years ago when he pointed out that the empowerment and connectedness of the post-industrial world made this inevitable.[1] I remind audiences that I'm old enough to remember being required to talk to a teller to get my money from my bank or to go to a licensed real estate broker to find out comparables on a new house I was interested in.

All good.

I'm also old enough to remember when only two nations were

able to take pictures from space and only one of them was really good at it. Now a laptop, Wi-Fi, and Google Earth can bring that to your home.

Mostly good.

I'm also old enough to remember that I never lost any sleep over a religious fanatic living in a cave in the Hindu Kush.

I do now and that's bad.

In many ways our security is now more at risk from ungoverned spaces and failed states than it is from actively hostile nations. So the collapse of the nation-state system in much of the Middle East should be very troubling. Simply put, Iraq, Syria, Libya, and perhaps even Lebanon have effectively ceased to exist and will never again return as unitary states.

The process is already under way. Parts of Iraqi Kurdistan have been a separate state in all but name for decades. Perhaps in a nod to inevitability, an Iraqi ambassador to the United States once observed that the only people in the world who want Iraq held together seem to be people who don't live in Iraq.

States melting down is important, but there is a lot more.

In normal times, the emergence of China would have already sucked all the analytic air out of the room. Or maybe China's potential failure should do that, since a lot of people like me spend as much time fretting over its failure as we do over its success, wringing our hands as much over Chinese weakness as we do over Chinese strength. There are daunting problems the Chinese juggernaut must inevitably face: a demographic pyramid with the point on the wrong end because of a three-decade one-child policy; a pending environmental catastrophe; social unrest; maldistribution of wealth; a democracy deficit; party corruption and the threat it creates to the legitimacy of party rule.

Graham Allison at Harvard reminds us[2] that China's emergence is a bit of an old movie, the major plotline being the question of how a status quo power (like us) accommodates the demands of an emergent power (like China). Allison holds this "emerging status quo" template up to sixteen examples from the last five centuries, ranging from Prince Henry the Navigator's Portugal dealing with the rising Spain of Ferdinand and Isabella through today's Britain and France accommodating a now unified Germany. Both of these challenges were actually resolved without war. Sadly, Allison points out, in twelve of his sixteen cases, the methodology used to get from an old to a new equilibrium goes by the popular name "global war."

And this case might be harder than average since the "emerging power" does not view this as emergence as all. For China, this is restoration, the inevitable correction of its unnatural decline in status that occurred in the century from the Opium Wars to the founding of the People's Republic.

Russia isn't in China's league as a resurgent power. Its extraction economy is crippled by low energy prices; its growth has been limited by a declining population; its wealth is exploited as a colony by its own native oligarchy (much of which prefers to live abroad). Vladimir Putin's Russia is far more revanchist than it is resurgent, with a cunning and aggressive leader playing a weak hand well, embracing considerable risk to assuage historic Russian grievances and keep himself in power—which might make him more of a danger, at least in the near term. Putin is working to restore Russian pride. Thus the resurrection of language about the third Rome, close ties with the Russian Orthodox Church, and a conspicuously conservative social policy. Russian-born American journalist Julia Ioffe describes Putin's approach as "classically Russian: using daring aggression to mask weakness, to avenge deep resentments, and, at all costs, to survive."[3] Thus the annexation of Crimea, the occupation of chunks of Georgia and Ukraine, a reassertion of power in the Middle East, pressure on the Baltics and states like Moldova and Kyrgyzstan, harassing tactics against NATO planes and warships in international spaces, and robust demonstrations of the power to politically obstruct whenever possible.

President Obama famously criticized Mitt Romney in 2012 for calling Russia the "greatest geopolitical threat" to this country: "The 1980s are now calling to ask for their foreign policy back," he chided. Mr. Obama may be forgiven a bit on this one. American intelligence appears to have been slow off the mark as well. As director of CIA from 2006 to early 2009 I visited almost fifty countries. Not one of them was Russia. And even later, American intelligence was slow to fully appreciate Russia's disinformation campaign against us. One first has to recognize a tectonic shift in order to deal with it.

With the inexorable proliferation of technology, we are also now faced with a group of states that can only be characterized as brittle, ambitious . . . and nuclear. The tectonic shift here is that efforts to stop nuclear proliferation have failed and these materials are now controlled (or worse, not controlled) by states like North Korea, Pakistan, and Iran—states that are paranoid, unstable, or messianic.

The Iranian program has been capped (temporarily and imperfectly) by the Obama Joint Comprehensive Plan of Action (JCPOA) negotiated with Tehran. But Pakistan, ranked by one respected Washington think tank as the seventeenth least stable country on earth (bracketed by such brittle entities as Burundi and Eritrea), is believed to have about 140 nuclear weapons, and the world's fastest-growing nuclear stockpile.[4]

And North Korea continues its march to strategic nuclear reach. We always figured we would be here one day, since North Korea's Kim dynasty sees this as a question of regime survival in a world Pyongyang has always viewed as relentlessly hostile. In fact, they *need* to see the world that way to justify the kind of regime the family has built: brutally autocratic, extravagantly militarized, self-consciously destitute.

Words unfamiliar to most westerners are holy writ in the Kims' hermit kingdom. *Juche*, self-reliance, is the doctrine that underpins keeping the rest of the world out while demanding incredible personal sacrifice within. *Songun*, putting the military first, was so pervasive that it insulated the regime from the worst effects of the "arduous march," the 1990s famine that killed half a million people. *Byungjin*, a nod to the need for economic development, was only made possible by the drive to nuclear weapons, a cheaper form of combat power than armor or infantry brigades.

So, in response to a later presidential tweet taunting Kim Jong-un after a missile launch—"Does this guy have anything better to do with his life?"—the answer is, "Well, no." Nuclear weapons and long-range delivery systems are as essential to regime identity as they are to regime survival. All of which tends to confirm my long-held belief that North Korea is not about to give up its nuclear status.

All of that's bad enough, but the biggest tectonic shift facing us—even in the eyes of a career intelligence officer—is not something beyond our borders, but rather changing American attitudes toward global challenges.

In early 2016, as America was turning its attention to the presidential campaign, I was on a panel at a hotel near Baltimore's Inner Harbor to discuss global security questions in front of the Republican caucus from both the House and Senate. The Republicans get together like this annually to try to hammer out some sort of consensus on key issues, and they had gathered a seasoned panel for this one, including General Ray Odierno, just retired after being chief of America's army; former secretary of homeland security Michael Chertoff; Ryan Crocker, six-time ambassador, including to Iraq, Afghanistan, and Pakistan; and historian Robert Kagan from Washington's Brookings Institution. That's a pretty big panel (five, including me), a broad topic, and an activist audience questioning us and one another, so it wasn't long before the discussion began to get a bit chaotic.

At one point, Kagan interrupted and announced, "Look! What's going on here is the melting down of the post–World War II, American liberal, Bretton Woods, World Bank, IMF world order. Get it?" Kagan's point was that the world has enjoyed nearly three-quarters of a century of relative peace, prosperity, and progress underpinned by institutions largely shaped (and nurtured) by American hands. But the industrialized, state-centered, less-well-connected world on which that American-created global structure was premised has changed dramatically, and now the question is: what role does America see for itself in creating and sustaining world order 2.0, given that the decades-long willingness of the United States to fulfill what has been its special role—which required it often to put global interests ahead of more narrowly defined national interests—is being challenged at every turn by our sitting president?

For people like me, such challenges aren't just about political theory. They are personal.

American intelligence professionals, through a process of self-selection and acculturation, much like their diplomatic counterparts, trend overwhelmingly internationalist. They view American involvement abroad as the natural order of things, and their life experience tells them that American disengagement rarely makes things better anywhere.

After all, this is what they do. It's all they ever wanted to do. OCONUS (outside the continental United States) is where they live a good portion of their adult lives. Many speak one or more foreign languages.

And in return, life has been good to them with the winds of globalization at their back, enhancing their role and increasing the importance, recognition, and rewards of their work.

Even the children are not immune. When they come home (and America *is* home), they find their less traveled classmates "different." Their classmates have the same view of them. At university many trend toward international students or settle in with groups of fellow "global nomads," composed of the children of businessmen, diplomats, and missionaries with similar backgrounds.

My personal experience was longer than most, but in this respect it wasn't atypical: some thirty-nine years, much of it lived abroad on Guam, in Korea (twice), Germany, and even in

Communist Bulgaria. There were challenges, but life was generally comfortable and the work was always rewarding.

Globalization has been good for people like me. Maybe too good. Edward Luce, the *Financial Times'* unflinching commentator on America, says the Western world's cities "have more in common with their international counterparts than with their national hinterlands." He adds that Marx got it wrong when he "predicted that capitalism would push the workers of the world to unite. . . . It is the elites who are loosening their allegiances and workers who are reaching for national flags."[5]

I personally don't relate to the "loosening allegiances" accusation, perhaps a factor of my almost forty years of military experience, and I have maintained contact with my own hinterland by braving the Pennsylvania Turnpike multiple times every fall to use my Steelers season tickets. But I admit that folks with my life experience are tempted to view our condition and our positive outcomes as the normal, near-universal state of affairs. And we have to visit our hometowns to see that for many of our contemporaries the winds of globalization are blowing in their faces, reducing opportunities, decapitalizing once thriving communities, and putting great stress on family bonds. Drive along the now clear waters of the Ohio River near Weirton and Steubenville and see the acres upon acres of America's industrial past and you will see what I mean.

So I resolved to reengage the "America First" issue, in the back room of a Pittsburgh sports bar over some Iron City beer. I asked my brother to arrange for several dozen of his friends, all Trump supporters, to meet with me for a couple of hours.

I knew many of the participants, indeed had grown up with several. But we could have been from different planets. They are angry. They feel abandoned and disadvantaged even though they work hard, pay their taxes, and struggle to raise their kids. They hate Hillary Clinton, I mean really hate her. And for them, it is still midnight on November 8, 2016. Donald Trump is still their guy. "He is an American . . . He is genuine . . . He is authentic . . . He doesn't filter everything or parse every word." They don't seem to be very interested in "facts," either. Or at least not in my "facts."

About two months after my Pittsburgh meeting, the *New York Times*' David Brooks wrote that political partisanship in America had become what he called "totalistic." It was no longer about better policies as it was with Eisenhower and Kennedy. Nor was it about better philosophy as it was with Reagan. Now "people often use partisan identity to fill the void left when other attachments wither away—religious, ethnic, communal and familial."[6]

Around the same time as the Brooks article, conservative ethicist Peter Wehner told me that in today's America, beliefs are really tied up with identities, and he pointed me to this: "If changing your belief means changing your identity, it comes at the risk of rejection from the community of people with whom you share that identity."[7] Wehner also reminded me that data is not particularly useful to argue a point that itself was not particularly data-derived (which is not quite the same distinction as true and untrue).

When I asked in that Pittsburgh back room if anyone really believed that Barack Obama had wiretapped Trump Tower, most hands shot up. I tried to explain how the relevant agencies (NSA and FBI) had said it wasn't true. When I asked why they still thought it was so, they simply replied, "Obama."

"Obama was against the country and did everything he could

to undermine it," concluded one participant. That was probably an extreme position, but it was clear to me that a lot of the reasons people voted for Trump had little to do with Trump.

From their point of view, the whole Russia-interference-in-the-election-thing is political theater, too. When I recited the intelligence community's high-confidence judgments on what the Russians had done, one boyhood friend told me that no business would ever make a decision based on that kind of information. He dismissed the high-confidence label with the characterization "I think I believe my opinion is . . . ."

Their grievances were less economic than they were cultural. Indeed, there were several successful small business people in the group. The mood in the room confirmed Edward Luce's broader observation that this is about "the psychology of dashed expectations rather than the decline in material comforts."[8]

It was also true that most in the room had spent their entire lives in or near Pittsburgh. National statistics say that Trump won by nine points among white voters who live within two hours of where they were born and by an overwhelming 26 percent among those who live in their hometown proper.[9] Everybody in the room in Pittsburgh was white, too.

When I asked what they thought "America First" meant, the answer was pretty simple. It meant that someone was paying attention to them.

Observers of the 2016 presidential election point to the declining relevance of traditional left-right, Democrat-Republican, liberal-conservative divides in American politics. Technological change, the explosion of information, and the erosion of borders have smothered old dividing lines over the size of government, family values, and the national debt. Changes in technology, information, and borders have created winners and losers, and these folks are in that group of Americans who are feeling left behind.

Collectively they view themselves as disadvantaged in a globalized world and they catalog refugees and immigrants as threatening their safety, trade deals as taking away their jobs, and political institutions as wasting their money. Hence the surge of a populism that claims "to speak in the people's place, in their name, and convey an undeniable shared truth on their behalf. In particular, populism claims to express the emotion of a people that feels beleaguered."[10]

Echoing David Brooks, J. D. Vance, author of *Hillbilly Elegy*, observed that with the decline of other social institutions like churches and clubs, politics now gives many people a core sense of their identity. Hence the unaccustomed intensity, and that intensity meant that in 2016, the United States—home of free markets and the world's largest, most integrated economy—went populist, nativist, and protectionist.[11] Another observer was more terse: "America had just elected a man who admired the way politics was done in Russia."[12]

The morning of my Iron City–fueled discussions in Pittsburgh, I had breakfast with a journalist, Salena Zito, the best chronicler of Trump's Rust Belt campaign and author of the insightful couplet that people like me took Donald Trump "literally, but not seriously," while Trump's supporters took him "seriously, but not literally." Besides being smart, Salena is from my old Pittsburgh neighborhood, so she knows the turf.

She offered the 1890s as a model to understand today. Both decades suffered major economic downturns (the Panic of 1893 and the 2008 meltdown) and both had iconoclastic New Yorkers (wilderness-loving, trust-busting Teddy Roosevelt and, of course, bureaucracy-smashing and norm-busting Donald Trump).

Conservative columnist and pundit Ron Fournier had already pointed me to the 1890s for parallels to our time. Late-nineteenth-century America, he said, was challenged to retool institutions that had served agrarian America well, but were no longer suited for the industrial giant the nation had become. Now, twenty-first-century America was doing the same thing: adjusting structures, processes, institutions, and even leaders suited for a more self-contained industrial nation and adapting all that to a post-industrial, globalized, interconnected country.

Salena reminded me that the icon of the 1890s was William Jennings Bryan, the nominally Democratic but thoroughly popu-list candidate in both 1896 and 1900. His "Cross of Gold" speech, one of the greatest in American political history, called for the weakening of the currency to help the victims of industrialization—a shrinking, indebted agricultural population—at the expense of the growing industrial, financial, global trading class.

I got the parallels suggested by Ron and Salena. It was good to view this in a broader historical context, to recognize that we have been here before.

But Bryan lost. Twice. His America opted for the future.

Not this time. And Bryan was a genuine populist: never a man of means, modestly educated, genuinely religious.

Today's populist is a ruthless Manhattan billionaire real estate developer, schooled in politics by Roy ("hit back ten times harder") Cohn, the uber-aggressive counsel for Joe McCarthy's Communist witch hunt of the early 1950s.

Whether Trump ranks as a genuine populist or this stance of

his is just a flag of convenience is a great question. And a very important one.

But it isn't exactly my question.

My field, after all, is security, and America was about to face its most fundamental foreign policy decisions in nearly three-quarters of a century.

What did Donald Trump mean for that?

Famed American academic Walter Russell Mead broke down the whole dynamic for me in terms of his four paradigms of the American presidency. He reminded me that there were *Hamiltonians,* wedded to the tough realism of America's first secretary of the treasury: America cannot be free unless America is prosperous, America cannot be prosperous unless America is strong. I had limited contact with Mitt Romney as an adviser during his 2012 campaign, but I suspect he would have trended Hamiltonian as president.

Hamilton's eighteenth-century rival offered another, *Jeffersonian,* model: America as a shining city on a hill, a shining city that demands nearly all of our attention. History pushed Jefferson into conflict in North Africa, and he did, after all, buy Louisiana, but fundamentally he was about turning inward and focusing here. Barack Obama, especially in his second term, showed a lot of Jefferson: "It is . . . time to do some nation building right here at home."

Wilsonian idealism offered a third approach driven by a sense of mission to share and sometimes impose American political values and the rule of law globally. Look no further than George

W. Bush's second inaugural: "So it is the policy of the United States to seek and support the growth of democratic movements and institutions in every nation and culture, with the ultimate goal of ending tyranny in our world."

And then there was Andrew Jackson: man of the people, frontiersman, Indian fighter, war hero—the first democrat in the White House whether you write it with a big D or a little d. *Jacksonian* foreign policy is shaped by an intense patriotism to an America defined by blood, soil, and shared history, and it is largely uninterested in international affairs unless, of course, somebody really ticks us off (like Japan in 1941, or al-Qaeda in 2001). Only half-jokingly do I describe it as a security policy organized around Robert De Niro's immortal line in Martin Scorsese's 1976 film *Taxi Driver:* "You talkin' to *me*?"

America's post–World War II internationalism has been largely shaped by Hamiltonian and Wilsonian concepts. In fact, the history of that era was often written as a struggle between the two factions, trying to balance American interests and American ideals in the conduct of our policy.

Jacksonians largely went along for this ride, frightened by the prospect of Soviet power and the reality of Soviet behavior. They started to withdraw from the consensus after the collapse of the Soviet Union, rallied to the colors once again after 9/11, and then retreated quickly after that as casualties mounted in unsatisfying wars in Iraq and Afghanistan, which is not surprising, since these were the people who disproportionally went or watched their kids go to fight the nation's wars. That crowd in the back room in Pittsburgh was overwhelmingly Jacksonian, and I suspect the proportion of military veterans in that room topped any green room or boardroom I have ever walked into.

Beyond the Jacksonians breaking consensus, Hamiltonians had their own return-on-investment problems with Bush-era interventions, and some Wilsonians were experiencing guilt over the by-products (civil wars, instability, autocracies) of American activism. Even from within the heavily guarded perimeters of the American intelligence community, it should have been clear that the post–World War II national security consensus was eroding. Indeed, some erosion had already taken place under President Obama.

Based on his life story, Barack Obama should have been the most internationalist of American presidents. Born of a Kenyan father and a globe-wandering American mother, raised for a time by her and an Indonesian stepfather, having spent four childhood years in Indonesia in Indonesian-language schools (while taking English-language correspondence courses from the Calvert School in Baltimore, as two of my own children did), traveling as a young man to Africa and South Asia, Barack Obama had his citizen-of-the-world ticket punched early.

From his parents, his stepfather, and his own experience, he often learned about America's overseas involvement through the lens of America "coming here" rather than our traditional view of our "going there." And the experiences, in the local view, weren't universally positive. America wasn't always well-intentioned, and even when it was, the results weren't always impressive.

During the transition in late 2008, beyond the usual "we're going to do this a lot better than you did" attitude, there was an undercurrent of America as part of the problem rather than part of a solution. It was palpable. Hence what many called the "apology tour" early in the administration: "America has shown arrogance"; "We went off course"; "At times we sought to dictate our terms."[13]

A few years later, while driving in downtown Washington and looking into the White House grounds while my car's satellite radio recounted some international crisis, I actually said aloud, "So, have you guys figured out yet that *we* weren't the problem?"

It must have been near Christmas, since it prompted me to compare the administration to the hero in Frank Capra's 1946 classic, *It's a Wonderful Life*. You know the story: a distraught George Bailey (Jimmy Stewart) is visited by his guardian angel, Clarence, and shown what the world would look like if there were no George Bailey. Clarence demonstrates what would have been the death of George's younger brother, the sinking of an American troopship, another death due to a pharmacist's error, the general deterioration of George's beloved Bedford Falls, and a variety of stunted personal relationships.

Of course, Bailey/Stewart got the message, saw the folly of his funk, faced his crisis supported by those around him, and everyone lived happily ever after (or at least through the final reel). Great moviemaking. So great that I suggested that in the national security realm, we were seeing life imitate art. We were getting to see what the world looked like if there were no America—or at least the America to which we and the world had become accustomed.

President Obama's belief that America had overreached, that we had become too involved, matched the national mood, and indeed there was evidence that it was true. Even Bob Gates, the Bush-era secretary of defense whom Mr. Obama kept on, no shrinking violet on the use of U.S. power, told West Point cadets in early 2011 that "any future defense secretary who advises the president to again send a big American land army into Asia or into the Middle East or Africa should have his head examined."[14]

In its best moments, Obama's retrenchment was about a necessary recalibration in the face of new realities; it was, at least at first, less about raw Jeffersonian isolationism than it was an attempt to better align the definition of American interests with the realities of American power. At other times, though, Obama's scaling back seemed more a cover for indecision and retreat. Policy seemed characterized by a willingness to bequeath to successors darkening circumstances that could only be redeemed by taking risky actions in the present. There was a real willingness to push consequences forward.

The failure to intervene in Syria in any meaningful way against the regime of Bashar al-Assad allowed the destruction of the Syrian state, the deaths of an estimated four hundred thousand people, the displacement of half of Syria's population, uncontrolled and destabilizing refugee flows into Europe, and the return of Russia as a power broker in the Middle East for the first time in nearly half a century. There were, of course, no easy choices in Syria, but it is fair to ask if any available choice could actually have made this worse. The people most responsible for the tragedy were still President Assad and ISIS caliph Abu Bakr al-Baghdadi, but, sadly, the one person who most could have prevented or ameliorated it was clearly Barack Obama.

The president's power ministries recognized this. His secretaries of state and defense urged him to embrace more robust actions, to arm the opposition, and to at least stabilize the battlefield if not outright overthrow Assad.

Nothing doing, or at least not much doing. The president even walked back from his own "red line" when Assad blatantly crossed it with his use of chemical weapons, a step that even an Obama supporter like Jane Harman, former congresswoman and now head of the prestigious Wilson Center, told me was "a major mistake. We lost prestige everywhere."

As the president steadfastly held his ground, he seems to have managed to suppress any inner Wilson (do something consistent with American ideals *there*) in favor of his inner Jefferson (but there is so much to do *here*).

We had seen a bit of the pattern earlier in the administration when the president's Afghan troop surge was given a strict time limit. We saw it again after Russia seized Crimea and the Donbas from Ukraine, in clear violation of treaty promises and international law. The United States responded with sanctions and a global effort to isolate Moscow, but the White House stopped short of providing Kiev with defensive arms, the kind of move urged on the administration by traditional internationalists like Zbigniew Brzezinski.

Mr. Obama was about ending American commitments, not taking on new ones. His much-celebrated 2011 withdrawal from Iraq fulfilled a campaign pledge just in time for his 2012 run for reelection. Predictably, perhaps inevitably, prematurely pulling the cork out of the ethnosectarian bottle there unleashed primal forces that directly led to the disintegration of the country, the (re)birth of the Islamic State, and the spread of Iranian hegemony. An immature, predatory, and now free-to-act Shia-dominated government began to settle old scores with Sunnis. As the last U.S. boots crossed into Kuwait, Shia prime minister Nouri al-Maliki issued an arrest warrant on murder charges for his Sunni vice president. The rest, as they say, is history.

Some, including occasionally even President Obama, blame

the 2011 deadline on George W. Bush, and indeed, 43 did negotiate with the Iraqis an agreed American presence *until* that date. But the Bush team never viewed 2011 as a fixed withdrawal calendar. We always saw this much like a lease on a property, negotiating hard to get a commitment as far forward as possible before we would have to renegotiate the arrangement. When it came time for the renegotiations, the Iraqis pushed hard on the legal status of remaining U.S. forces (the so-called status of forces agreement, or SOFA), President Obama declined to get personally involved, and the talks collapsed. Obama then celebrated the withdrawal of U.S. forces as a campaign promise kept rather than the resistance of a balky ally. Amazingly, when all the wheels flew off three years later, the president rushed substantial U.S. combat forces back to Iraq without a formal SOFA.

One wonders how good (or firm) intelligence was in pushing back against some of these policy decisions, or at least making their downsides known. On Iraq, I suspect intelligence would have framed the question less as "stay or go" and more like "pay me now or pay me later." It was a choice between a modest, largely in-garrison training force (in 2011 the number was around fifteen thousand) that would occasionally track down al-Qaeda wannabes, but mostly keep a stopper in Iraq's still toxic bottle of ethnic and sectarian tensions . . . or an inevitably far more kinetic, actively engaged long-term combat force that would have to return after a withdrawal when the sectarian shit really hit the fan.

Most of the senior intelligence folks I have talked to told me that their relationship with President Obama and his administration was positive. The community had an analytic impact on the president; he was a faithful reader of the PDB (President's Daily Brief) and often made direct references to PDB articles in policy discussions. One intelligence senior said the image of the president fixed in his mind is Obama sitting quietly, finger on chin, reflecting while he was briefed. The president also insisted on hearing out analysts even when members of his staff were trying to cut them short for one policy reason or another.

That said, no one claimed that Obama and the intelligence community were intimate. The president was always a bit distant and occasionally moody. He also wasn't above a little hanging the IC out to dry for personal political cover, as when he defended his response to ISIS in a *60 Minutes* interview with the claim that *the intelligence community* had underestimated the movement. There was also a political speed bump early in the administration with lots of talk from the new team about fighting terrorism consistent with American values, an implicit swipe not just at the political team they were replacing, but also at the community that had been conducting the fight.

Over time the president, who came into office with a liberal Democrat's distrust of an intelligence community around which multiple controversies had been swirling, grew more comfortable with both the institutions and the people who were serving him. Obama also came to office with little intelligence background, since he had not served on the Intelligence Committee while in the Senate. He had a steep learning curve, but gradually absorbed both the capabilities and the limits of the community. The PDB in the president's second term was described to me as often a ten- to fifteen-minute tactical update for someone who was now quite familiar with the issues. Both John Brennan and Jim Clapper recall Obama as genuinely appreciative. Jim said the president was gracious and complimentary during his last meeting with him in the Oval Office.

When needed, Dennis McDonough, who held several positions within the White House and ended as Obama's chief of staff, was always a dependable go-to guy for the intelligence folks. In the internal debate over the Syrian use of chemical weapons in 2013, for example, the White House kept raising the evidentiary bar for the IC. Finally, intelligence leadership just cornered McDonough and told him to tell folks to stop being in denial since the evidence was overwhelming.

Lurking in the background, perhaps, was a broader philosophical difference that one community veteran described to me. Intelligence, he reminded me, is generally Hobbesian in its worldview, subscribing to that philosopher's description of the state of nature absent controlling power as a "war of all against all." Barack Obama seemed to instinctively trend Lockean, believing that human nature was more characterized by reason and tolerance. It was perhaps the belief that people were fundamentally good and that, given an even playing field, governments would bend toward wisdom that allowed him to have faith in his nuclear agreement with Iran. Take the nuclear portfolio off the table, allow more normal diplomatic and commercial contact, and Iran would inevitably act more like a "normal" state.[15]

That Lockean trend showed itself, too, after the revelations of Edward Snowden, the NSA contractor who created a hemorrhage of disclosures about how the United States conducted electronic surveillance. As the revelations piled up, President Obama seemed to have an instinctive aversion to the process that was providing him intelligence that he clearly appreciated. "You're doing what?" was a common response, according to one intelligence senior. The president had an evident discomfort with some intelligence tradecraft, and it was visible in his demeanor, body language, and choice of words.

There may have been more of that Lockean worldview present in Obama's discounting Russian activity in Ukraine since it put Moscow "on the wrong side of history," a history seemingly governed by a built-in inevitability responding to unseen laws. Luce, the *Financial Times* columnist, says that "the idea of history as a separate force with a mind of its own is a bedtime story to help us sleep." Most intelligence professionals would agree; they subscribe to a more circular view of folly and correction rather than any inevitable progress upward.[16]

One former National Security Council staffer confirmed that it was really hard to stir team Obama into greater action over Russia. They were committed to reset. They were still thinking of Moscow as a declining power. They were still thinking they could put the Ukraine issue off in a corner. Intelligence reported faithfully on events, this staffer conceded, but also seemed to know what the market would bear. Many briefers became what the staffer labeled as Russian *Verstehers*, explainers of Russian actions. Often they were asked whether this or that American action would provoke Moscow—a frequent question from "don't do stupid shit" administration seniors. It wasn't especially hard to describe to a skeptic on providing arms to the Ukrainians the variety of ways that the Russians could amp up the pressure if we did that.

That's not quite the politicization of intelligence, but when the views of policymakers are strongly held and widely known, a subtle form of self-censorship sometimes takes place. "You can't say it like that," was how one officer described the self-policing. Knowing the blowback that some positions could generate, there is always the temptation to hold them back until they are "ready for prime time"—in other words, until the evidence is too compelling to refute.

That's one reason why, on many issues (and Russia was prominent among them), there seems to have been an endless series of meetings within the Obama NSC. Although it was hard to move those at the top off of their positions, contrary data and views were never far away, and that generated cause to reconsider this or that aspect of a question. From the American intelligence community, the complaint was often, "How many times are we going to meet on this?" One NSC veteran whose experience spanned two administrations quipped, while waiting for such a session to start, that "at least under Bush the fake meetings started on time."

There may have been another, more subtle factor at work here, too. One IC veteran described the Obama team to me as the first "Google White House," where people were accustomed to searching for their own information. "Google doesn't require a series of questions like PIRs (Priority Intelligence Requirements)," is how the veteran put it to me. "Google lets you wander and explore. They really didn't know how to search intelligence and we didn't know how to make it available to them that way. And because they weren't satisfied, their answer was to call another meeting. You ended up with more meetings and more people in them because you didn't know the questions."

There is more here than just the quirkiness of a particular staff. Gillian Tett of the *Financial Times* tells of searching for a good restaurant in an unfamiliar New York neighborhood and abandoning the older, *vertical* axis of trust (check Fodor's) in favor of going *horizontally* online (for recommendations from people who had eaten in the area). She preferred advice from a peer group rather than an authority and concluded, "We live in a world where we increasingly trust our Facebook friends and the Twitter crowd more than we do the IMF or the prime minister."[17]

Or, it appears in some cases, more than we trust the intelligence community. And that's a trend that is generational and will likely not be confined to one administration.

The complaint I heard from America's friends during the Obama administration, reflecting their sense of America's absence, was "where are you guys?" As I've suggested, the president's Jeffersonian tendencies seemed more and more to win out over any Wilsonian instincts. But retrenchment wasn't a phenomenon confined to one party or one branch of government.

In January 2011, I was asked to brief the incoming Tea Party wave of nearly ninety new Republican members of Congress. The venue was a downtown Washington hotel, and my wife and I made the rounds over cocktails, answering questions from the new arrivals and their spouses about schools, churches, neighborhoods, mass transit, and the like.

I had been invited there to speak to global threats to the United States and give the new members a strong dose of traditional Republican internationalism. They listened with interest and respect, but I wasn't sure a lot of it was sticking.

Reading the audience, I decided against asking the group a question I had formed during my preparation: "How many of you have passports?" It had been a pleasant evening and I don't think they would have appreciated the tone of my question. I also suspect that I wouldn't have liked their answer. They were polite, patriotic, sincere, and enthusiastic, but foreign affairs wasn't a strong suit or strong interest.

I wasn't alone in my concern. Not long after the 2012 election, many of the foreign affairs, defense, and intelligence practitioners and scholars who had gathered to support a potential Romney transition self-organized into a loose confederation called the Hay Initiative (after former secretary of state John Hay, who had served in Republican administrations from Lincoln to Teddy Roosevelt). We had a sense of what was coming, so we made a commitment to strengthen the Republican Party's internationalist tradition and an "economically and militarily strong United States, globally engaged . . . and dedicated to free trade, good governance and liberty secured by individual rights."

The initiative was intended to keep the band together, the "band" in this case being "a durable network of responsible, internationalist Republican foreign policy advisers" who could educate the new Republicans in Congress and serve as an advisory bullpen for Republican candidates in the 2016 presidential election.

With nearly four decades in the armed forces, I always tried to avoid political labels. I was a Bill Clinton appointee to NSA, a George W. Bush appointee to CIA. Still, I had been asked to advise the Romney campaign, did so willingly, and stayed with the effort in the Hay Initiative.

I headed the counterterrorism team; our work included some papers complaining about Obama administration timidity and self-imposed constraints. More broadly, the group addressed the tension "between American ideals and American interests": the perennial challenge for American internationalists, especially Republicans, to balance their Wilsonian and Hamiltonian instincts.

A few from the Hay Initiative ended up in the Trump administration. Many more became "never Trumpers," because the Republican nominee was neither internationalist, Wilsonian, nor Hamiltonian.

Walter Russell Mead described Donald Trump as pure Jacksonian: nationalist, populist, nativist, suspicious of the outside world—and willing to use force to beat it back.[18] In fact, he may be the most Jacksonian occupant of the White House since, well, Andrew Jackson.

Although his actual knowledge of Jackson was suspect, Trump visibly identified with the seventh president. A portrait of Jackson appeared in the Oval Office the first week of the administration, and before two months were out Mr. Trump had made a pilgrimage to Jackson's plantation home, the Hermitage, outside Nashville. And Trump channeled his Jacksonian instincts or at least his Jacksonian brand with an unrelenting "America First" mantra throughout the campaign.

There were echoes of Obama's retrenchment here even if expressed via inelegant bumper-sticker-like shout-outs at rallies rather than in thoughtful paragraph-length sentences. And Trump doubled down on the Obama administration's disdain for the Washington foreign policy establishment (the mother ship of American internationalism), describing it as a threatening "deep state" and not just the "Washington blob." But otherwise, the contrasts were stark.

Internationalist—nativist. Nuanced—blunt. Informed—instinctive. No drama—all drama. Studied—spontaneous. Fully formed paragraphs—140 characters. America as idea—America as blood and soil. Free trader—protectionist.

And then there was the issue of truth. All candidates shape their message, but Trump just seemed to say whatever came into his head. Was he uninformed, lazy, dishonest . . . or did he simply reject the premise that objective reality even existed or mattered?

Little wonder folks like me were concerned about the disruption that a Trump presidency would cause. We had our issues with some Obama policies and practices, but a lot of the Trump stuff looked like it would be off the charts. If he was genuinely Jacksonian, his overall approach would have some legitimate roots in American history, but it seemed an inappropriate model for America's needs today. One keen observer told me that in order to make his Jacksonian-populist story work (beyond just manipulative, crowd-pleasing rhetoric), Trump would have to reject, reinterpret, or simply ignore many of today's realities and a good deal of yesterday's history.

The same observer, deeply knowledgeable of the Middle East, also suggested that as jihadists have hijacked some of the authentic historical narratives of Islam for their own purposes, so too has Mr. Trump hijacked the narratives of Jacksonian foreign and security policy for his own ends.

Scary proposition.

Next, the source of all these concerns: Donald J. Trump, the candidate.

THREE

THE CANDIDATE AND THE CAMPAIGN

My little email universe was steadily lit up in the spring and summer of 2016 with commentary on the Trump campaign. That universe comprised a lot of people with backgrounds like mine: intelligence, security, military, diplomatic, and related fields. We had lots of issues, but the key themes of truth, inclusion, and lawfulness quickly emerged.

The most intense buzz was about telling the *truth*, or, more specifically, about Donald Trump *not* telling the truth. Or at least not bothering to find the truth in order to speak accurately.

We noted to one another that Russia really wasn't fighting ISIS in Syria; that American alliances were a national competitive advantage, which Russia and China, which didn't have any friends that mattered much, actually envied; that defending Latvia or Estonia wasn't just a matter of their having paid their bills; that the Trans-Pacific Partnership (TPP) was really an alignment of twelve nations bordering the Pacific (*none of them named*

China) in an American-facing rules-based order, not a rip-off of American workers.

We had a long list of out-and-out lies, too, like the candidate's claim that there were pan-Islamic legions celebrating wildly on the streets of New Jersey as the Twin Towers were aflame and collapsing. And then there was the moment Mr. Trump, hammering Obama-era political correctness, departed from prepared remarks to say that the neighbors of the San Bernardino terrorist couple, beyond seeing suspicious behavior, "saw bombs on the floor," a claim for which there was absolutely no evidence.

In March he defended the intentional killing of terrorists' families because "they knew what was happening. . . . They left two days early, with respect to the World Trade Center, and they went back to where they went, and they watched their husband on television flying into the World Trade Center, flying into the Pentagon."

None of that really happened, of course. Few of the 9/11 hijackers were married. None had family in the United States. We know of no family members, even overseas, who were flown *anywhere* before or after 9/11.

Before election day, candidate Trump had also managed to insinuate that Ted Cruz's father had a hand in the Kennedy assassination and that Supreme Court justice Antonin Scalia had been murdered at a Texas hunting lodge. He also "clarified" that he had put to rest Hillary Clinton's scurrilous accusation that Barack Obama had not been born in the United States.

I think it fair to say that the Trump campaign normalized lying to an unprecedented degree, and when pressed on specifics it routinely tried to delegitimize those who would disagree with countercharges about the "lyin' media," "intelligence" (in accusatory quotation marks), "so-called judges," fake news, Washington insiders, and the deep state.

One undisclosed CIA location in the United States has T-shirts emblazoned with the words *Deny Everything. Admit Nothing. Make Counter-Accusations.* But it is meant to be a joke.

The candidate himself had earlier suggested that in real estate, a little stretching—what Mr. Trump called "truthful hyperbole"—never hurt. In our view, though, it would really hurt him in the job he was pursuing. The day would come when the president would need others to take him at his word about something he would not be able to prove beyond a reasonable doubt. For us the bottom line was clear: the Oval Office was no place for routine exaggeration, much less for "alternative facts."

There may (and I emphasize *may*—I have only undergraduate psychology courses in my portfolio) have been something more involved here as well, something even more troubling: the candidate often didn't know what he was talking about, and he may not have known that he didn't know.

Tom Nichols, a professor of national security affairs at the Naval War College, laments the post-truth world in his 2017 book *The Death of Expertise.* Nichols is pretty aggressive: "The United States is now a country obsessed with the worship of its own ignorance . . . Google-fueled, Wikipedia-based, blog sodden . . . [with] an insistence that strongly held opinions are indistinguishable from facts."[1] Early in the work he introduces the concept of metacognition, essentially the ability to think about thinking, which leads to the "ability to know when you're not good at something." He cites a singer knowing when she has hit a sour note, a director knowing when a scene isn't working. If you lack metacognition, those discoveries are beyond you.

Nichols credits a 1999 study by Justin Kruger and David Dunning, research psychologists at Cornell, with driving home this point. Nichols writes, "The lack of metacognition sets up a vicious loop in which people who do not know much about a subject do not know when they're in over their head . . . and there is no way to educate or inform people who, when in doubt, will make stuff up."

I was not terribly familiar with the concept of metacognition when I heard candidate Trump talk about celebratory Muslims in New Jersey on September 11 or fleeing terrorist family members on September 9, but incidents like that came to mind as I read and reread Nichols's words.

The concept came to mind again when after a year in office the president riffed on climate change with British journalist Piers Morgan: "There is a cooling, and there's a heating. I mean, look, it used to not be climate change, it used to be global warming. That wasn't working too well because it was getting too cold all over the place. The ice caps were going to melt, they were going to be gone by now, but now they're setting records. They're at a record level."[2] For the sake of history and science, I should add that arctic sea ice levels were at record lows as the president spoke (a generally well-known and accepted fact regardless of your views on *human*-caused climate change).

None of which explains why the American people would *accept* post-truth, alternative-facts narratives. The answer to that lies elsewhere. A decade ago, long before "post-truth," comedian Stephen Colbert had coined a new word, "truthiness," while criticizing the Bush administration. He said, "We're not talking about the truth, we're talking about something that seems like truth—the truth we want to exist." The Wikipedia entry for the word

(word of the year in 2005!) characterized it as a truth "known" intuitively by the user without regard to evidence, logic, intellectual examination, or facts.

Trumpism was a long time coming.

Beyond the lack of *truth* telling, there was the question of *inclusion*, with the campaign's emphasis on the politically convenient but somewhat amorphous "other"—immigrants, illegals, Mexicans, Muslims, and so on—as the root of our problems. The campaign broadcast a palpable sense of America less as a welcoming Madisonian "we the people" than a nation defined by blood and soil and shared history. If the campaign hadn't been conducted in English, we would have routinely heard words that evoked blood and soil like the German *Volk* or the Slavic *narod*. Lacking a good English equivalent, the campaign settled on "hardworking Americans" as an adequate dog-whistle equivalent. The label preferred by some in the alt-right was "awakened whites."

There were lots of reasons why we worried about the nativism: alienation of a friendly and important neighbor to the south; limiting the bounty we harvested from the youthful, entrepreneurial vigor of new arrivals; distancing ourselves from important allies and cooperative foreign sources; even redefining the essence and values of the nation.

In one particularly divisive campaign shtick, Trump would dramatically read a poem about a kindhearted woman who responds to the plea of a nearly frozen snake and nurses it back to health. Revived, the snake bites and kills her. It was an anti-immigrant crowd pleaser, and when Trump reprised the act in

Harrisburg, Pennsylvania, a hundred days into his presidency, David Gergen called it "deeply disturbing . . . the most divisive speech I've ever heard from a sitting American president."[3]

Concerns about this clearly went beyond my narrow band of American internationalists to include a cross section of American and global society. Candidate Trump, as the old Catholic joke goes, was so exclusionary he "pissed off the pope" . . . literally. Trump's rhetoric on illegal immigration, particularly a wall on the Mexican border, prompted Pope Francis to bluntly counter, "A person who thinks only about building walls, wherever they may be, and not building bridges, is not Christian. This is not the gospel." The pope later warned about leaders who exploit fear, and cautioned the faithful not to rely on "the false security of walls—physical or social."[4]

The influential Jesuit publication *La Civiltà Cattolica* continued the skirmish well after the election, accusing some American Catholics and evangelicals of becoming a "community of combatants," fostering an "ecumenism of conflict" with a "xenophobic and Islamophobic vision that wants walls and purifying deportations."[5] The authors, close to Pope Francis, suggested that exclusionists were fostering a latter-day Manichaean vision of the world, with the forces of darkness now including "the migrants and the Muslims."[6]

As a practicing American Catholic, I have never experienced the counterimmigrant narrative in my faith community. *Never.* I *have* occasionally stumbled across a more general them-versus-us, as when the last prayer at Sunday mass—the one right before we leave church—is a call for Saint Michael the Archangel to defend us in battle. I actually like the prayer; it is the oft-used entreaty for Catholics in the armed forces. But in a civilian parish, it is admittedly a bit distant, at least in tone, from Saint Francis's call to be an instrument of the Lord's peace.

And I fear that among even my coreligionists there is a minority that views Islam as part of a hostile world: "Some Muslims may be tolerant, but one cannot meet the definition of being a good Muslim and be tolerant at the same time," is how one put it to me. This is all discomforting enough on a human basis, but folks like me zero in on what such attitudes might mean for America's relationship with the world's 1.6 billion Muslims, one-fifth of the globe's population and a majority in some fifty countries.

During the campaign Donald Trump suggested that he would create a database on Muslims and would "certainly look at" the idea of closing mosques. He called for "a total and complete shutdown of Muslims entering the United States" all because "Islam hates us. There's something there that—there's a tremendous hatred there. There's a tremendous hatred. . . . There's an unbelievable hatred of us."[7]

I don't think that Mr. Trump needed any help getting to his "Islam hates us," clash-of-civilizations paradigm. Certainly his base seems to welcome it. During the discussion in that back room in Pittsburgh, there were moments when Islam and terrorism were dangerously close to being viewed as synonyms by some in the group.

And there were plenty of civilizational warriors on team Trump. In 2014, strategist Steve Bannon said that "the Judeo-Christian West" was "in the very beginning stages of a very brutal and bloody conflict . . . an outright war against jihadist Islamic fascism" that threatened to "completely eradicate everything that we've been bequeathed over the last 2,000, 2,500 years."[8] The candidate's favorite soldier, former defense intelligence director

Mike Flynn, once famously tweeted, "Fear of Muslims is RATIO-NAL."

I thought that was dangerous. For me, the center of gravity of this conflict is not a war *between* civilizations (Christians versus Muslims), but rather a war *within* a civilization, within Islam it-self. Brussels, Berlin, Manchester, Barcelona, San Bernardino, and other attacks invite the former conclusion, but the reality is that the victims of jihadist terrorism have overwhelmingly been Muslim and to confine our understanding of this conflict to the former (a war between civilizations) will make the resolution of the latter (a war within a civilization) delayed, tougher to achieve, and less satisfying.

And until the latter is resolved, *all* the killing continues.

Islam is experiencing a conflict that parallels Christendom's struggle in the seventeenth century, trying to arbitrate a balance between faith and reason, between the sacred and the secular. Christendom's Thirty Years' War, the last great war of religion in the West, was incredibly bloody—the death rate in Germanic lands approached 20 percent—and led to the separation of the secular from the sacred, broadly divorcing the coercive power of the state from matters of faith.

George W. Bush's senior speechwriter, Michael Gerson, sum-marized it this way: "Over time—at least since Calvin's Geneva and Cromwell's England—Christians have learned that too close a relationship between church and state is highly damaging to both. Associating the reputation of the Christian gospel with the fortunes of any politician or movement is bound to dishonor sa-cred things."[9] That principle has been unevenly applied over the past three and a half centuries, but the principle remains.

The three great monotheisms—Judaism, Christianity, and

Islam—all revere and profess to be children of Abraham, and all come out of the same desert. Islam traditionally refers to adherents of the other two faiths as "people of the book," a nod to the Torah and the Bible that Mohammed allegedly perfected.

Despite these parallels, it may be more difficult for Islam to approach Christendom's compromise of separating church and state since, at least in its fundamentalist forms, Islam is a more transcendental faith, allowing human reason less space to interfere with the purported will of God. Men are capable of terrible things when they believe they are doing his will.

The British academic A. C. Grayling, a frequent commentator on religion in modern society, agrees that there are parallels between modern Islam and seventeenth-century Christendom. He told me that the ferocity of today's fundamentalists is a marker of the depth of distress within Islam and that what we see in the West is a sad "splash over" from Islam's internal struggle.

Grayling stressed to me that the core of Christendom's transformation—the Reformation and the Enlightenment—was less about shifting religious doctrine than it was the growth of tolerance. Unable to enforce orthodoxy because of the fracturing caused by the Reformation, Christendom made a virtue of necessity. We tolerated because we had to. He suggests that pushing similar concepts of pluralism and toleration would do more to heal the Muslim world than any effort to reinterpret the tenets of Islam.[10]

That will be a heavy lift, but before we too quickly condemn our fellow monotheists, we should remember that the Western democracy that most allows the "will of God" into the public square is our own. Believers of many faiths (including members of my family) march for life in Washington to overturn what the

Supreme Court says is a constitutional right, and they do so on largely religious grounds. American Catholicism in effect set up its own justice system in the recent priest sex abuse scandal. Opting for ecclesiastical judgment while avoiding criminal courts is not quite the same as imposing sharia, but there are parallels. And American evangelicals make up the biggest pro-Israel bloc in the United States, supporting the Jewish state not for reasons of policy but because of biblical teaching. One evangelical leader (Reverend John Hagee, pastor of a San Antonio megachurch) labeled support for Israel "God's foreign policy"[11] and personally lobbied President Trump to move the U.S. embassy to Jerusalem.

None of which should tempt anyone to equate American belief with jihadist fanaticism nor to suggest that we should tolerate or condone violence. We must do what we need to do to defend ourselves. The physical destruction of ISIS, al-Qaeda, and their affiliates is a short-term necessity and a crucial precondition for long-term success since these groups claim to represent both the hand and the will of God and they have pointed to battlefield victories to buttress those claims. Battlefield defeats, on the other hand, undercut their jihadist credibility as well as their tactical situation. Those defeats cannot come quickly enough as we mourn the destruction of ancient civilizations.

Three summers ago, shortly after the fall of Mosul, my wife and I attended mass in Aspen on the margins of a rather despondent Aspen Security Conference. There the priest reminded the local faithful that, for the first Sunday since the time of the apostles, holy mass would not be said that weekend in Mosul (ancient Nineveh), a characterization that saddened me more deeply than anything I had heard over the preceding three days at the Aspen Institute.

The human terrain of the Middle East is being irrevocably altered as Christian communities that have existed there for more than a millennium (often under tolerant Islamic rulers) are being eradicated or simply depopulated as those who can, flee from ancestral homes that predate the birth of Islam. Jihadists painting the letter N (for followers of the Nazarene) on local homes have accelerated a broader decline in the Christian population of the region from 14 percent a century ago to only 4 percent today. Iraq's Christian population is estimated to be a third of what it was shortly after the American invasion, and Christianity has all but disappeared from Iran and Turkey.

Still, grief and righteous anger are thin reeds on which to base policy, and we need to keep the big ideas straight or the limited power we have to influence outcomes will be misplaced at best and destructive of our purposes at worst.

When we describe this struggle—as the Trump campaign did—as a struggle between civilizations, we adopt the narrative of ISIS and al-Qaeda that there is undying enmity between Islam and the West. We strengthen the hand of our adversary. I said publicly during the campaign that the candidate's language *as a candidate* already had made us less safe as a nation.

The Obama administration erred in the other direction, I think, refusing even to say the words "radical Islam," seeming to suggest that today's violent extremists were just self-generating free electrons or something. That's just silly. As the *Atlantic*'s Graeme Wood (author of the highly acclaimed 2015 article "What ISIS Really Wants") has said, terrorist groups take strength from some authentic narratives within Islamic history. They *do* have something to do with Islam. It's just not by any means all of Islam and all Muslims.

President Obama's own life experience exposed him to the complexities of Islamic history, both the good and the bad, and should have positioned him for a rather nuanced public discussion of this topic. That never came, perhaps because he did not want to offend Muslims; perhaps he felt it dignified the terrorists too much; perhaps he feared feeding the worst instincts of some on the American right. In any event, it was an opportunity lost and it practically invited the harsh rhetoric of candidate Trump and, in the eyes of some, gave it legitimacy.

Reuel Marc Gerecht is a former CIA analyst, a keen observer, an unabashed hawk on questions of terrorism, and a friend. He dismisses the Obama approach that "needlessly got itself into trouble by avoiding an adult conversation about the problems in the Muslim world. Muslims aren't children. They don't need Western affirmative action programs."

But he saves his strongest language for the religious warriors on team Trump, saying he has "a really big problem when certain individuals attempt to paint Islam, in all its 1400-plus years of glorious complexity, as a deranged civilization and faith, whose denizens and practitioners are somehow uniquely capable of violence because they are hard-wired to do so, via the Koran, the holy law, and whatever else the anti-Islam crowd thinks makes Muslims tick. This is just historically atrocious. It is often obscene."[12]

Put me down as voting with Marc, as would most American intelligence professionals I know. Which is why a counterterrorism strategy defined solely by the promise to "bomb the shit" out of ISIS frankly scares the shit out of us and was one of the most frightening things to come out of the Trump campaign.

Then there was the question of *lawfulness*, with candidate Trump promising to push past traditional restraints on American behavior, bringing back waterboarding "and a lot worse" while killing not just terrorists but their families. The campaign also explicitly regretted that earlier presidents had passed on another war crime, plunder: "We should have kept the oil in Iraq. . . . In the old days, when we won a war, to the victor belonged the spoils."

As this was playing out, in the spring of 2016, I was on a book tour for *Playing to the Edge,* my unapologetic account of Bush-era tactics that included electronic surveillance, metadata collection, renditions, detentions, interrogations, and targeted killings. I expected that with those topics and that attitude, I would be spending a lot of time playing defense as I traveled the country, that I would have to explain why we thought we *had* to play to the legal and ethical edge given the circumstances we were in after 9/11.

As it turned out, I didn't have to do much defending. In fact, given the tone of the Republican primaries—mostly set by Trump, though Ted Cruz did have a "carpet bombing" moment—I spent more time explaining that there *were* edges, that there were things we should *not* do, that there were lines beyond which we should *not* go.

There was a moment on Bill Maher's HBO comedy/commentary show *Real Time* when the host asked me about Trump's promise to intentionally target and kill the families of suspected terrorists. The candidate had actually said on *Fox and Friends,* "The other thing with the terrorists is you have to take out their families, when you get these terrorists, you have to take out their families."[13]

In answering Maher, I really didn't think I was making news. It was more like an observation, akin to saying that things that are dropped tend to move toward the center of the earth. "God no," I said. "If he were to order that once in government, the American armed forces would refuse to act."

"That's quite a statement there. I thought the whole thing was, you had to follow orders," Maher replied.

"You cannot—in fact, you are required *not* to follow an unlawful order. That would be in violation of all the international laws of conflict." Although I quickly dismissed Maher's comedic overstatement about "a coup in this country," I was serious that the U.S. military's traditional deference to civilian control would not include agreeing to or committing such a blatant war crime.

During a Republican debate the following week, Fox News' Bret Baier asked Trump specifically about my comments on the armed forces' unwillingness to do such things. The candidate responded, "They won't refuse. They're not going to refuse, believe me. . . . I'm a leader, I've always been a leader. I've never had any problem leading people. If I say do it, they're going to do it."

I quickly translated candidate Trump's words in my own mind: "I'm going to use the power of my office and the force of my personality to direct twenty-somethings in America's armed forces to commit war crimes."

The Trump campaign uncharacteristically walked that back the next day when they tossed a written statement through the transom to the *Wall Street Journal* claiming that the candidate understood "that the United States is bound by laws and treaties" and that he would "not order our military or other officials to violate those laws and will seek their advice on such matters."

It wasn't really much of a walk back. It was a press release, after all, not the candidate personally saying it. At rallies Trump quickly returned to the theme that we had to be tougher, much tougher. And at the first opportunity, he chafed at the restrictions of the Geneva Conventions, telling CNN's Anderson Cooper, "Let me explain something. We are playing at this level and they don't care. . . . [I]t's interesting what happens with the Geneva Convention. Everybody believes in the Geneva Convention until they start losing."

Then there was Mr. Trump's promise to bring back waterboarding. He said to loud approval during a rally in Ohio, "Would I approve waterboarding? You bet your ass I would—in a heartbeat. . . . Believe me, it works. And you know what? If it doesn't work, they deserve it anyway, for what they're doing."[14]

I objected to that, too, although the argument was a little harder to make. After all, my book *Playing to the Edge* defended those who had done waterboarding and maintained that it had worked. But neither I nor the Agency were calling for its return. It had last been used in early 2003 (under circumstances far different from those of 2016), and it was the Bush administration that had formally taken the technique off the table in 2006. Besides, we never did it "because they deserve it," and certainly not with the enthusiasm the candidate was exhibiting. It was done reluctantly (on a total of three detainees) to get information about possible *future* attacks, not to punish for previous ones.

Ben Wittes, curator of the redoubtable *Lawfare* blog, approached me later to coauthor a piece for the site on "The Special

Obligation of the Advocates of Strong National Security Measures." Ben and I noted that we had spoken out against some of the rhetoric of the Trump campaign and some people had seemed surprised. We were surprised that they were surprised. We admitted to a certain comfort level with legitimate surveillance, detention, interrogation, and targeted killings, but quickly added that that gave us a special duty to speak up about policies that were neither necessary nor beneficial. Indeed, we felt a burden that civil libertarians and human rights advocates—who opposed such policies across the board—did not have.

If you believe, as we did, that the national security community had formed a consensus around certain tools because they were effective, and that part of that effectiveness lay in the rejection of more extreme measures, then candidate Trump's words were particularly harmful. We concluded that *because* we believed in a series of hard measures, we had "a special obligation to rigorously and publicly distinguish between the tools we advocate and measures we abhor." We believed that opposition to what the candidate was saying was in "no sense a recalibrating of our judgments or a revisitation of our values. It [was] an expression of them." And we resolved to continue to express them.

By early March 2016, Eliot Cohen had done enough suffering in silence. Eliot's no shrinking violet, but he's not a bomb thrower either. So I was a little surprised when he emailed me (along with scores of others) to "join in an effort to inform the American people of our concerns about Mr. Trump's candidacy and our resolve not to support him."

He attached a pretty hard-hitting draft letter describing the candidate as, among other things, "unmoored in principle . . . fundamentally dishonest . . . [and] a distinct threat to civil liberty." Eliot also set a pretty tight timeline, requesting "a clear statement of support within the next 72 hours . . . [and] because of the speed with which this effort must proceed, we regretfully cannot submit the statement to additional editing." The latter was likely intended to avoid the editing nightmare certain to occur with a group that loved nothing better that to tinker with somebody else's prose.

In the end, Eliot got 122 signatures, a pretty powerful list of security professionals who had served in Republican administrations. It was a disparate list, too—for and against the Iraq War, for and against intervention in Syria. The roster included several folks with intelligence experience, like David Shedd (deputy director, DIA), Fran Townsend (head of Coast Guard intelligence before becoming homeland security adviser), and Reuel Marc Gerecht (CIA).

I was not among them. I told Eliot that I agreed strongly with the thought, but had a personal and a larger concern. The personal concern was that I was on the book tour and feared that going public might be viewed as a commercial move on my part. Possibly bad for me, but certainly bad for our objective.

I also feared that Trump would use this as just another talking point about how Washington insiders reflexively opposed him and needed to be swept out. Our public opposition could actually make this worse. Although the Trump campaign ultimately was surprisingly (and wisely) subdued about the whole thing, one influential (but unidentified) Republican did point out the obvious:

"The people signing that letter will be the establishment—the very people that Trump is running against. It will make Trump's day."[15]

Finally, I conceded to Eliot that if anyone deserved an ad hominem attack, it was Donald Trump (who certainly was not above making them: "Lyin' Ted," "Crooked Hillary," and so on). Tactically, though, I suggested it might be more productive to hammer him on specifics, rather than make an outright rejection of the man.

Eliot fully understood all my concerns, but pressed ahead. For him, he said, it was really pretty simple. "This is really drawing a bright moral line and saying that if we're going to keep our souls, we can't cross it."[16] He reminded me that he had three grandchildren and "when they ask me what I did when Donald Trump ran for president, I want to have a good answer." He conceded, "Tactically it won't make a particle of difference to the outcome, which I fully accept."

Quixotic or not, the letter actually did make a splash. The site on which it was originally posted, War on the Rocks, promptly saw its server crash.[17] There was plenty of press commentary drawing attention to the letter, too.

The issue simmered throughout the summer. I tried to cabin my public commentary by simply observing that *if* Mr. Trump governed in a way consistent with how he spoke during the campaign, we had a lot to worry about. Inserting the *if* was my trying to leave some room for hope, at least publicly.

I also made it clear that my choice for president was former Florida governor Jeb Bush and made no secret that I had joined a small group to brief him on national security matters in Coral Gables. That was a pretty straightforward session. There were things the governor thought he knew and things he knew he did not know. He tested the former and inquired about the latter.

When Bush dropped out, I endorsed fellow Pittsburgh native John Kasich, now governor of Ohio, and pretty much the last centrist standing, although I never met with the candidate.

Some clear lines were now being drawn and folks were being challenged to decide on which side of them they wanted to be. In midsummer, I received a call from a retired senior colleague who had been invited by a friend of his—a close, near-original member of the Trump team—to come help expand the candidate's thinking on security matters.

The close adviser making the request understood the candidate's obvious limits on security questions. There had been a few examples of embarrassing ignorance when, for instance, he seemed unaware of the substantial contribution NATO forces were making against terrorism in Afghanistan.

My friend could surely help. But my friend wasn't sure that he wanted to help, and so he asked my advice. I simply said that there was a difference between helping a man who wanted to be president of the United States and helping a man who had been elected president. In other words, if there was a time to help Mr. Trump, it would be *after* he had won an election, not before. I think I said something like "helping a badly flawed man to become president was one thing, trying to fix those flaws post-election was another."

Maybe that should have been a tougher call for me to make. Aren't all candidates entitled to advice and preparation? In this case I doubted that the advice would have made a difference, and, despite promises made to guarantee the anonymity of my friend (promising anonymity to entice someone to advise a candidate suggests how weird this whole campaign was), I warned that this could be played as some kind of endorsement of the candidate. He thanked me for my counsel. I don't think he signed on before the election, but I don't know for sure. He is not currently in government.

It really wasn't clear that Mr. Trump actually wanted much advice anyway. He told MSNBC's *Morning Joe* in March, "My primary consultant is myself and I have a good instinct for this stuff, I'm speaking with myself, number one, because I have a very good brain."[18]

He had earlier identified the source of his foreign policy thinking to Chuck Todd of NBC: "Well, I really watch the shows. You really see a lot of great, you know, when you watch your show and all of the other shows, and you have the generals and you have certain people that you like."[19]

Indeed, there were only a few military or national security officials close to the Trump campaign. Lebanese-born Middle East scholar Walid Phares was a well-known hawk in counterterrorism circles. Keith Kellogg had had a successful Army career, commander of a division and of U.S. special operations forces in Europe, before retiring as a three-star general. Keith and I shared time in the headquarters of U.S. European command in the early 1990s and occasionally saw one another at the Fort Myer chapel in retirement.

The rest of the "team" prompted observers and journalists to go to the web to help identify them: energy consultant George Papadopoulos; former Defense Department inspector general Joe Schmitz; managing partner of Global Energy Capital Carter Page, who had done work in Moscow. None of these could be considered leading figures in the Republican foreign policy establishment.

Most of that group had preemptively thinned the bench available to Trump by signing that March letter declaring that he was unfit for the office he was seeking.[20]

Mike Flynn was one security expert in the Trump camp who was already well known. Mike had more than thirty years in the Army, much at the operational level, and built the innovative intelligence engine behind Stan McChrystal's relentless counterterrorist raids in Iraq and Afghanistan. Flynn was aggressive, iconoclastic, intolerant of bureaucracy, and impatient with people and institutions he saw as dated.

Translating those traits to running a large D.C.-based organization like the Defense Intelligence Agency proved difficult. Flynn's creative mind spun out far more ideas than his bureaucracy could digest, and his inventive interpretation of events (dubbed "Flynn facts" by his workforce) taxed his analysts' credulity as well. DIA—the blue-collar, steady-as-you-go, workmanlike element of the intelligence community—was in turmoil being run by a self-described "maverick, an atypical square peg in a round hole." The director of national intelligence and his Defense Department counterpart jointly requested that Flynn resign about a year earlier than he or most people had expected.

Mike left angry. Over time he contributed to the story that he had been canned by the Obama White House because his take on Iraq, Syria, and ISIS had less of a happy face on it than the administration preferred. DIA had indeed taken a darker view of the battlefield (a somber view with which I agreed) than much of the rest of the IC, but that was not the cause for his dismissal. This was about management, pure and simple, and the decision was made within the Pentagon and within the intelligence community, not in the White House.

Conservative media also struck up the theme that in two years at DIA, General Flynn had never once had a chance to express his more pessimistic views personally to President Obama. Some have read that as political suppression of intelligence dissent. I and most of the intelligence community wondered why anyone would expect the head of DIA (who worked for the secretary of defense) to ever have a meeting with the president. That's just not how it works.

In civilian life, Mike quickly hit the usual speaking and TV commentator circuit and also teamed up with Michael Ledeen, a controversial neoconservative historian, to write *The Field of Fight*, which aligned radical Islamists with North Korea, Russia, China, Cuba, and Venezuela in an axis of hate against the United States. The work's harsh tone (one of my students described it as a book-length blog post) and its central premise that "Islam is a political ideology based on a religion" converged easily with the tone and substance of the Trump campaign, and Mike soon became the candidate's toughest and most enthusiastic surrogate.

And he apparently could not see how people like me could stand on the sidelines with such important issues in play. He tracked me down through my George Mason University email account in August 2016 to ask, "Mike, Seriously, you believe HRC will make a better President?" He continued, "I have been disappointed in the 'national security experts' and the entire republican establishment to date for their lack of character and disloyalty to the tens of millions of Americans who want to see DT win and who desperately want change in our country (as do I). The 'experts' and 'establishment' must take those Americans for idiots."

I simply responded with a caution about the lack-of-character accusation. "Honest people can have honest differences," I replied. I declined to add that at that point many more millions of Americans had voted for somebody other than Donald Trump and that supporting someone else was not actually "disloyalty" to Trump voters.

Trump campaign outreach had better success with some other retired generals and admirals. In early September the campaign published a letter of support with eighty-eight such signatures. I recognized some names, considered a few on the list as friends, and also noted that fully three-fourths of the signatories had retired before the 9/11 attacks. The letter reflected the larger Trump following in demographics (trending older) and issues: rebuild the military, secure the border, defeat Islamist supremacists, restore law and order. Their letter certainly echoed Trump's dystopian view of the current world.

Not to be outdone, there was another "never Trump" letter brewing, this one organized by John Bellinger. John had been senior legal adviser to Condoleezza Rice when she was national security adviser and again when she became secretary of state. He was always considered a moderate in the Bush White House and often had the unenviable task of squaring the circle between our tough response to the 9/11 attacks and our allies' views of international law.

John had not participated in Eliot Cohen's earlier effort because he thought it was too overtly Republican, but he kept the idea of a separate letter in his head and was now strongly motivated by what he called Trump's continued "over the top comments." He had also been put off by Trump's audacity in criticizing candidate Ben Carson's ignorance about foreign affairs.

John told me that he talked to a lot of folks who had similar views. A few sympathized but were reluctant to sign on, fearing that this played into Trump's hands and would effectively be dialing themselves out of the game. Most were more enthusiastic. There was a growing consensus to do something together and not just continue the individual, private grousing in our email exchanges.

Like Eliot Cohen in March, John knew that this would not affect many of Trump's supporters, but his goal here was to affect the middle, the folks who were saying things like, "I like a lot about what Trump is saying, but I hope he doesn't get us into a war."

Word of the effort leaked to the Democrat side and John Podesta quickly asked if this could be parlayed into an endorsement for Hillary Clinton. Bellinger responded that it could not, and although the ultimate letter explicitly said, "None of us will vote for Donald Trump," some of us insisted that it include as well, "We also know that many have doubts about Hillary Clinton, as do many of us."

The thrust of the letter was the candidate's general unfitness for office (would be the "most reckless president in American history" was the macro judgment). In making his case Bellinger researched literature from President Reagan's advisers on what it takes to be president. He highlighted virtues like the ability to listen and to exhibit trust.

John felt that the best timing for the letter would be to wait until after the convention when Trump would have formally been made the candidate and more people were paying attention. By the end of June, though, he felt he had to move. He characterized it to me as an ethical and moral decision. The unanswered language of the campaign had already done enough damage.

John originally sent his draft to about twenty people, eighteen of whom said they were in. In early August he sent it to a larger group and again the response was positive. When he got to fifty, he figured he had enough and was ready to publish.

John compiled an impressive list of signatories. Although there were a few like me who had clearly done their last stint in government, many were younger folks who had just approached senior status at the end of the Bush administration and would be prime candidates for the next Republican White House—but not this one. The team back at Trump Tower was keeping book. There were no illusions that a President Trump, who valued loyalty above all, would ever forgive, forget, or reconcile with anyone whose name was at the bottom of this letter.

One of the complaints that we cataloged was that Mr. Trump "has shown no interest in educating himself. He continues to display an alarming ignorance of basic facts of contemporary international politics. Despite his lack of knowledge, Mr. Trump claims that he understands foreign affairs and 'knows more about ISIS than the generals do.'"

A little more than a week after we published those words, candidate Trump was scheduled for his first formal intelligence briefing. These briefings after the nominating conventions are American political ritual. They were started by Harry Truman in 1952 and are usually seen as signs of our stability and maturity as a democracy: *all* candidates get the *same* briefing. Governor Romney got two in 2012 and would have had more had Hurricane Sandy not intervened. His vice presidential pick, Paul Ryan, actually got four.

In 2016 it was different. There was absolutely unprecedented media attention, including press stakeouts. Then there were grand debates on cable news over whether or not Mr. Trump should be trusted with classified information; former Senate majority leader Harry Reid suggested that Mr. Trump be given "fake" information during briefings because he couldn't be counted on. Some Republicans raised the identical question for Secretary Clinton.

My view was simple: get the nomination, get the briefing. No need to make it more complicated than that. Just brief.

The morning of the first Trump briefing on August 17, he was asked on Trump-friendly Fox News whether he trusted U.S. intelligence. He replied, "Not so much from the people that have been doing it for our country. I mean, . . . look what's happened over the years. I mean, it's been catastrophic. In fact, I won't use some of the people that are standards—you know, just use them, use them, use them, very easy to use them, but I won't use them because they've made such bad decisions."

That last was probably a reference to the people like me who had signed the early August letter, but it still set off some alarm bells within the intelligence community.

Since Mr. Trump had no background in national security, this would be his first real impression of intelligence. The IC wanted to get off on the right foot. The DNI's transition team hoped the pessimistic Fox News exchange had just reflected Trump's habit of reacting to questions without much thought.

The intelligence folks had been preparing for this moment since at least mid-July. They had gamed out potentially difficult scenarios that might arise before, during, and after the candidate briefing. They put the briefers though a "murder board," a mock session where every imaginable unpleasantness was thrown at them.

One senior intelligence official began calling friends of the candidate. They conceded that he had little background on global affairs or on the structure of the intelligence community, but predicted that he would be attentive. The official also pulsed the community on the role that Mike Flynn might play in the session. One official formerly close to the departed DIA director warned, "If he starts talking, he'll never shut up." In the event, Flynn was active but far from obnoxious, and appeared to be most interested in impressing Trump.

By all accounts, the August intelligence briefing went well. These are generally broad overview briefings, "scene setters" in the language of the community, and there appears to have been a good give-and-take. Admittedly, the bar is low here. Just getting acquainted is a pretty good day.

Mike Flynn went out onto Fifth Avenue after the session to give the briefers high marks in front of the press, probably to blunt Trump's extemporaneous criticism of the intelligence community that morning on Fox.

In fact, the second time around, in September, Mr. Trump went out of his way to tell the briefers himself that the sharp things he had said earlier didn't apply to them, at least not personally. In essence, he seemed to be saying that he had been caught off guard by the Fox News reporter and that he respected the briefers and wanted them to know that.

The second briefing on September 7 seems to have gone well, too, but then the wheels started to fly off. That evening Matt Lauer interviewed the two candidates (sequentially) aboard the

USS *Intrepid* in the Hudson River on NBC's "Commander-in-Chief Forum." Lauer asked Trump about the intelligence briefing earlier in the day. "Did you learn new things in that briefing?"

The candidate started well: "I have great respect for the people that gave us the briefings . . . they were terrific people." Indeed, one of the IC participants later told me that the candidate walked into the September 7 meeting with a decidedly respectful air, the way a layman would walk into a conference of experts or specialists. But then Mr. Trump alleged that despite the great advice these professionals had given them, "President Obama and Hillary Clinton and John Kerry, who is another total disaster, did exactly the opposite."

When pressed on how he knew that, the candidate responded, "In almost every instance. And I could tell you. I have pretty good with the body language [*sic*]. I could tell they were not happy. Our leaders did not follow what they were recommending."[21]

From an intelligence point of view, there was just so much wrong with that exchange. First, it broke the seal of the sacrament, so to speak. Candidate briefings are not required. They are offered by the incumbent as a matter of good governance, good faith, and courtesy. Prior to this night, it was unimaginable that such a meeting would be used against the one who had offered it.

Second, it turned the candidate's intelligence briefers into political props and campaign tools.

Third, it was almost certainly wrong. I know the kind of people who do these briefings (I actually know some of the people who did *this* briefing). They never would have allowed their body language to betray any internal views, even if they had them. They're too professional. They do this all the time. Trump's commentary was pure bullshit.

Finally, the candidate's comments set off a press feeding frenzy for the "inside baseball" account of that day's meeting at Trump Tower. And, unhappily, some of the subsequent articles appeared to be sourced, at least in part, to current intelligence officials—an extremely troubling component of the 2016 race.

As someone might have tweeted: "Sad."

And then there were the Russians. Lurking in the background of what was always going to be a difficult candidate–intelligence community relationship was the specter of Russian involvement in the American electoral process.

We now know that American intelligence was consumed by this well before it became public knowledge. Analysts started to pick up troubling indicators in the spring, part of a broader pattern of Russian assertiveness in Crimea, eastern Ukraine, Syria, the Baltics, and even in European elections. By late July there was mounting evidence that Russian meddling in the American election, especially in the theft and weaponizing of data, was different in quantity and quality from previous efforts, that it was more coherent in design and was being directed from the very top of the Russian government. And there were growing fears about how much the intelligence community was not yet seeing.

The director of national intelligence and the director of CIA worked to impose urgency about the issue on a reluctant incumbent political leadership. In early August, John Brennan got White House permission to phone his Russian counterpart, FSB[22] director Alexander Bortnikov, and deliver what John later described to me as a "brushback pitch—high, hard and inside," a warning that the Russian behavior was unacceptable.

President Obama issued another warning to Putin in September on the margins of a G20 meeting in China, and in early October Clapper and Homeland Security Secretary Jeh Johnson publicly announced that they were "confident that the Russian government directed the recent compromises of emails from U.S. persons and institutions, including from U.S. political organizations" and they did so "to interfere with the U.S. election process."[23]

Candidate Trump would have none of it: "I notice, anytime anything wrong happens, they like to say the Russians are. . . . Maybe there is no hacking. But they always blame Russia. And the reason they blame Russia is because they think they're trying to tarnish me with Russia."[24]

Rejecting a fact-based intelligence assessment—not because of compelling contrarian data, but because it was inconsistent with a preexisting worldview or because it was politically inconvenient—is the stuff of ideological authoritarianism, not pragmatic democracy. And for the American intelligence community, seeing that from someone who could be president would have been very discomfiting.

And this was against the backdrop of other, difficult-to-explain behavior. I know I wasn't the only one to notice, but candidate Trump really did sound a lot like Vladimir Putin. There was always a sympathetic authoritarian chord between them. Both were on record as admiring a strong leader. They've even complimented one another on the trait. Putin could have been humming along when Trump was claiming, "I alone can fix it," during his Cleveland acceptance speech.

Both seemed to have a pretty conspiratorial view of the world. Putin comes by his naturally. He's a product of a KGB Marxist philosophy in which the *other*—any other—is reflexively identified as hostile, created by immutable forces of history, something to be feared and ultimately crushed.

Sounding a little bit the conspiratorial Marxist himself, Mr. Trump claimed that there were forces that could rig the U.S. election. It's a theme that Putin was happy to echo. Indeed, it's a theme that his intelligence services were always happy to propagate.

And the American presidential candidate routinely came to the defense of his Russian soul mate. He echoed Mr. Putin when it came to Syria and ISIS. His second debate formulation—"I don't like Assad at all, but Assad is killing ISIS"—was precisely the one that the Russian and Syrian presidents had been attempting to craft. "It's me or the terrorists" has been Assad's false choice. It's hard to explain how the candidate of a major American political party could have gotten there, especially after receiving classified intelligence briefings.

Perhaps some of this could be explained by the murky ties of some on team Trump to things Russian. There is certainly a history there, and perhaps a comfort level as well. Former campaign manager Paul Manafort did consulting work for the ousted pro-Russian regime of Viktor Yanukovych in Ukraine, and revelations from Kiev stoked questions about whether he should have registered here as working on behalf of a foreign power. Before 2017 was out, Manafort and a protégé would be indicted for conspiracy, money laundering, failure to register as an agent of a foreign power, and failure to report foreign bank and financial accounts—all linked to Manafort's ties to Putin's man in Kiev.

Manafort denied any role in suppressing a Republican platform commitment to send lethal defensive weapons to the Ukrainians in their battle against separatists and the Russian army. Although it's clear that the suppression was initiated by Trump staffers, Trump has denied any *personal* responsibility for it. The whole episode begs explanation.

Then there was Carter Page, an adviser with intermittent contacts with the campaign, but with deep ties to Russian money, oil, and gas, who blamed aggressive Western policies for the mess in Ukraine and what he described as the "so-called" annexation of Crimea. *So-called?*

And what about the money? Although Trump claimed that "I have zero investments in Russia," his son boasted in 2008 that "Russians make up a pretty disproportionate cross-section of a lot of our assets. . . . [W]e see a lot of money pouring in from Russia." Absent more detailed data (like tax returns), who knows?

We've really never seen anything like this before. Former acting CIA director Mike Morell said that Putin had cleverly recruited Trump as an *unwitting agent* of the Russian Federation. I preferred another term drawn from the arcana of the Soviet era: *polezni durak.* That's the *useful idiot,* some naïf, manipulated by Moscow, secretly held in contempt, but whose blind support is happily accepted and exploited. That's the term I used in the *Washington Post* the Friday before the election. I admitted that it was a pretty harsh characterization and conceded that Trump supporters would be offended, but offered that it was the most benign interpretation of all this that I could come up with.

We didn't know it then, of course, but that now infamous June meeting at Trump Tower that had Jared Kushner, Donald Trump, Jr., and Manafort on one side and two Russian lawyers, an interpreter, and two representatives of the Agalarov family (the Russian fixers for the meeting) on the other perfectly fits the useful idiot scenario. The Trump team had accepted the meeting expecting Russian government dirt on Hillary Clinton.

For veteran CIA case officers, the offer constituted a Russian soft approach, using people who did not have "SVR"[25] on their business cards, but whose historical connections to the Russian government were clear. That made the meeting easier to accept from the American side while allowing the Russians plausible deniability should they need that in the future.

And the Russians accomplished several things with the session. First, they established the willingness of the Trump campaign to deal with the Russian government for dirt on Hillary Clinton. Second was confirming that the Trump campaign would not report such approaches and meetings to the U.S. government (otherwise they would have detected increased counterintelligence activity from the FBI). Third, since the two Russian negotiators had made a career of fighting for sanctions relief, I think the Russians would have fairly assessed that the Trumps were open to that linkage. Finally, the Trumps' accepting the meeting created a potential point of leverage on the campaign and the later administration. It was the first down payment on a bit of Russian *kompromat,* as it were.

We now also know that another "adviser" to the campaign, twenty-nine-year-old George Papadopoulos, was approached by a Maltese academic fronting for the Russians and offered email dirt on Hillary Clinton. President Trump later dismissed Papadopoulos as a bit player in the campaign, a "coffee boy" according to one campaign official. But it was Trump who, when pressed by the *Washington Post* to name *anyone* advising him on foreign affairs, volunteered Papadopoulos as "an energy and oil consultant" and an "excellent guy."[26] I suspect that Papadopoulos *was* a bit player, but his actions put the lie to earlier categorical denials by the campaign about contacts with Russia, and the episode displays the costs of Trump's "say anything" response to queries, a near-nonexistent vetting program, and the perils of chaos as a campaign organizing principle.

Then there was Donald Trump Jr.'s sporadic contacts via Twitter Direct Messaging with WikiLeaks, likely Julian Assange himself. The younger Trump spread the word throughout the senior campaign staff and seemed to synchronize campaign actions (Trump Sr. shout-outs for WikiLeaks; complaints about the press not following WikiLeaks' exposés; directing followers to a WikiLeaks website) with the actions of WikiLeaks. Some of the synchronizing came even after American intelligence had publicly linked WikiLeaks to Russian efforts to interfere with the election.

There seemed no limits for the campaign with regard to propriety, appropriateness, or acting in a way consistent with American political values.

Those with more political or security experience might have warned team Trump about the Russians and told them that WikiLeaks was a "non-state hostile intelligence service" (as Trump CIA chief Mike Pompeo later put it), but this was a campaign and a candidate with an almost preternatural confidence, disdain for experts or expertise, and contempt, not just for their political opponents but also for much of the government they would eventually inherit.

That suggested some serious challenges for American intelligence as the news networks began to paint Pennsylvania, Ohio, Michigan, and Wisconsin a deep red late on the evening of November 8.

It was going to be a challenging transition.

FOUR

THE TRANSITION

During that August discussion in the back room of the sports bar in Pittsburgh, someone asked me, "Mike, in this Trump-intelligence thing, who drew first blood?" It was a great question. And like most great questions, it was tough to answer.

Intelligence is always challenged to establish a relationship with the chief executive. That's really nobody's fault. It's far more structural than personal (although personalities do matter). The goal, of course, is for intelligence to get into the head of the president, to meaningfully contribute to his deliberations. But intelligence and the president come at this from different perspectives. Metaphorically, they enter the Oval Office through different doors.

The intelligence door is labeled "facts"—the kind of data that intelligence steals, elicits, or otherwise acquires to inform decision making. The president's door—any president's—is labeled "vision," specifically the one that people voted for in the first place.

Intelligence is fixated on the world as it is. The president and his policy team dream of the world as they want it to be. Intelligence is inherently inductive, swimming in a sea of data and attempting to draw generalized conclusions. Policymakers are inherently deductive, trying to apply their first principles, the ones you voted for, to specific situations. And intelligence analysts trend pessimistic. It comes with the turf. Bob Gates, director of central intelligence well before he became secretary of defense, says that when a CIA analyst stops to smell the flowers, she looks around for the hearse. Policymakers have to be optimistic; otherwise they never would have pursued the job.

So there is always some relationship building when a new president comes on board. The intelligence folks have to get into the head of the policymaker without crossing a line and breaking the tether to their fact-based, inductive, pessimistic worldview. After all, that's their only legitimate reason to be in the room. The president (whether he knows it or not) needs keen and impartial observers, not cheerleaders.

The intelligence community also needs to know the character of the first customer and especially how he learns. President Bush was a voracious reader, but it seemed to me that he best learned in the dialogue, which was always lively and intense. Present Obama appeared to be more reflective, preferring to read, and learning in the private moment.

There was going to be another adjustment in 2016 either way, although adjusting to a President Hillary Clinton would probably have been a light lift. She had gotten the President's Daily Brief for four years as secretary of state. The briefers would have known her and been familiar with her worldview, and she in turn would have understood the intelligence baseline on which any day's material was being presented. It's not too far off to say that she might have introduced her first briefing by simply asking, "Now, where were we?"

A President Trump was a different matter, of course. Not only was he less familiar with government, the structure of intelligence, and the global situation, but the creator had also given him a few extra doses of those deductive, world-as-we-would-like-it-to-be, vision-based attributes described above. He seemed purely instinctive, spontaneous, even impulsive, and although he had little background on the substance or processes of international affairs, he also had little patience with written or even verbal presentations. He seemed to have an eerie confidence in his own a priori narrative of how the world worked.

He also seemed disinclined to learn more, even at first pushing back on the very concept of a daily intelligence briefing, saying that he was a very smart person and did not need to be told the same things over and over again every day, itself a hideous mischaracterization of the PDB.

Mr. Trump puts a great deal of stock in personal relationships. No surprise there. I suspect we all do. But he does so to an extraordinary degree, weighing loyalty to him as an absolutely essential virtue, and giving greater weight to a conclusion based on who is presenting it to him rather than any evidentiary trail supporting it.

And if all this wasn't daunting enough, the first time American intelligence really had to try to force its way through Mr. Trump's bubble of skepticism, they had to engage him on a matter that was being used by other Americans to challenge his very legitimacy as president of the United States: the Russian interference in the U.S. election. That was a tragedy for the IC and it created an almost perfect storm of hostility between a rejectionist president and an intelligence community that was there to tell him the truth.

So I didn't have a good answer for my Pittsburgh friend's question about who drew first blood. And maybe it just doesn't matter. It all ended up with a lot of blood on the floor.

John McLaughlin was one of the best analysts ever to work at CIA. After heading up all analysis at the Agency and then serving as deputy director, John ended his thirty-plus-year career as the acting director of central intelligence following George Tenet's departure in 2004.

John stays plugged in, and in his calm rational way, he says that Mr. Trump's relationship with the intelligence community has evolved over four distinct phases. The first was characterized by the candidate's and the president-elect's ignorance of the community and its structure, its ethos, even its purpose. There was, for example, an inordinate focus on CIA as if it comprised all (or all that was important) in the IC.

As the transition wore on and the Russia interference story moved to center stage, the president-elect slipped into an attitude of overt hostility toward the community. Hence the tweet barrage comparing intelligence professionals to "Nazis" and such.

But intelligence is essential to good governance, so as inauguration day came and the needs of governing set in, the new president seemed to more and more appreciate that he *had* to rely on the intelligence community. Briefings became more frequent as the realities of North Korean ICBMs and Syrian chemical weapons became unavoidable.

The first three stages blended together, of course, and even today powerful elements of each (ignorance, hostility, unavoidability) seem to weirdly coexist in the president's worldview. That evolution is an important and fascinating story. I will work to describe it in this chapter and the next.

Of course, John said there were four stages in the Trump–intelligence community story. Stage four, John predicts, will begin when Bob Mueller reports out on his investigation of potential collusion by the president's campaign with Russians interfering in the U.S. election. No matter what Mueller recommends, the impact of that will be immense.

Presidential transitions display both the strengths and the weaknesses of American democracy. The strengths are obvious: every four or eight years we conduct a peaceful transfer of power for the most powerful office on the planet. The weaknesses largely deal with the effects of massive changes—changes in senior personnel certainly and, very often, in policy as well—and the resulting tensions.

The incoming team is focused on change. After all, they won and believe they have a mandate.

The government they will inherit is focused on stability. After all, they believe they know how things are best done.

That puts a great burden on the transition team—that body of folks loyal to the incoming administration, but wise and experienced in the ways of Washington—to build bridges to the outgoing administration as well as to those officials in the departments and agencies who aren't going anywhere.

One veteran of the Trump transition drew a sketch on the back of a breakfast napkin to demonstrate to me the always large information gap between an incoming political/policy team and permanent institutions like the intelligence community. In normal circumstances, he said, there is enough trust (or at least a sufficient lack of hostility) for the two sides to get together, close the information gap, and in the process form the relationships needed to eventually assemble a national security team—always an amalgam of political/policy types and career professionals.

Barack Obama pretty much campaigned in 2008 as not being George Bush, but his team gave the Bush folks high marks for how they handed off the reins of government. And the incoming Obama team was populated by a legion of seasoned Washington hands who had been waiting eight years in the wilderness for this moment. It was a pretty smooth transition.

Not so much in 2016. During the Republican primaries, Florida governor Jeb Bush predicted that Donald Trump would be a chaos president.[1] It was certainly a chaos transition.

First, there was good evidence that team Trump really didn't expect to have to come to work the day after the election.

They certainly hadn't prepared to govern. Developing policy is usually done before the primaries kick off in Iowa. There is some time then to think a bit, to put some purpose to the campaign, even to identify key intellectual influencers. None of that happened with the Trump campaign.

There is traditionally a second shot at this between the conventions and election day. There we normally see massive policy teams turning out papers on a variety of issues. That didn't happen with the Trump campaign, either. Nada. Nothing.

More than any other candidate in the modern era, Donald Trump ran on attitude, not policy. One intelligence senior said the incoming team was as weakly anchored on facts and on the artifacts of governance as any he had ever seen. While quick to point out that he wasn't talking about *everybody*, he added that he saw some of the wackiest stuff he had ever seen during any transition. Another senior observed that the new team was so ignorant of the institutions and processes of government, it seemed like "the Wild West."

That meant that in November 2016 the demands of manning a government (the usual transition task) were compounded with the demands to decide with some specificity what the new government actually intended to do and how they intended to do it.

The chaos was aggravated by the de facto excommunication of 172 experienced foreign policy specialists who had signed those letters condemning Trump in March and August 2016, plus some 75 retired diplomats who had signed a similar letter in September describing Trump as "entirely unqualified to serve as President and Commander-in-Chief."[2] All that left a pretty thin bench to call on.

Then there was the chasm of distrust that team Trump brought with it to the transition. Trump had run, after all, on a promise to drain the Washington swamp, and it was the swamp dwellers who were putting together the briefing books and trying to schedule meetings and to identify their counterparts on the incoming team. One senior intelligence official told me that those closest to the candidate seemed to believe that "inherently governmental" structures were second-tier compared to the private sector. Hence the lack of interest in the structure and processes of the intelligence community.

Mike Flynn could have been a bridge, but the putative national security adviser seemed more and more alienated from the community to which he once belonged. His views on al-Qaeda and ISIS were increasingly radicalized, his words on the outgoing administration increasingly condemnatory, and his zeal to restructure the entire intelligence community, with a special emphasis on CIA, increasingly obvious.

At the policy level, the far right news and opinion website Breitbart seemed to enjoy an outsized influence. Its former executive chair, Steve Bannon, was now chief strategist and senior counselor, and he would later surprise no one when he promised to battle tirelessly for the "deconstruction of the administrative state."

Closer to the intelligence community, Bannon acolyte Sebastian Gorka, who had been editor for national security affairs at Breitbart, met with Trump as early as 2015 and provided the soon-to-be candidate with a variety of position papers on Islam and terrorism.[3] One intelligence insider confided to me that Gorka was viewed as weak on analysis, someone who had made his mark as a grenade thrower, purposefully provocative, committed to ideologically driven disruption and in the vanguard of the no-peace-with-Islam movement.

All of this had the air of a hostile corporate takeover.[4] I have also heard it compared within the intelligence community to explorers landing in a suspicious and hostile environment, looking to make alliances with some tribes in order to subdue all the others. Resistance to the ways of the incoming team was quickly identified as evidence of the "deep state," a phrase previously used to describe murky military and security power centers that secretly work to thwart the democratic will in countries like Turkey.

Trump supporters like Breitbart News and Fox News' Sean Hannity made frequent references to it. Newt Gingrich, the former House Speaker, said, "Of course, the deep state exists. . . . They create a lie, spread a lie, fail to check the lie, and then deny that they were behind the lie."[5]

The Russians were happy to push a version of this idea, too. Julia Ioffe, the Russian-born American journalist, told a crowd of security specialists at Aspen that Russia liked Trump and wanted to circumvent the mostly hostile or at least suspicious American national security establishment. She colorfully described the Russian view as Trump being Gulliver tied down by an army of American establishment Lilliputians.[6]

The issue created really odd bedfellows. Self-described advocacy journalist Glenn Greenwald joined in against "the neoliberal and neoconservative guardians" of the current consensus, "with their sprawling network of agencies, think tanks . . . and media outlets," and then railed against "the unelected agenda of [National Security Adviser Lieutenant General H. R.] McMaster and [Homeland Security Secretary and later White House chief of staff Marine general John] Kelly."[7]

I have worked in intelligence for over three decades. I know what antidemocratic forces look like. I have seen them in multiple foreign countries. There is no "deep state" in the American Republic. There is merely "the state," or, as I characterize it, career professionals doing their best within the rule of law.

Not that they always play nice or quietly sit in their cubicles waiting to be called on. Many of the leaks that have plagued the

Trump administration have come from internal White House factions vying for advantage, but there is no doubt that some have come from career professionals. My journalist friends admit to me in a generalized sort of way that a lot of folks are certainly more willing to talk to them.

That can be bad, but painting this as a dystopian government universe inhabited by secret malevolent forces is simply inaccurate. Trump routinely defines himself against caricatured enemies. Mexicans are murderers and rapists; intelligence professionals are Nazis; immigrants are deeply unfair; refugees are dangerous; and Muslims hate us. Now the organs of the government that he was about to inherit were the secret, antidemocratic, all-powerful, conspiratorial "deep state." It is not a particularly useful description, frankly one that enhanced rather than dampened internal opposition, and one especially ill-suited to effective governance.

On several occasions, when I have made such remarks, folks recommended that I read Michael J. Glennon. Glennon laid out a kinder, gentler "deep state" theory in a 2014 article, "National Security and Double Government," explicitly dismissing secret collusion in some dark plot, but nonetheless expressing deep concerns about the antidemocratic *effects* of America's national security establishment.

Glennon bases his theory on the writings of nineteenth-century British journalist Walter Bagehot, widely credited as editor of the *Economist* with pushing that magazine to political prominence. Glennon cites Bagehot's reflections on British government where he describes dual institutions, one public and the other concealed, evolving side by side to maximize both legitimacy and efficiency. "Dignified" institutions like the monarchy and the House of Lords gave legitimacy to "efficient" institutions like the House of Commons and the cabinet that actually did the real work of government.[8]

Glennon transfers this duality to the modern American government. He labels our "dignified" institutions as *Madisonian*—the courts, Congress, and the executive that draw their powers from constitutional processes. These bodies are dignified and public, fulfilling necessary forms, endorsing decisions, and granting authority and legitimacy to governing.

But in our foreign and security policy, he says, we are more and more actually governed by the *"Trumanite"* entities that comprise our national security structure. *Trumanite,* of course, refers to the internationalist consensus that has governed American policy since 1947. Glennon sees these bodies as opaque but efficient, making decisions anchored in expertise and focusing on substance.

Glennon believes that "the *Trumanite* network survives by living in the *Madisonian* institutions' glow," but he also sees effective Madisonian control as fading, largely a product of the growing complexity of security issues as well as an increasingly ill-informed electorate and political class.[9] He supports his argument by demonstrating the continuity in counterterrorism, surveillance, and other policies between presidents as different as George Bush and Barack Obama and the strong carryover of personnel from one administration to the next. The Trumanites still determine things even as the Madisonians swap out, he reasons.

Of course, the apparent continuity could simply reflect limited options in the face of hard international realities, and personnel staying in place the admirable depoliticization of key jobs like chairman of the Joint Chiefs of Staff or director of the FBI.

Glennon also overachieves in his description of Trumanite control and initiative. His account of expanding electronic surveillance after 9/11, for example, is inaccurate in what was done and in who first pushed it.[10]

Still, Glennon raises serious questions, does not feel compelled to create villains or ill intent where none exists, and makes an effort to prove his case. This sets him apart from the reflexive conspiracy-mongering crowd that identifies opposition to any Trump initiative as proof of malevolent intent by a unified cabal committed to overturning the results of the election.

There is no doubt that large bureaucracies are set in their ways, and I can aver from personal experience that it is hard to get them to change course. But the "deep state" calumny is neither accurate nor useful. And all it did was to harden the lines that presidential transitions are designed to soften and eventually merge.

To make matters worse, the pure mechanics of this transition were awful.

Take communication. The transition would happen in Washington, but decision making was still tightly held at Trump Tower in New York. Even after a formal intelligence transition team was stood up in Washington, it was the view of the intelligence community that New York was still a powerful, controlling, distant, and not particularly communicative lord.

A lot of intelligence veterans were encouraged that former congressman Mike Rogers had the national security portfolio under New Jersey governor Chris Christie's overall transition effort. Rogers had been head of the House Intelligence Committee, was a known and trusted quantity, and got high marks for his knowledgeable and bipartisan leadership of the committee with Maryland Democrat Dutch Ruppersberger.

I cornered Rogers a week after the election during a party he was hosting at his house for America Abroad Media, an organization that promotes American values in popular culture overseas and that night was hosting the cast and writers of *Homeland*, Showtime's hit CIA drama. I began to tell Rogers how much we in the community were counting on him as a bridge and a voice of reason when he interrupted to tell me that he was no longer with the campaign.

That wasn't very comforting. Rogers didn't volunteer a reason, but he had been attached to Christie, who himself was being shoved off the island, erasing what little preparation for governing that the Trump team had done. Rogers wasn't really part of any of the evolving administration power centers, and Republican hard-liners (who were in the ascendency at that moment) had never forgiven him for what the intelligence community had viewed as his committee's reasonable report on Benghazi.

Retired Army lieutenant general Ron Burgess, Mike Flynn's predecessor at the Defense Intelligence Agency, had been quietly assembling an intelligence transition team tucked under Rogers's larger national security effort. Burgess had retired to a comfortable position at his alma mater, Auburn, but had been asked by his friend Alabama senator Jeff Sessions (Trump establishment Republican supporter number 00001) to lend his effort to the transition. More to prevent harm than to advance any agenda, Ron agreed.

Burgess put together an impressive team of (non-letter-signing) IC veterans, bided his time until the election, and then orchestrated a twenty-page paper on the things that the incoming administration should look at in the intelligence community. Ron told me that it was what *any* of us would have told *any* incoming administration: what was going well; where challenges remained; even prosaic questions like the right number of senior intelligence executives.

With Mike Rogers out at the top, the buzz at Washington transition headquarters was that Burgess could step up to head the national security portfolio, something that he did not seek and made clear that he would not accept. No matter. Within a few days Mike Flynn descended on the Washington office from the New York campaign headquarters, set up his own team and meeting schedule, and effectively froze Burgess out of the process. Burgess, already wary of Flynn, quietly informed Sessions and Vice President Elect Pence that he would be leaving and returned home to Alabama, unsure if anyone had actually read the paper his team had prepared.

All transitions tend chaotic. Two weeks after the election, this one was chaos on steroids.

On Monday of Thanksgiving week, for example, the president-elect appeared in a video announcing his day one plans in office. The video was clearly designed to sustain some political momentum and to fill the news void over the long holiday weekend. As part of his list, Trump promised to rip up the Trans-Pacific Partnership trade agreement, which he later did. The president-elect also said that he would direct the Defense Department and the chairman of the Joint Chiefs of Staff "to develop a comprehensive plan to protect America's vital infrastructure from cyber attacks and all other form of attacks."

No one currently or formerly in government had any idea what this meant. It bypassed the Department of Homeland Security's statutory responsibility to protect critical infrastructure and put America's armed forces in an unusual and likely illegal domestic defense role. A transition senior later told me that somebody just said that "we gotta say cyber and it's gotta sound tough." The team went into what he described as campaign mode and drafted the statement based on their gut. Thankfully the idea was never heard of again. I suspect that the Department of Defense and the Joint Staff made sure that it died a quick and inglorious death.

There was one important and notable exception to the transition chaos: the nomination of Mike Pompeo to be the director of CIA and the process that secured Pompeo's confirmation from the Senate. This was especially impressive since three days after the president-elect deconstructed his transition team, with nothing in place to replace it, he announced that the Kansas Tea Party Republican would be his man at Langley.

One senses the hand of Vice President Elect Pence in this surprisingly early pick. Pence had had confidence in the now departed Ron Burgess (former DIA chief) and had actually urged him to stay on despite the reshuffling of the security team. Now he seemed uncomfortable with Flynn's sudden ascendency, a condition that did not improve with time. Indeed, within three months Flynn would be fired from his national security adviser post for lying to Pence.

Pompeo could act as a counterweight, or at least deny the CIA post to a Flynn acolyte, a choice that would almost certainly have turned the Agency and much of the IC into a war zone. Pence knew Pompeo from their together time in the House, and Pence, who once said that he was "a Christian, a conservative, and a Republican, in that order,"[11] found in Pompeo a kindred spirit who also fit that description.

As a member of the House Intelligence Committee, Pompeo had taken an uncompromising and politically high-profile position condemning Hillary Clinton and the Obama administration for the 2012 terrorist attack in Benghazi. It was a bone he had locked his jaws around and would not let go of. He was also reliably and publicly hawkish on hot-button issues like surveillance, detentions, and interrogations.

But while he was filling the public political role of a tough Tea Party Republican, Pompeo earned high marks from intelligence professionals for his serious study of their work. He visited multiple stations, asked good questions, and stayed late.

Shortly after his nomination had been announced, Pompeo began contacting his predecessors in the CIA post. I met with him privately in his congressional office for over an hour and was impressed with his genuine enthusiasm for the job. He seemed to understand the challenges of the task, but he wasn't intimidated by them either.

Since the director-designate was a West Point graduate and had spent six years on active duty as a cavalry officer, I asked him if his wife intended to be active at the Agency. Although it is never required (at least not in the modern age), military spouses often sacrifice a great deal of their time and energy on behalf of the command. Once he confirmed that she did indeed want to be involved at the Agency, I offered that my wife had also played that role and volunteered that she would be happy to talk with her about it. I was impressed that Susan Pompeo was in my kitchen that afternoon for an extended conversation with my wife, Jeanine.

Pompeo's confirmation team was led by two Bush administration veterans, Ben Powell, former associate White House counsel and general counsel for the director of national intelligence, and Juan Zarate, former deputy national security adviser for combating terrorism and first-ever assistant secretary of the treasury for terrorist financing and financial crimes. Neither man could be viewed as a Trump partisan, but neither had signed any "never Trump" letters; neither had ambitions to serve in the Trump administration. Their team was focused, pragmatic, and largely autonomous within the larger transition kerfuffle. They also intentionally held back, letting the Agency tell its own story to the DCIA-designate, in effect letting the Agency adopt him as their own.

They coached the nominee smoothly through the Senate confirmation process. Even though candidate Trump had talked about bringing back waterboarding and more and Pompeo as a congressman had advocated tougher interrogations, at his hearing he wisely noted current law, said he would abide by it, and promised to come back to Congress for changes if he felt that his current authorities were insufficient to keep America safe. He even committed to disobeying any order to resume waterboarding. This was very different from other aspects of the transition. Simple. Nonideological. Pragmatic. Successful.

The Pompeo confirmation team made some other important contributions. They counseled Pompeo to get out of the car alone when he arrived at Langley. In other words, don't bring congressional staff with you. Depend on the team you are inheriting. I don't think Pompeo needed much coaching on that. He had already developed a healthy respect for the Agency.

Powell, Zarate, and team also insisted that Pompeo pick a deputy from within the organization, almost a given since Pompeo had no experience at Langley. They then recommended a specific Agency veteran, Gina Haspel. Gina was an inspired choice. The Agency exhaled when Pompeo was nominated. When Gina was announced, they exulted. I was certainly heartened when informally approached by the transition team for my views on the choice.

The Agency's bland press release noted Gina's thirty years of service, work as chief of station, and a stint working counterterrorism. Actually, her duties had taken her into some of the most controversial programs of the Agency's recent past. Her choice would provoke some on the outside, which is why the press release was accompanied by enthusiastic endorsements from five Agency veterans (including me), a DNI (Jim Clapper), and a member of Congress (former House intelligence chair Mike Rogers).

On a larger message, Gina's choice was pitch perfect: CIA intended to neither repeat nor repudiate its past.

With Pompeo and Haspel at the top, the Agency seemed in good hands. On this question, at least, many at Langley believed they had dodged a bullet.

Vice President Pence also had a hand in the selection of fellow Indianan and former ambassador to Germany Senator Dan Coats to be the new director of national intelligence. Coats was viewed by the community as a solid choice: sober, experienced, reluctant—the last viewed as an important virtue since there were rumors swirling that the Trump team was enlisting the billionaire head of Cerberus Capital Management (and friend of Steve Bannon), Steve Feinberg, to redo the intelligence community and the office of the DNI. Many in the IC suspected that was an overt attempt to impose more administration loyalty on the community.

I told the *New York Times* at the time that I was having trouble wrapping my head around "the idea of a D.N.I. nominee in the confirmation process while others consider retooling the position."[12] I suspect that Senator Coats thought so, too, and there were press accounts that he pushed back hard against anything like this being done except under his auspices . . . and only once he had been confirmed.[13] He seems to have carried the day. If a Feinberg review was ever the plan, the administration quietly backed away from it.

Coats's nomination came nearly two months after Pompeo's name had been announced, even though the law says that the DNI should nominate the head of CIA to the president. The timing of the nominations and confirmations gave Mike Pompeo a leg up on establishing Oval Office relationships. It also likely reflected the president's and his team's focus on CIA and perhaps a bias on the part of the incoming team toward action (which only CIA was authorized to do) versus intelligence advice (which was the statutory responsibility of the DNI). The timing, the relevant personalities, and the statutory limits on his office promised significant challenges for the incoming DNI.

More broadly in the overall intelligence community transition, retired admiral Paul Becker had come on board the transition team when Flynn descended from New York. Becker was a Flynn associate, but also a well-regarded intelligence veteran in his own right and an island of relative calm in all of this. He worked hard to limit damage and reduce the impression that this was a hostile takeover. His team was the outward face of the transition to the IC, and they dutifully took their formal informational briefings from all the big agencies.

But these were largely "listen and learn sessions," unconnected to the all-powerful New York transition office and whatever decisions were being made there. They weren't really preparation sessions for an incoming team, and each meeting seemed to have its own logic rather than being part of a whole. As one senior intelligence official said to me, "We waited for *the* knock on the door, but it never came." One despondent official described it as "all small ball."

Absent too were the substantive briefings, usually rather extensive deep dives, given to the incoming team on key topics like Iran or Syria or North Korea. There were two dozen such formal sessions in 2008, hardly any in 2016. There wasn't much interest, and there weren't many named incoming officials either.

One exception was the new secretary of defense, Marine general Jim Mattis, always an avid consumer of intelligence, who was described as gracious and appreciative throughout. But overall, the closing of that information gap between the outgoing and incoming team never really happened and so the relationship of trust between the new governors and their future staffs was never built.

The day after the inaugural, the same day as the infamous Trump speech in front of the wall honoring the fallen at CIA, a DNI officer entered the Situation Room to preview what one official described to me as "IC 101." Never really satisfied with their day-to-day linkages with the now departed Obama team, intelligence seniors wanted the new guys to understand the nuts and bolts of the intelligence community and its support for the incoming national security team.

The briefer was greeted by Ezra Cohen-Watnick, the thirty-year-old newly appointed NSC senior director for intelligence programs, whose qualifications for the job appeared to be his devotion to his former boss at the Defense Intelligence Agency, now national security adviser, Mike Flynn. Cohen-Watnick's position had traditionally been filled by a senior CIA officer or, in one case, a future CIA director (George Tenet), so his appointment was an unambiguous slap at the Agency. On this day, Cohen-Watnick did not disappoint, filling the space with what was described to me as a rant against CIA, and promising, among other things, to take covert action authority away from the Agency.

Hostility at a personal level was a bad sign. Things would be harder than they had to be. More important, at the institutional level, the transition was truly opportunity lost. Concerns were high. Confusion persisted. Building teamwork was deferred.

And then there was that deteriorating personal relationship with the new president.

John Helgerson, CIA's inspector general during my time at the Agency, has written the definitive history on presidential transitions. In it, he concludes that although all transitions have their own character, "overall it has proved easier to help the new president become well informed than to establish an enduring relationship" with him. There have always been these two tasks: informing the president-elect and forming a positive relationship with him. This transition was tough on both counts.[14]

Donald Trump had been a successful businessman; he clearly

understood the ground rules that enabled success in real estate. Since it couldn't have *all* been about bluster, bluff, bullying, energy, and ambition, he must have had to rely on some form of "intelligence." But this was a new world for him and no one should have expected Mr. Trump to have a solid base of knowledge about international affairs and security questions. These issues were not really part of his life experience as a real estate developer, and he frankly showed little interest in substance even as he campaigned. When asked in the summer of 2016 if he read much, Trump replied, "I never have. I'm always busy doing a lot."[15]

He was stumped by the meaning of the word "triad" when asked about nuclear forces by Hugh Hewitt during a debate. Earlier, in a phone-in interview with the same conservative talk show host, he admitted to not knowing the names Nasrallah, Zawahiri, or Baghdadi, the leaders of Hezbollah, al-Qaeda, and ISIS, nor knowing the distinctions between their murderous organizations. He later accused Hewitt of throwing a bunch of "Arab" names at him. Unfamiliar with the Quds Force under Iran's ruthless general Qassem Suleimani, he confused it with America's friends in the region, the Kurds.

All of which presented a problem for intelligence. Where do you begin if you want to "well inform" the incoming president? Intelligence briefings can be a bit like teaching or journalism, a journey from what the client knows to what he does not yet know. Where should that journey begin with a President-Elect Trump? Probably a little too basic to launch with, "Let's start with Iraq today, Mr. President-Elect. It's the one on the left." But what should you assume he knows about the Sunni-Shia split and the struggle over succession to the Prophet in 632, which actually is not a trivial element in understanding today's Middle East?

And what constitutes success? Since this isn't a client who favors objective analysis, history, or explanation, the bar may be very different here: can you use the venue to get one level deeper with him, to get him to do better and reflect more than he otherwise would?

Although it's not an intelligence matter, I often wonder what happened after that session with Piers Morgan where the president created in his own mind a global ice pack expanding at record levels. He had been president a year and would have been accompanied by the usual entourage of handlers and advisers. Did anyone approach him afterward to tell him of his mistake? If someone did, how did he respond? Did he welcome it? Did he even care? Did the new data matter?

Director of National Intelligence Coats suggested some broad success in this regard when he said at the 2017 Aspen Security Conference that the president has ended some sessions with, "I got it. It's not what I thought. It's not what I heard. But I got it." That is essentially the challenge, since intelligence is less about predicting than it is about understanding, about providing the context within which wise policy can be made. As one PDB veteran told me about President Trump, "How do you connect for him things that he does not connect himself?" And that comes less out of any personal ignorance about a particular topic (although that *is* important) and more from the personality of the first client, whom former White House speechwriter Michael Gerson once described as living in the "eternal now," a personal world without history or consequence—the antithesis of the intelligence task of delivering context.[16]

In his PDB sessions, Mr. Trump fit the mold of a populist leader that A. C. Grayling describes as someone who favors

"simple slogans . . . instead of attention span, the immediate instead of the long term, the local and obvious instead of the larger
picture and all . . . in the form of attitudes rather than worked-out
ideas."[17]

Briefing sessions for the president-elect were described to me
as simple, visual, and chaotic: a few sentences from the briefer, a
question, then a tangent with frequent interventions about intelligence, policy, and current press all competing for attention. One
familiar with the sessions told me that a literal transcript would
read like a James Joyce novel: a series of thoughts that appear as
they come to mind.[18]

Early sessions often went long, in one sense a measure of the
president's interest, in another sense a reflection of the difficulty
of staying on topic. It was not unheard of for the president to
tweet during sessions (probably *not* about the intelligence content) or to get unhelpful nods of agreements from some in the
room when he made controversial comments (like "We should
have kept the oil in Iraq!").

A fairly common question that intelligence people ask themselves after an important briefing session is: did they adequately
explain and clearly distinguish what they knew, what they
thought, and what they did not know? To that was now added,
"Do you think he got that?" It's not that we have never asked that
question before, it's just now more routine.

The incoming president was impatient with detail and demonstrably prone to action, so there was the added burden of not creating circumstances where decisions were made before adequate
data was available, before complete context had been discovered
and presented.

That can be challenging. There were reports that National

Security Adviser H. R. McMaster irritated the president because he lectured Trump and didn't allow him to ask questions.[19] But how far can you tailor a message before you can be fairly charged with "leading the witness"? Clearly you always have to "know" your client, but how much should you have to cater to a unique personality? At what point does packaging, simplifying, or shortening become self-defeating? Or just dishonest?

Then there was the larger question of whether objective reality, even well presented, was decisive. The veteran PDB briefer cited above agreed with my suggestion that the president-elect has a verbal tic—phrases like "people are telling me," "people are saying," "many people are saying"—that allows whatever statement that follows to function as if it were therefore true for him.

Later, during the administration, CBS News' John Dickerson was interviewing the president and pressing him about his charge that Barack Obama had wiretapped Trump Tower in New York. He asked him if he stood by the charge.

"I don't stand by anything," Trump replied. "I just—you can take it the way you want. I think our side's been proven very strongly. And everybody's talking about it."[20]

We saw the same thing in an interview with ABC News about alleged voter fraud. Anchor David Muir asked the president, "Do you think that talking about millions of illegal votes is dangerous to this country, without presenting the evidence?"

"No, not at all, because many people feel the same way that I do. . . . Millions of people agree with me when I say that."[21]

Many people feel the same way I do. Everybody's talking about it. QED. Thus it has been demonstrated. You have your proof. Whether or not it actually happened, it is still demonstrably true.

The veteran briefer ruminated with me over whether or not

the president made a distinction in his own mind between true and untrue. He raised the controversial speech the president had given in the summer of 2017 to a Boy Scout jamboree in Virginia. The speech was overly political for an audience like the Boy Scouts and occasionally tasteless to boot.

In the face of some pretty sharp criticism, the president said that Scout leadership had called him later to say that it was "the greatest speech that was ever made to them."[22] Of course, no such call ever occurred. The former briefer then asked me if I thought that the president knew that, if I thought that his mind actually made the distinction between the past that actually happened and the past that he needed to claim at that moment. His point was that you could sometimes convince a liar that he was wrong. But what do you do with someone who does not distinguish between truth and untruth? We have had obstinate first customers in the past. We have had argumentative customers. He cited President Nixon as someone who disparaged the Agency's views, and then added that analysts often welcomed such challenges. But we never had a first customer for whom ground truth really didn't matter or who simply might not embrace the concept that there *is* objective truth.

One junior observer was more direct: she said they were going to have to rechisel that quote from Saint John in the Agency lobby: *And ye shall know the alternative facts, and they shall make you free.*

It will take an insider's true memoir for us to learn the actual effect that intelligence had on the president-elect. He quickly discarded his brief foray into abandoning the one-China policy that has dominated American diplomacy since Nixon, for example, but it's unclear that intelligence had any role in that recanting. It's also unclear that he even understood the policy he had challenged or that he had actually challenged it.

If intelligence raised the downsides of cutting loose from the Trans-Pacific Partnership—a strategic arrangement masquerading as a trade deal—it certainly didn't stick. The United States withdrew from the treaty four days into the administration, in my eyes one of the most destructive steps taken by the administration so far. It was also the most stunning example of a red-meat, emotional campaign promise being enacted without considering the broader context and seemingly ignorant of or indifferent to the implications of that step, not just for American prosperity, but also for American security. During the campaign, it appears that Mr. Trump actually believed that TPP enabled China, rather than isolating it: "It's a deal that was designed for China to come in, as they always do, through the back door and totally take advantage of everyone."[23] There is no record that intelligence or any other part of the government, for that matter, was consulted before this dramatic decision was made.

There was also a lot of tough talk during the transition by the president-elect that we were now going to settle things in the Middle East by defeating ISIS quickly and ruthlessly. One wonders if any analyst ever tried to respond with, "Yes sir, and we'll do that, but you need to know that we believe strongly that you can't kill your way out of this mess," or was he or she too cowed, intimidated, or polite to say so?

So I have my doubts about how "well informed" the president-elect was by inauguration day.

There is no doubt, however, about where the intelligence

community stood on the second task that Helgerson had laid out: establishing "an enduring relationship" with him. That one was in the toilet.

Director of National Intelligence Jim Clapper and Secretary of Homeland Security Jeh Johnson had announced in early October that Russia was interfering in the U.S. election, and doing so under the direction of the senior leadership of the Russian Federation. FBI director Jim Comey had been scheduled to be there for the release of the report, but opted out because of his ongoing investigation. He feared the optic.

Clapper's and Johnson's short announcement was a bombshell.

For thirty minutes.

Then the *Washington Post* published a video of Trump speaking in explicit and vulgar terms about groping and kissing women, bragging about what sounded like sexual assault.

Thirty minutes after that, WikiLeaks seemed to toss a lifeline to the Trump campaign by dumping emails hacked from Clinton campaign chairman John Podesta. Eventually, twenty thousand pages of emails were dribbled out, backfooting the Clinton campaign on a variety of issues through election day. Trump actually referenced WikiLeaks 164 times during the last month of the election.

With two major scandals already burying what they viewed as a major intelligence discovery, Clapper and Johnson went back to the relative obscurity of the intelligence community where President Obama had directed that a detailed ICA (Intelligence

Community Assessment) be prepared on the Russian interference. The rationale here was simple: they wanted a single agreed-upon document for the next administration and Congress to refer to. The assumption was that it would be a Clinton administration, so the work took on added urgency (and drama) with Donald Trump's election victory.

It is hard to overestimate the importance of DNI Jim Clapper to this effort. To be sure, CIA director John Brennan had become equally alarmed in the summer when it became clear that this was *not* like previous Russian efforts. But it was Clapper as the head of the community who made things happen. One senior told me that they would not have gotten the Russian report out without the director of national intelligence marshaling resources and making sure that everyone had full access to arguments, sources, and methods.

And *everyone* in this context means the Federal Bureau of Investigation (counterintelligence), the Central Intelligence Agency (human intelligence and analysis), the National Security Agency (intercepted communications), and the DNI (overall leadership).

Later President Trump would downplay the report, saying, "Let me just start off by saying I heard it was 17 agencies, I said, 'Boy, that's a lot.' Do we even have that many intelligence agencies, right? Let's check it. And we did some very heavy research. It turned out to be three or four—it wasn't 17."[24]

There is so much misleading in that verbal smokescreen. The report bore the title "ICA—Intelligence Community Assessment." It was prepared by the three relevant agencies listed above, but it represented the community's view (all seventeen agencies), and if the Drug Enforcement Agency or the intelligence arm at the

Department of Energy or anyone else had an objection or had something to contribute, they would have been included in the authorship as well.

In early December the *Washington Post* began reporting that the draft ICA was concluding that the Russians had intervened in the election to try to help Trump win the presidency, not "just" to undermine Americans' confidence in their electoral systems.

Trump predictably responded via Twitter and (equally predictably) tried to delegitimize the report's authors rather than argue its content: "These are the same people that said Saddam Hussein had weapons of mass destruction. The election ended a long time ago in one of the biggest Electoral College victories in history. It's now time to move on and 'Make America Great Again.'"[25]

Two days later on *Fox News Sunday*, the president-elect continued, "They have no idea if it's Russia or China or somebody. It could be somebody sitting in a bed someplace. I mean, they have no idea."

This would all have to be hammered out at a meeting with the president-elect and his team that was scheduled for Friday, January 6, at Trump Tower. Even that became Twitter fuel; the president-elect tweeted on Tuesday of that week, "The 'Intelligence' briefing on so-called 'Russian hacking' was delayed until Friday, perhaps more time needed to build a case. Very strange!"

Since the briefing had always been scheduled for Friday, this sounded a little like pregame taunting to get into the head of an *opponent*. Which is not how the intelligence leadership viewed itself.

The president-elect was back at it the next day with some more digital trash talk, this time preemptively undercutting what he was likely to hear: "Julian Assange said 'a 14 year old could have hacked Podesta'—why was DNC so careless? Also said Russians did not give him the info!"

To underscore the obvious: this is not normal. American intelligence had never before seen such behavior in an important client, and certainly never in a president. January 6 was going to be a big day.

That day began for the intelligence leadership (minus Comey, who was already in New York) with a briefing in Washington to the congressional Gang of Eight: the leadership of the two intelligence committees and the senior members of both chambers. The members were told that the intelligence community had high confidence that the Russians, operating under the direction of Vladimir Putin, had hacked several email accounts in the United States, including those of the Democratic National Committee, and had weaponized that information by pushing it back through platforms like DCLeaks and WikiLeaks into the American information space to sow confusion here. The effort was aided by overt Russian information platforms like RT and Sputnik as well as by a covert army of trolls who treated the data in such a way as to make it appear trending to the algorithms of a variety of search engines. (We later learned that the Russians had a sophisticated use of social media sites like Facebook and Twitter in their repertoire, too.)

This covert influence campaign appeared to be designed, at first, simply to mess with our heads, but as time went on and more information became available, it became clear that Putin wanted to punish Hillary Clinton, whom he hated, and weaken the legitimacy of what he expected ultimately to be her presidency. Eventually, however, there was more and more evidence that the Russian campaign was working to push votes in the direction of Donald Trump.

The report made no effort to judge the effect the Russian effort had on the election and specifically said that it had found no evidence of vote tampering—which is a far cry from the later claim by some Trump supporters and some members of his administration that the IC had said that the Russians did not affect the election.

The congressional Democrats in the room for the briefing seemed happy enough with the presentation. Senate intelligence chair Richard Burr asked some good questions. Speaker of the House Paul Ryan was largely quiet, but attentive. House intelligence chair Devin Nunes and Senate majority leader Mitch McConnell seemed less pleased, but said nothing.

The intelligence team then headed for Trump Tower via the airport at Newark, where they were met by a large police escort that guaranteed they would not arrive in Manhattan unobserved. They admit that they were fairly tense as they had no idea how the president-elect would respond to their message.

At Trump Tower, Jim Comey (FBI), Jim Clapper (DNI), Mike Rogers (NSA), and John Brennan (CIA) filed in and took their seats at a small conference table. Also in the room back-benching from the president-elect's team were Mike Flynn and K. T. McFarland (national security adviser and deputy), Tom Bossert (homeland security adviser), Sean Spicer (communications), Reince Priebus (chief of staff), Mike Pompeo (CIA director designate), and Vice President Elect Pence.

For about an hour the intelligence officials laid out their case. The briefing went well. The president was affable and sociable. He and his team were in a listening mood. The intel folks had to beat back only one tangent, a short discussion about how the Republican National Committee *had* protected its data. Given all the buildup, the actual session felt a little anticlimactic.

The intelligence directors also explained a bit of why they were so confident in their conclusions, each of them relying on their own collection discipline to make the case. The identity of the hackers, the tools employed, the infrastructure used, and the targets selected all pointed to Moscow. To that was added technical and human intelligence that went "behind the screen" (so to speak) to give additional evidence for the high-confidence findings. And then there was their deep knowledge of how things worked in Russia, knowing the kinds of things that can only happen with Putin's approval, for example.

There were some limits on how detailed the sourcing could go during the briefing. This was actually a fairly large group and the Russians were already in max counterintelligence mode, launching their CI apparatus in an effort to discover how we knew so much.

The president-elect disparaged HUMINT a bit, saying it relied on what he called "sellouts," but overall there was no real pushback.

The IC script then called for Jim Comey, the FBI director, to stay behind for one more item. Priebus asked the president-elect if he wanted anyone else to stay, but Trump declined.

Comey was there to brief Trump on the infamous "Steele dossier," a compendium of opposition research that Chris Steele, a former British MI6 case officer, had compiled on Trump's alleged ties with Russia. There were no precedents to guide the leadership on this; it was just one more "off the chart" episode in the 2016 transition. Jim Clapper later said that he believed it rightly fell under the rubric of a "responsibility to warn," and they felt that the best, low-key way to share this with the president-elect was a Comey stay-behind.

I did not know Steele, but he was described to me as a competent and honest officer. Still, I was cautioned to be careful and not to automatically overrate him or his report. I was also reminded that writing a commercial intelligence document for a commercial client was different from intelligence service reporting. The client was usually less knowledgeable, less aware of the importance of vetting sources, and perhaps more needful of a "useful" document. When I finally read Steele's report it did have the feel of a genuine intelligence product; the language and syntax and pace were all very familiar. "This is actually how we write this stuff," I reflected. The dossier runs the gamut from the obviously true (Russia was trying to influence the American political process), to the possibly true (suspicious contacts between members of team Trump and team Putin), to the hard-to-believe-it's-true (lurid sexual encounters in a Moscow hotel).

But far from being definitive, it was most useful as an indicator of things that needed to be further investigated. If this had actually been an American intelligence product, it would have been boldly labeled: THIS IS RAW, UNEVALUATED INFORMATION. THIS IS NOT A FINISHED INTELLIGENCE PRODUCT. We then would have gone through it line by line asking, for each assertion: Who is the source? Would the source logically have had access to this kind of information? Has this source reported reliably in the past? Do we have other information that would tend to confirm or deny this particular tidbit?

Comey, of course, didn't address any of that. The Steele dossier had not been used for the Intelligence Community Assessment on Russian interference. The community had no views on its findings. The community just wanted the president-elect to know that it was out there.

The Trump team's statement later that day avoided any comment on the Steele dossier, of course. The statement actually began with dutiful praise for the intelligence community, then cataloged the ongoing and multifaceted cyber threat to the nation (which was true enough, but was not the focus of the briefing), and then claimed—without any reference to the sustained Russian efforts—that "there was absolutely no effect on the outcome of the election." That last part . . . that was actually so misleading and so untethered to the briefing that Trump had just received that it warranted a description I learned in the third grade. That was a lie. Without publicly challenging the intelligence community findings, team Trump attempted to mischaracterize and then bury them.

The president has never really accepted them. Most egregiously, in a foreign country, standing next to a foreign leader, he said in midsummer 2017, "I think it could very well have been Russia but I think it could very well have been other countries, and I won't be specific. But I think a lot of people interfere."[26] He later tweeted in September 2017 that the "Russian hoax continues."[27]

So the president never accepted the findings of his intelligence community that January afternoon. Even in the face of arguments that Russian actions are not just past but present, he remains in a different place, neither inspiring nor directing his government to decisive action. There has rarely been as much distance between an urgent intelligence community judgment and a government's response.

The Steele dossier, by the way, didn't stay secret very long.

When the Internet media site BuzzFeed published the dossier in its entirety four days after the Trump Tower meeting, the president-elect immediately tweeted, "Intelligence agencies should never have allowed this fake news to 'leak' into the public. One last shot at me. Are we living in Nazi Germany?"[28]

Actually, the dossier was more or less common knowledge in D.C. circles throughout the summer and fall of 2016. I had multiple newsmen buy me breakfast in the hope I might know something about the mysterious report. (I didn't.) It is a matter of public record that Senator John McCain had the dossier, which he forwarded to the FBI in early December 2016.[29]

So Trump was wrong to implicate the intelligence community in this one, and everyone in the IC, especially Jim Clapper, was incensed at the Nazi reference. As Clapper put it to me, the Nazi tweet made him see red, and so he put a call in to Trump. Jim was surprised that he took it. Jim told me that he tried to appeal to Trump's higher instincts, reminding the president-elect that he was inheriting a national treasure that intended to support and enlighten him. You should treat it accordingly, Jim advised.

Mr. Trump listened attentively and then asked the director of national intelligence to publicly rebut the Steele dossier. Clapper simply said that was not his job and thanked the president-elect for his time.

Donald Trump would be president in about a week, and wise heads in the transition office like Ben Powell (who had honchoed Pompeo's confirmation) urged him to go to CIA, meet the workforce, and reboot his relationship with the IC.

So the president went to Langley the day after the inauguration.

And conducted the worst presidential visit to an intelligence agency in the history of the American Republic.

The original concept had been that this would be a swearing-in event for the new CIA director, Mike Pompeo, but the Senate had not yet acted to confirm him. Still, the president had a productive meeting with senior Agency leadership and then went to the concourse armed with talking points designed to calm the waters between him and the intelligence community.

That never happened. Perhaps sensing the cameras that were broadcasting the event live, the president shifted into full political riff mode. In a disjointed, nearly stream-of-consciousness speech in front of the wall of 117 stars honoring the Agency's fallen, the president never quite managed to recognize their sacrifice while finding time to resurrect his bromide about keeping Iraq's oil and dragging Director-Designate Pompeo into the discussion: "But if you think about it, Mike, if we kept the oil you probably wouldn't have ISIS . . ."

He also claimed that "almost everybody in this room voted for me," that he had caught the media in a beauty of a lie about inaugural crowd size, and that "they're going to pay a big price," and then announced that he had been on the cover of *Time* magazine more than anyone, even Tom Brady.

The president also announced that the media "are among the most dishonest human beings on earth. And they sort of made it sound like I had a feud with the intelligence community. And I just want to let you know, the reason you're the number one stop is exactly the opposite—exactly."

That to an institution of fact-based analysts.

To be fair, there was some whooping and hollering in the CIA concourse as the president spoke. CIA reflects America, and no doubt there were Trump voters in the Agency. And this was a self-selected crowd. An Agency-all email had gone out the day before asking people to come in on a Saturday to be part of the event.

But CIA seniors sat stone-faced in the front row. At the Farm, the Agency's clandestine training site that had the ceremony piped in via direct video link, many officers simply walked out. It's hard to imagine a deeper hole from which to begin an administration.

FIVE

THE FIRST HUNDRED DAYS

(MORE OR LESS)

A few weeks after the inauguration I was sitting in a Miami ballroom waiting to appear on a panel with General Ray Odierno, former Army chief of staff. Ray and I were going to talk about security, but the panel in front of us on the agenda was composed of journalists—two from a recently launched news website and the other a U.S.-based correspondent from Europe—so I came down to the ballroom early to sit in and hear the latest Trump buzz from the press.

At one point the foreign correspondent paraphrased Salena Zito's summary of the campaign, about Trump supporters taking him seriously but not literally, and then added, "But he seems to be governing *literally*."

In that back room in Pittsburgh, a friend of mine had asked the group how many actually believed that President Trump was going to build a physical wall along the Mexican border and that Mexico was going to pay for it. No hands went up. I later heard in another, similar conversation with some military officers that for Trump supporters it was only important that what he said "rhymed" with a larger truth they cared about—in this case, apparently, tighter border security.

It was that "literally" and "seriously" issue again.

Except that I, at least, feared that Donald Trump sometimes meant what he said. Literally.

So, apparently, did a bunch of Mexicans. More Mexicans now view the United States unfavorably than at any time in the past fifteen years. Nearly two-thirds (65 percent) express a negative opinion of the United States, more than double the number of two years ago (29 percent).[1]

And of course, we have also been treated to former Mexican president Vicente Fox, actually a friend of America, saying in English on the American cable channel Fusion, "I'm not going to pay for that fucking wall. He should pay for it. He's got the money."

Eliot Cohen reminds that much of "diplomacy is about words, and many of Trump's words are profoundly toxic."[2]

But by the time of that Miami conference, we were also seeing the consequences of administration steps that went beyond words. Trump had already ripped up the Trans-Pacific Partnership, signed an executive order banning immigration to America from seven Muslim-majority countries, and signed another order directing the Department of Homeland Security to construct a wall along the southwestern border.

It was always hard during the campaign to piece together what a President Trump would actually *do*. There had been so many tweets, so many offhand remarks, so many contradictory statements that it was hard to really predict presidential behavior.

Some campaign advisers must have been concerned about

that, because the candidate made an attempt to lay out a somewhat more coherent foreign vision in two speeches, one at the
Madison Hotel in downtown Washington in April at the height of
the campaign, and a second in Youngstown, Ohio, a few weeks
after the Republican convention. The speech in Washington was
more subdued than Trump's usual rally rhetoric, although he did
find plenty of time to condemn the Obama/Clinton team for Benghazi, the failed Syrian red line, a "disastrous deal with Iran," the
"total disaster" of NAFTA, "senseless immigration policies," and
a "reckless, rudderless and aimless foreign policy" that created
friends who cannot depend on us and adversaries who no longer
respected us.[3] The candidate firmly trashed "the false song of
globalism," praised the nation-state as "the true foundation for
happiness," and rejected "international unions that tie us up and
bring America down."

The overall tone was so "America First," so concerned with
American overextension, and so critical of freeloading allies that
the Brookings Institution's Thomas Wright suggested that it pres-
aged the end of America's alliances in Europe and Asia.[4] Mr.
Trump's remarks were far more critical of China than of Russia,
but he struck a more threatening tone toward American companies that moved jobs out of the United States than he did toward
either Moscow or Beijing.

The commentariat was pretty critical after the speech: "inco-
herent," "disconnected," "confused," and "muddled" were some of
the words used in the reviews. It may have been personal since
Trump had threatened in his talk, "We have to look to new people because many of the old people frankly don't know what
they're doing, even though they may look awfully good writing in
the *New York Times* or being watched on television."

Mr. Trump was also contemptuous of the "dangerous idea that we could make Western democracies out of countries that had no experience or interests in becoming a western democracy" and pledged as his first foreign policy goal to "work with any nation in the region that is threatened by the rise of radical Islam."

The later Youngstown speech was totally focused on just that: defeating radical Islam. It was another important speech, even if you had to slog your way once again through Mr. Trump's imputing near criminal conduct to the Obama/Clinton team as well as having to navigate a series of self-justifying pronouncements that he (Mr. Trump) had been right all along about so many things.[5]

Political campaigns cry out for simplification and differentiation. Make it clear. Make it different. Repeat. So Mr. Trump's differentiation was stark: his predecessors were weak, stupid, and corrupt. He was strong and smart. And he was straightforward. No babble about nation building. We're going to solve ISIS quickly by being very, very tough. And then we're coming home. Case closed.

I tried to read through and sometimes between Trump's lines. It was clear that at least for *candidate* Trump, defeating ISIS and halting the spread of radical Islam was the core foreign policy objective of the United States. It was a goal so important that he promised to subordinate other policy goals to it. He actually said—without condition—that any country that shared that goal would be our ally. Trump specifically mentioned Jordan and Israel, fairly noncontroversial entries for such an enterprise.

He also listed President Abdel Fattah el-Sisi of Egypt, who had given a powerful speech to the faculty of the prestigious Al-Azhar University in Cairo two years earlier in which he told Islamic scholars essentially that they had better get their act together and delegitimize the crazies of ISIS.

But Sisi had cracked down on civil society (especially pro-democracy groups, including American-based NGOs) even harder than his predecessors, and there was already a good case that it was Hosni Mubarak's repression that drove *his* political opposition toward the relative safe haven of the mosque and eventually into the hands of the Muslim Brotherhood. How free a hand would Mr. Trump offer Mr. Sisi in return for support?

Later, in office, President Trump would downplay human rights concerns in Egypt[6] and do much the same with Turkey. The president made a remarkable congratulatory phone call to Turkish president Recep Tayyip Erdoğan after Erdoğan's heavy hand in a referendum to expand his authority as president may well have ended Turkey's ninety-year experiment with secular democracy, a heavy strategic price to pay for continued access to ten thousand feet of runway at Incirlik Air Base from where anti-ISIS raids are being conducted.

In the Youngstown speech Mr. Trump also returned to the point that "we could find common ground with Russia in the fight against ISIS." That was even more complicated than Egypt. How much of Russia's behavior in Crimea—in eastern Ukraine, in its cyber theft and doxing to affect the American election, in its dangerous buzzing of American aircraft and ships—was he willing to ignore or downplay to align Russia as an ally in his core struggle against radical Islam?

And would it even work? Russia certainly had a terrorist problem, and Moscow was certainly bombing in Syria, but it had *not really been bombing ISIS*. Russian strikes were carefully coordinated with the fire and movement of Assad's forces to expand

Syrian government control against the rebel opposition, including factions armed and supported by the United States. Russia's goals in Syria were more about regime survival, Russian spheres of influence, and East-West competition than they were about jihadists.

Aligning with Moscow would also put us somewhat in league with *their* allies in Syria, like Iran's militias and Revolutionary Guard forces, and that alignment would also include Iran's proxies, the Shia terrorist group Hezbollah, even though Mr. Trump had pointedly included both Tehran and Hezbollah in his catalog of radical Islamists.

Although Mr. Trump did not mention it, if you followed his logic, we should have also left some space on our bench for Bashar al-Assad. His government, though brutal, was unmistakably secular before the revolution and he had since labeled all of his opposition as terrorists. And to be fair, the longer the war went on, the more fundamentalist his opposition had actually become. If opposing radical Islam was the core criteria, could Assad be our friend?

Maybe, apparently. Later, in an October presidential debate with Hillary Clinton, Trump said, "I don't like Assad at all, but Assad is killing ISIS. Russia is killing ISIS and Iran is killing ISIS." It sounded like grounds for an alliance or at least an arrangement.

But it was Assad who triggered all of this in the first place, suppressing the legitimate democratic opposition so violently that it was driven into the hands of waiting jihadists. And it was Russia and Iran that were sustaining Assad.

Which brought me back to Mr. Trump's simple first premise: we are indifferent to what nations otherwise do as long as they are willing to help us kill jihadists. Which, perversely, may actually be a pretty good formula for ensuring that we are going to have to kill jihadists for a very long time.

In my internationalist mind, the speeches raised more questions than they answered, and frankly that was true of the whole campaign. Still, I worked to map out what I thought comprised the Trump strategy (or maybe the Trump emphasis or at least the Trump attitude). I feared that I was no more than a fortune-teller, just reading the bones that the candidate had strewn about the campaign, but the following was my take on where the centerline would be shifting in American foreign and security policy under a President Trump:

Immigration will be treated more as a threat to American well-being than as a strategic advantage. We have had nativist, anti-immigrant periods in our past, so this would not be unprecedented; the "Know-Nothing" party gained significant prominence and prowled the streets of America throughout the 1850s. Today extreme vetting, beautiful walls, and deportation forces would add up to a similarly less welcoming country, alienate adherents of one of the world's great monotheisms, slow the entry of people who keep our population youthful and entrepreneurial, and reduce the number of foreign students in the country—many of whom in the past have mastered English and been imbued with American values before later becoming prime minister or such back home.

Foreign military engagements will be reluctant and short, but more violent. Despite a great deal of campaign talk about strengthening the military, the president-elect's critiques of Iraq, Afghanistan, and nation building anywhere almost guaranteed that there would be no long-term commitments. In this he was a contrast with his predecessor, who was enamored of low-key military and covert actions but comfortable with extending these actions over long periods (think drones and special forces). Trump intended to "bomb the shit out of them" and then leave. Bigger effort. Shorter time.

Alliances will be seen more as transactional than as strategic relationships. Actually, the candidate spoke of American allies and alliances more as burdens than as strategic advantages. Amazingly, he complained about arming other militaries rather than our own, as if this was some sort of national weakness or madness. In reality, it was enabling friends to do things that young Americans would otherwise have to do were the allies not so well prepared. He also consistently tied America living up to its treaty commitments to its allies being "fully paid up." I doubt that burden-sharing talks would exactly mirror a Staten Island protection racket ("It'd be a shame if something happened to your pretty little country"), but we were likely to alienate our friends and embolden our enemies. (By the way, countries like Japan, Korea, and Germany contribute billions each year to the upkeep of U.S. forces stationed there, and the United States could ill afford to keep those forces if they were to be returned home.)

Despite being the global champion of free trade for three-quarters of a century, the United States will turn more protectionist. Trying to opt out of rather than manage globalization might seem an odd position for the world's most integrated, most powerful, and still most envied economy. But the candidate's language condemning NAFTA as one of the worst deals ever made, promising to tear up the Trans-Pacific Partnership, and claiming that we were weak negotiators and did not know how to win anymore—all that promised a transactional trade relationship with the world, with each deal viewed in narrow, zero-sum terms.

The administration will reset relationships with the near peer and the pretender. In short, China down, Russia up. China down largely for alleged currency manipulation and product dumping rather than for its sandcastles and aggressive territorial claims in the South China Sea or its human rights record. Russia up, it would seem, with a strange affinity for the leadership strength and style of Vladimir Putin, but without demands for him to amend his conduct in Ukraine, Syria, cyberspace, or elsewhere. "Wouldn't it be great to be friends with Russia?" was the meme, with nil said about changing Putin's behavior.

The fight against terrorism will fundamentally be about more combat power. Most in the American security community would actually welcome this, as they viewed the Obama administration as indecisive and when action finally was taken it was often overregulated and underresourced. The community would also add, however, that you really can't kill your way to a solution here.

Let me go out on a limb and suggest that none of these lines of action, none of these shifts in the centerline of American policy, were anchored on the judgments of the American intelligence community. In fact, in many cases there would be strong intelligence-based arguments to moderate if not reverse these policies.

And, as discussed in the last chapter, the shifts in emphasis were not the product of a thoughtful, deliberative policy process conducted by a wide-ranging transition team. They were, more or less, the attitudes and habits of thought picked up throughout his life as a Manhattan businessman who occasionally watched the

Sunday morning talk shows, but who freely confessed that he did not read very much.

Middle East expert Robin Wright wrote a caustic article about six months into the administration, asking rhetorically in her title, "Why Is Donald Trump Still So Horribly Witless About the World?" and then cataloging a series of foreign policy gaffes like congratulating the prime minister of Lebanon for fighting Hezbollah, which as a political party was part of the Lebanese government with cabinet posts and seats in its parliament. Wright quotes John McLaughlin, the former CIA acting director, as characterizing Trump coming in "as the least prepared President we've had on foreign policy."[7]

Moreover, whatever the new president knew or didn't know, his preexisting instincts and attitudes were surprisingly at variance with the thoughts and the life experience of the powerful team that he selected to lead the Departments of State, Defense, and Homeland Security.

To cite but one example, in his confirmation hearings for secretary of defense, Marine general Jim Mattis strongly backed the president-elect's call for more military spending, but also gave a full-throated endorsement of American alliances, saying that "nations with strong allies thrive." He was also markedly pessimistic about improved relations with the Russian Federation and said that even if the Iranian nuclear deal had its flaws, a nation's word (i.e., the United States agreeing to the deal) had to mean something in international affairs.[8]

Mattis had settled in as a visiting fellow at the Hoover Institution at Stanford after his retirement from the Marine Corps. Three months before election day, Hoover published an essay ("Restoring Our National Security") that Mattis had penned along with retired admiral Jim Ellis (former commander of STRAT-COM) and Kori Schake (a Stanford fellow and veteran of the Departments of State and Defense and the George W. Bush NSC) as part of the institution's *Blueprint for America.*

The piece ranked the priority challenges the United States would confront: first, Russian belligerence; then, Chinese activities in the South China Sea; followed by ISIS and Iranian aggressiveness; and finally drug-gang activity south of our border.[9]

If Donald Trump had ever been cornered and forced to catalog his "dangers to America" list, I am convinced its order would have been precisely the opposite of the one signed off on by his incoming secretary of defense. Trump had made southern border security issue number one throughout the campaign, followed closely by his much-discussed commitment to defeating ISIS. From time to time he would also complain about China, more often for commercial practices than island building in the South China Sea. But there was nary a mention during the campaign of threats from Russia. Indeed, the incoming president had often appeared to be a Putin apologist, while his incoming SECDEF (and I should add the chairman of the Joint Chiefs that he would inherit) listed the Russians as job one.

Mattis's and Trump's threat matrices were mirror images of one another. No wonder we and others around the world were confused and anxious.

Just when I thought it couldn't get worse, it did.

The Trump administration committed, in my eyes and in the eyes of many intelligence community veterans, a variety of unforced errors in its first six weeks.

There was the president insulting the prime minister of our best intelligence partner in the Pacific and perhaps in the world (Australia) in what was supposed to have been a get-acquainted phone call. "I have had it. I have been making these calls all day, and this is the most unpleasant call all day," was Trump's response to PM Malcolm Turnbull's reminder that the United States had previously agreed to take 1,250 refugees who were then in Australia.[10]

And then there was the president's tweeting habit, which raised lots of issues, but one with specific intelligence implications.

All intelligence services create leadership profiles—biographical sketches on personality, preferences, habits, quirks, and the like. Usually public records form the base of these profiles and then tidbits from collection and personal encounters are added. They're quite useful to gauge how a leader will react, or to develop a game plan to guide encounters with him or her.

Nada Bakos, a highly regarded career analyst, commented on the president's tweets in June. She said that she used to track terrorists and other enemies at CIA, but "never had such a rich source of raw intelligence about a world leader, and we certainly never had the opportunity that our adversaries (and our allies) have now—to get a real-time glimpse of a major world leader's preoccupations, personality quirks and habits of mind."[11]

The president's twitter tsunami must have been a gold mine for foreign services. Pressable buttons, loyalties, exposed nerves, responses to pressure, sleep habits, even his unfiltered id were pretty much on full display. And surely the contents of some tweets would tempt some foreign services to conclude that the president bluffs and bends the truth to meet the needs of the moment. You can almost anticipate the language in the report: "Mr. Prime Minister, you need to know that President Trump appears to be what the Americans call a bullshitter." Good stuff for adversaries to know in upcoming sessions with POTUS and hardly designed to maximize the president's leverage.

The tweets also threatened to inject a certain amount of uncertainty and danger into the proceedings. If a foreign leader has reason to believe that the president doesn't mean what he says, that leader may choose to ignore it, and if he is right, he wins the hand, so to speak. If he is wrong, though, he could trigger American responses that both he and we would have preferred to avoid. Neither are good outcomes. Little wonder that the president's best advisers wanted him to keep his thumbs off the smartphone.

Then there was the administration's ill-conceived, poorly implemented, and ill-explained executive order that looked to the world and to much of America like a Muslim ban. It actually would have been hard to explain the executive order since it was not the product of intelligence and security professionals recommending change, but rather policy, political, and ideological personalities close to the president fulfilling a campaign promise to deal with a threat that they had overhyped. One intelligence senior told me that when the ban was announced internally, everyone was simply told to get on board.

"Donald J. Trump is calling for a total and complete shutdown of Muslims entering the United States until our country's representatives can figure out what is going on," he said in December 2015.[12] The threat from Muslim immigrants and the ineffectiveness of American vetting was a staple for the rest of the campaign. It was a powerful and recurring note in the campaign chorus of America as a grim and failing country.

The January 27 executive order suspended immigration into the United States from seven Muslim-majority countries for 90 days, banned all refugees for 120 days, and Syrian refugees indefinitely. Since it was created and imposed by the incoming political team and not developed by those who would implement it, chaos erupted at points of entry here and points of departure abroad. Legions of lawyers descended on American airports to assist those caught up in the order's arbitrary (and unclear) provisions.

My wife and I landed at Dulles Airport near Washington at the height of all this and could see the tables set up just outside the international arrivals hall. She walked over to congratulate the volunteers. I hung back, supportive in spirit, but wary of the effect the image of a former CIA chief might create.

I did sign up a few days later to an amicus curiae brief supporting the court challenge to the order. I wasn't alone. Five former directors and acting directors of CIA (myself, John Brennan, Leon Panetta, Michael Morell, and John McLaughlin); former director of national intelligence Jim Clapper; and former head of the National Counterterrorism Center Matt Olsen all eventually joined in. These people represented about two centuries of experience across multiple Republican and Democratic administrations.

Our arguments weren't that this was unjust (which it was), but that it was unfounded, that nothing in objective reality justified such an action. The order had not been based on an assessment of the real threat (no such assessment would have justified it), but on feelings, attitudes, and preferences that had actually been stoked by the campaign: the very definition of post-truth decision making.

And the order was worse than unnecessary. It was dangerous, since its premise implied agreement with the very jihadist forces we were trying to defeat—that there was undying enmity between Islam and the West—and would fuel the recruitment and commitment of those forces.

Within government a thousand foreign service officers used the State Department's formal dissent channel to register their opposition to the ban on similar grounds as well.[13] I also privately heard from intelligence professionals who focused on the operational consequences of this action. They noted that six of the seven countries in the ban (Iran being somewhat an exception) were troubled, fragmented states where human sources were essential to our understanding and defeating threats to America. Paradoxically, they pointed out how the executive order breached faith with those very sources, many of whom they had persuaded and promised to always protect with the full might of our government and our people, sources who had risked much if not all to keep Americans safe.

I understood the case officers' angst. In a sense, I had helped create it, since as CIA director I had reminded them at their graduations that when they recruited a source, they would likely be the only face of America that source would ever see. And that in the act of recruitment they would assume a powerful and permanent moral responsibility for the well-being of the source and his or her loved ones. The case officers believed that they were empowered to offer the full faith and credit of the American nation for that task, and now, they told me, that promise was eroding. The ultimate sanctuary, America, was being denied to their sources and to anyone those sources cared about.

One former station chief put it this way: "How would you look him [a source or a partner] in the eye these days and promise him we'd take care of him and the men who follow him? What do you tell him to tell those men? We won't leave them behind? We'll take care of them no matter what? That our president is shoulder to shoulder with them?"

Some would quibble that this, at least technically, was not really the case. That this was a temporary ban (maybe) and exceptions could be made (possibly). But as the former station chief told me, in the places where intelligence officers operate, rumor, whisper, and conspiratorial chatter rule people's lives. And it doesn't take paranoia to connect the actions of the executive order with the broader hateful anti-Islamic language of the campaign.

The station chief continued that in the Middle East, you are dealing with honor-based cultures. Shooting at someone is one thing (we might still be able to recruit *him*), but dishonoring a man, or his family, or his entire society . . . well, that's a big red line. He reminded me that the fundamental posture of an intelligence service looking for sources was, "We welcome you, you count, you have value. Our society respects you. More than your own." He feared that would no longer be the powerful American message that it once was.

The simple *idea* of America didn't hurt either. The station chief said that one of the fundamentals of his business was selling the dream. The Soviets "had a hard time with that. We had it easy. A lot of intelligence targets—officials, military figures, African revolutionaries, tribal leaders—railed against our policies, our interventions, many things . . . *but they loved America*. It was the idea of the country as a special place. They didn't necessarily want to go there, but it was a place they kept in their minds where they would be welcome." He told me about one Arab source who would linger dangerously long after meetings just to talk about America: "He loved the idea of belonging to America in his own, clandestine way."

The travel ban was stopped by the courts, the amicus comments from security professionals being cited as one of the reasons for its rejection, before a modified version was allowed to proceed. But the effects of even attempting to impose such a ban will not pass quickly. These are not short-term, transactional societies. Insults rarely just fade away. Honor patiently waits to be satisfied.

In the meantime CIA will be left with more of the weak and the merely avaricious, agents who will cut a deal just for the money, the worst kind of sources—and ISIS and al-Qaeda will (with more justification than they once had) claim that America and Islam are inevitable enemies. And all of this, I firmly believe, is based on a false, post-truth premise.

The intelligence community got another jolt of a post-truth world in the early morning hours of March 4 when without warning the president tweeted, "Terrible! Just found out that Obama had my 'wires tapped' in Trump Tower just before the victory. Nothing found. This is McCarthyism!" He followed that up a few minutes later with, "How low has President Obama gone to tapp [*sic*] my phones during the very sacred election process. This is Nixon/Watergate. Bad (or sick) guy!"

Note: the president has offered no evidence (then or since) of his spectacular charges.

A few days after the tweets I was on Stephen Colbert's late night show pushing the paperback rollout of my book. The comedian asked me about the tweets and I suggested that Mr. Trump had awakened in Mar-a-Lago that Saturday morning and had simply forgotten that he was president. Otherwise, he would have reached for the landline rather than his smartphone and directed that his FBI and NSA directors (the organizations in the government that actually tap phones) join him for lunch to answer some questions that had occurred to him. The case would have been closed before the president started the back nine.

Of course, that didn't happen, because this wasn't about closing the case.

On ABC's *This Week* the day after the original tweets, White House deputy press secretary Sarah Huckabee Sanders proliferated the conspiracy theory: "Everybody acts like President Trump is the one that came up with this idea. . . . There are multiple news outlets that have reported" that President Obama ordered the wiretapping of Trump.[14]

That wasn't true either, but it didn't stop Sean Spicer from doubling down the next day with "there is no question something happened. The question is, is it surveillance, is it a wiretap, or whatever," and then refusing further comment "until such oversight is continued [*sic*]."[15]

The president joined in the everybody's-talking-about-it meme in mid-March, telling Fox News' Tucker Carlson, "Well, I've been reading about things," before he mischaracterized a January *New York Times* report that actually did *not* in any way say that President Obama had wiretapped him.[16]

Then the next day Spicer picked up an allegation from Fox News' Judge Andrew Napolitano that Obama had actually outsourced the tapping to Britain's GCHQ, a charge so outlandish that even Fox News shot it down the following day.[17]

This story still takes my breath away, even retelling it months later. It is very scary.

And not unfamiliar. In the mid-1980s I lived in Communist Bulgaria as the air attaché at our embassy in Sofia. One of my duties was simply to keep track of the local news, so I would tune in to the tediously repetitive evening broadcasts on state TV and scan the daily newspaper, Работническо дело (*The Workers' Deed*), the mass-circulation organ of the Communist Party.

A fairly common technique for them was to make reference to a story from "Western sources," sources that were pretty hard to track down and if tracked down were often from clearly fringe outlets. Then those stories were given legs by repeating them with great seriousness in state media. Then it was somberly announced that the matter was now in the hands of the appropriate organs of the state.

Of course, Bulgaria didn't have a free press to raise the *bullshit* flag on stuff like this, although occasional Bulgarian citizens would do so for me in chance, informal contacts.

But here in twenty-first-century America we have a free press, and it was pushing pretty hard for evidence—*any* evidence—that *any* of the wiretap accusations were true. That was especially so after FBI director Jim Comey and NSA director Mike Rogers denied the allegations in open congressional session just a few days after Spicer's GCHQ innuendo.

Comey and Rogers were in the witness chair for a remarkable hearing in front of the House Intelligence Committee. The confirmation hearings for Supreme Court nominee Neil Gorsuch began the same day. It should have been hard to push round one of the most important Court nomination in half a century below the fold of the next day's newspapers, but that's exactly what happened, as Comey and Rogers contradicted the president they were serving on his charge that President Obama and/or our British friends had tapped his phone.

At the time, I wrote that this "was what happens when BS runs into the confidence, competence and courage of professionals. I suspect that neither Comey nor Rogers envied an opportunity to contradict the President, and I know, having been there myself, that neither wanted to spend a day on national TV in that setting. But my reading of their body language and tone tells me that both welcomed the opportunity to set the record straight and defend the institutions they lead and represent."[18]

For Rogers's part, there was a remarkable change in the timbre of his voice when he defended GCHQ, his British counterpart, passionately adding to his denial that spying on the president-elect would be "expressly against the construct of the Five Eyes agreement."

The Five Eyes agreement is an intelligence-sharing alliance between the United States, the United Kingdom, Canada, Australia, and New Zealand. And in case you didn't know, the National Security Agency often seems closer to GCHQ than to CIA. I know. I've headed both American agencies. So Rogers's comment about NSA not doing this was a straightforward denial of the charge. His response to the charge against GCHQ was akin to defending a sister or other close relative against some gross calumny. GCHQ, for its part, broke its traditional silence to label the accusations "utterly ridiculous" and "nonsense," a powerful commentary from a normally voiceless institution.[19]

Boxed in by what I would call objective reality, the Trump administration began to look for an off-ramp, but certainly not a back-down from its outrageous claims. Two weeks after the president's original tweets and two days before the Comey-Rogers denials, I was on fellow Pennsylvanian Michael Smerconish's Saturday morning CNN talk show and predicted that the off-ramp was going to be an attempt to criminalize what's called the "unmasking" of U.S. identities in intelligence reporting. I claimed no special knowledge, no private heads-up, just an instinct.

Turned out I was right. Devin Nunes, chair of the House Intelligence Committee, took a call from the White House three days later, left his staffer in the car in which they had been traveling, summoned another vehicle, and went to the White House grounds to receive information on Obama-era privacy violations.[20]

The next day, without telling the rest of the Intelligence Committee, Nunes held a press conference expressing his concerns and then hurried back to the White House to talk to the president *about what the president's staff had given him the night before.* Mr. Trump, when later asked about his conversation with the congressman, said that he now felt "somewhat vindicated" in his Obama-wiretapped-me charge. Needless to say, he hadn't been.

Before the week was out, Chairman Nunes would cancel a planned appearance before his committee of a trio of what would have been "fact witnesses"—former director of national intelligence Jim Clapper, former director of CIA John Brennan, and former acting attorney general Sally Yates—but appeared on Trump-friendly and guaranteed-no-pushback Sean Hannity's Fox News talk show to express his continuing concerns.

Nunes had explained a bit about these concerns in an impromptu press conference on the North Lawn of the White House after visiting with the president. He said that under FISA court warrants, NSA had lawfully collected foreign intelligence in

November, December, and January related to the presidential transition. He emphasized that the collection was not about Russia and not related to any investigation. To repeat, he said it was about *foreign intelligence*.

He was careful in his language, and in several instances he seemed to go out of his way to say that he was referring primarily to information in reports "about" U.S. persons, not communications to or from such persons.

Barely reading between the lines of Chairman Nunes's comments, it was clear to this former NSA director (who was there for the 2000 and 2004 elections) that the chairman was referring to what must have been overwhelming foreign speculation as to the future course of the United States following Mr. Trump's victory. After all, foreign capitals were as surprised as most of us at the election's outcome.

In the normal course of its intelligence work, NSA would have collected, processed, translated, analyzed, and reported on these communications when they revealed significant foreign intelligence . . . like what country X thought about, or how it planned to respond to, policy Y or rumored appointee Z. Or where country X saw weakness or leverage it could exploit. Taken in its entirety, this is called *intelligence*. It's why all of this is done in the first place.

The NSA reporting would not have been a transcript of intercepted conversations. It is routinely an appreciation of the communication (or multiple communications) by an analyst who would point out the intelligence meaning of what had been said. Since the agency was reporting on what foreigners were saying about us and our processes, this NSA reporting would have unavoidably included information about what the agency calls "protected persons"—that's you, me, any American anywhere, and any legal long-term resident of the United States—and that would include the president-elect and his team.

NSA is notoriously conservative in revealing the identity of protected persons, so it would have instinctively defaulted in most cases to simply "named U.S. person number one" when making these references. That's not required by law or the Constitution, and occasionally the U.S. identity is so critical to the intelligence that it is included in the original report, but that is not the norm. NSA reasons that once an identity is out there, it's out there, so it is bureaucratically wiser (and safer) to mask the identity (i.e., "named U.S. person") and then see who might have cause to ask for more.

So when a senior consumer got one of these intelligence reports, a report we know by definition that NSA already had judged to be of intelligence value (otherwise the report would not exist), it would not have been surprising to ask for more detail on masked U.S. persons, or at least a more clear descriptor, if not an actual name.

To cite a purely illustrative example, say two foreign officials were reported to be in conversation discussing someone they speculated would be the next secretary of state. The more knowledgeable party then opines that this individual—identified by the official but only "named U.S. person number one" in the report—was ill-suited for the job and would be a disaster for relations with the United States. It does not strain credulity that a serving U.S. official would then legitimately request the name of the U.S. person so as to better evaluate the intelligence. The request would then be adjudicated at NSA and the agency would make the judgment about whether or not more detail was warranted. Unmasking can be requested by any of the recipients of the original report, even a junior analyst at, say, CIA.

Susan Rice, an all-purpose villain for some since the Benghazi debacle, was frequently identified in press accounts as requesting unmasking. It would not have been surprising for even a departing national security adviser to be interested in this. What was surprising was that the incoming president was not. After all, he and his team *could* have asked for reflections of what foreign capitals were saying about him, his team, his policies. It might have been useful.

Certainly an unmasking request from a national security adviser would have carried great weight, but in *all* cases the decision to unmask is NSA's and it is based on whether or not the requester needs the detail to do his or her job. NSA director Rogers said that about twenty folks were empowered to make that decision. And if unmasking did take place, the identity was revealed only to the specific requestor.

I could not read Susan Rice's heart, and surely any legitimate government authority is subject to abuse, but from what I could see, hers and the other alleged requests to unmask U.S. person information were well short of a smoking gun. In fact, on their face they appeared to be lawful, appropriate, and even numbingly routine.

And it should have been a simple matter to judge whether the unmasking requests themselves were within or beyond traditional norms. NSA has an audit trail on this that rivals the way Irish parishes husband baptismal records. That allowed me in early 2005 to refute Democrat charges that John Bolton, then nominated to be UN ambassador, had abused American privacy by asking for the unmasking of U.S. identities in about a dozen intelligence reports.

A group of trusted agents—perhaps a bipartisan group of respected former security and intelligence officials—could have made quick work of this and delivered a verdict that would have put the affair behind us. Of course, that assumed that all parties wanted a resolution of the issue, rather than a festering, distracting political sore.

There are plenty of things here that should concern all Americans, but there is a special tariff to be paid by the intelligence community. Despite the popularity of TV shows like *Homeland* and *24* and movies like *Zero Dark Thirty*, intelligence rests uneasily inside the broader American political culture. Good espionage relies on two things for its success: power and secrecy. And those are the very characteristics most distrusted by our society.

Still, American espionage survives. Most people recognize that although it may from time to time be distasteful, it is almost always necessary. And it has rarely been turned inward against the very political processes it is designed to defend.

But that was the very essence of the Trump accusation: that American intelligence agencies had been used by one political entity to spy on another. And the president seemed unaware of and indifferent to the corrosive effects of what was, at the end of the day, a baseless allegation. The president had used the American intelligence community as a handy political prop, and an ugly one at that, suggesting it was an unconstrained, politically motivated gang of lawbreakers. He had had an urge, a need, an uncontrolled impulse. He wanted to accuse, to distract, to taunt. The rest be damned.

When I reflected on what impact this might have on American intelligence, I could not help but think of Rudyard Kipling's mistreated British soldier, Tommy Atkins, and the poet's final line: "You bet that Tommy sees."

In March, at about the same time that Jim Comey announced his investigation into potential collusion between Russia and the Trump campaign, the president asked two top U.S. intelligence officials to push back against the FBI's effort. Director of National Intelligence Dan Coats and National Security Agency director Mike Rogers both declined.[21] Although both refused to talk about the president's calls when asked about them in open congressional session, the magnitude and inappropriateness of the president's "ask" could not have been lost on either man. All the more so because the president was already using the power of his office to enshrine loyalty, defined as absolute loyalty to him, above any other consideration, as the core measure of merit within his administration.

The president's handling of FBI director Jim Comey, Attorney General Jeff Sessions, and (to a lesser extent) Acting Attorney General Sally Yates were already creating cringe-worthy and ominous moments for the intelligence community.

Yates had pressed upon the White House her concerns about General Mike Flynn and had then directed the Department of Justice not to defend the controversial travel ban the administration had applied to seven Muslim-majority nations. And so she was fired.

But Yates was not a member of the intelligence community, and was serving in an acting position. Folks in the IC understood that defying a presidential executive order (however justified she might have believed that to be) was probably going to elicit a tough White House response.

Comey was different. As the director of the FBI he *was* a member of the intelligence community and a member in good standing. He sat at the table when the director of national intelligence gathered his executive committee. He worked hand in glove with NSA and CIA in crafting the community assessment on Russian interference in the election. So there was a sense of identity and kinship when Comey was suddenly dismissed. And some sense of "when am I going to find myself in these same circumstances?"

I didn't ask around and I certainly didn't take a survey, but I suspect that I was reflecting intelligence community consensus when I told a reporter for the *Times* of London that the president had fired Comey because "[t]he Oval Office, right now, is an unfriendly climate for truth." I added that the president "fired Comey because he was a free electron, with insufficient loyalty in the narrow sense of the word to the Administration and the President. Comey was too much his own man . . . he was too independent, too uncontrolled . . . which is exactly what he was supposed to be."[22]

There are lingering questions, of course, with regard to the president's motives and potential legal liabilities in firing the FBI director, but I am concerned here with the impact on American intelligence. What lessons should have been drawn from this episode by others who should also be committed to telling the truth in the Oval? Not comforting ones.

From Comey's account, the president demanded loyalty of a type that no legitimate FBI director should ever be able to give him. Comey's refusal triggered his firing and a presidential attempt at public humiliation. Trump told Oval Office visitor Sergei Lavrov, the Russian foreign minister, that "I just fired the head of the F.B.I. He was crazy, a real nut job. I faced great pressure because of Russia. That's taken off."[23]

The president treated his attorney general and longtime supporter Jeff Sessions in much the same way. The AG had recused himself from the Russia investigation, prompting the president to declare, "It's extremely unfair—and that's a mild word—to the president," and then added that he would not have picked Sessions for attorney general had he thought Sessions would have done such a thing.

To just review the basics here, the president's metric was not appropriateness, not the rule of law, not avoiding conflict of interest. The president's metric was only loyalty, loyalty to him.

And then there was the genuinely embarrassing June cabinet meeting where reporters were brought in to witness the vice president and department and agency heads singing their president's praises: "The greatest privilege of my life . . . I am privileged to be here—deeply honored . . . We thank you for the opportunity and the blessing to serve your agenda."[24] For people in the intelligence community it must have looked every inch like a lift from the DNI's Open Source Center of North Korean TV coverage of a similar session with Kim Jong-un where no functionary wants to be the first one to stop clapping for the "Dear Leader." DNI Coats and DCIA Pompeo dodged a bullet by choosing to praise their workforce, and Pompeo got offstage by adding, "In the finest traditions of the CIA, I'm not going to share a damn thing in front of the media."

But the core question remained. What standards of "loyalty" should the leaders of the intelligence community expect the president to eventually impose on *them*? And what might that ultimately mean for what the president is told or not told, or, for that matter, who might be left around to make that decision?

And how would other elements of the president's character—his challenged relationship with the truth, for example, or his undisciplined tweeting on matters that should demand great precision, or his continued public rejection of judgments about Russian behavior—have an impact on the practice and productivity of intelligence?

How was all of this being read by a community that measures itself on how completely, accurately, and candidly it is telling the truth to the president and on how that helps protect the Republic they serve and he leads? It clearly presented great challenges to the community's leadership.

Asked bluntly at the Aspen Security Conference why the president rejected aspects of the Russia story, DCIA Mike Pompeo could only respond that his team was fully engaged, that policymakers argue a lot with intelligence, that the Agency has lots of clients, and that many issues are close calls.

NBC's Lester Holt asked DNI Dan Coats at the same conference if he ever told the president that his comments were hurting morale in the intelligence community. Coats said that he hadn't, but he often did tell the president about the community, and on the Russia question he had reminded Trump that there was "no dissent."

I don't envy their task.

In midsummer 2017, a truly iconic CIA veteran, retired after doing some of the Agency's toughest work in the world's most austere places, told me that he had always been proud of his work, proud "to take the king's shilling for doing the king's work," as he put it. But, he confided, he had "never been more concerned about where we are and what we might be asked to do."

Another equally iconic veteran suggested that for the president there are "moments of sanity and even purpose, but these are washed away by vindictive behavior and childlike behavior—and an unbelievable narcissism."

A third, just-retired senior officer characterized it this way to me. More than at any other time in his decades at the Agency, he said, the people he described as being "belowdecks" (younger officers focused on mission, but more likely to digest a lot of news, especially from social media) are asking, "Am I part of a good thing?" And for the people "abovedecks" (midlevel and senior leaders), the question he was hearing more than at any other time in his experience was, "Does what I do still make a difference?"

Former director John Brennan told that security conference in Aspen in July that his fears were not just immediate effects on decision making: he feared real effects on families, real effects on potential recruits, long-term corrosive effects on the intelligence community in general.

The just-retired veteran case officer volunteered the harsh judgment that while he would have recruited someone like Donald Trump as an agent of influence (since he was always selling something), he would never have recruited someone like him as a source: you could never believe what he told you, he said, and if presented with a threat or an opportunity, he would have rolled on you and your network in an instant. And a former allied intelligence chief summarized rather nicely for me what seemed the core dilemma: "The intelligence mission falls apart without an ethical core for its conduct and purpose."

My most important meetings with President Bush had dealt

with covert action—edgy proposals where the operational, legal, and ethical way ahead was often unclear—and I wanted to know that the man across the table from me was honest and broadly shared my and my nation's values.[25] I also wanted to be sure that the particular proposal, whatever it might be, actually fit into the president's broader, well-thought-out, coherent strategy since there were too many temptations to embrace covert action instead of patiently creating and implementing such a strategy. Finally, I wanted to know that the president was the kind of man who would have the Agency's back when the action went to shit, which many do, even if backing the Agency would carry a political price for him.

I have never met Donald Trump, but based on the public persona he has displayed, I would have thought long and hard about each of those criteria before any meeting with *this* president.

This is all the more important because this president's personality bends him toward action more than reflection, and CIA director Pompeo has reflected the administration's bias toward "doing" with remarks in Aspen about separating Kim Jong-un from his nuclear capacity[26] and finding a "platform which could uniformly push back" against the Revolutionary Guard Corps' leadership in Iran.[27]

Where DNI Coats has promised not to be policy prescriptive, Director Pompeo has been more comfortable infusing policy into his public remarks, sounding a bit like his boss—describing an apocalyptic past, inheriting a mess, accusing past administrations of whistling past graveyards, talking tough—and thereby inviting press accusations of being "political," a very unwelcome headline at Langley.[28] But Pompeo has been a politician, after all, and he has gotten to spend a lot of time with the president, something that the Agency really values. Any internal concerns were about the challenges of retaining that access (and influence) *and* telling the president what he doesn't want to hear.

Director Pompeo told that July Colorado audience that the administration would have to work hard to unwind the situation they had walked into. He told an audience in Austin in October, "We can't perform our mission if we're not aggressive. This is unforgiving, relentless. You pick the word. Every minute, we have to be focused on crushing our enemies."[29]

And the president was supportive. Pompeo told veteran security beat reporter Bill Gertz that the president frequently asked, "What do you need to go get it done?" And when the CIA director outlined where the gap in authorities might be, "Every time he's said, 'Go do it.'"[30]

There were a lot of officers in the Agency who welcomed the more aggressive posture. They had chafed at the restrictions, overlayering, and indecision of the Obama years. This was just what they had been waiting for. But others were less certain. One Agency veteran of covert action told me that in the eyes of some, the new administration seemed to be leashing in those you would want to be unleashed (namely analysts, by insisting that refugees were *really* dangerous and the Russia thing *was* a hoax), but unleashing those over whom you always wanted to have a little more control (like the special activities center and covert action offices).

'm not there and I don't know, but these are all certainly important and weighty issues, and I *do* know that intelligence officers talk about them among themselves at the water cooler, and at the

Starbucks and Dunkin' Donuts in the Agency cafeteria, and at diners and steakhouses near the Agency.

But CIA officers don't spend all of their time at local escapes. They spend most of it at Langley. And since they know how the Electoral College works and they know how to count, they know who represents the sovereign choice of the American people.

So when they are at work—whatever philosophical issues might be in the air or in their heads—they tend to just keep their heads down and do their jobs. They know that they are there to serve the president and they are in the habit of just grabbing an oar and rowing. Still, unaccustomed questions remain.

SIX

GETTING ON WITH IT

At the hundred-day mark of the administration I was invited by a news outlet to write an op-ed and give the administration a grade for its foreign and security policy. I began the piece by observing that we were all still here, which belied the worst fears that had been suggested during the campaign and transition. And I grudgingly admitted that the administration had clawed its way up to accepting much that I thought should have been obvious: that China was not currently a currency manipulator; that NATO was not obsolete; that maybe Vladimir Putin sometimes did bad things.

I attributed a lot of that to the strong national security team that the president had set in place, a team that was not just strong for a Manhattan real estate developer, but would have been considered so for any president. And the president had wisely cleared the security policy decks with the removal of his war-of-civilizations prophet Steve Bannon from the National Security Council.

Mike Flynn, of course, was also gone. There was little mourning in the intelligence community when Flynn was asked to resign after only weeks on the job, and there was probably intelligence community leaking that poured oil on this fire. But Flynn was fired for lying to the vice president, and many of the leaks about his Russia connection could easily have been the by-product of internal White House maneuvering.

The president, typically, though, put the blame squarely on a version of the deep state when he tweeted two days after the dismissal, "Information is being illegally given to the failing @nytimes & @washingtonpost by the intelligence community (NSA and FBI?). Just like Russia."[1]

Flynn's firing made the new national security adviser, Army lieutenant general H. R. McMaster, the last-arriving senior on the security team. Flynn in his Army career may have been an American hero, but I knew few who thought him a good fit for the national security adviser role, and almost everyone I knew thought that the president had traded up with McMaster.

As an Army major, H.R. had literally written the book on "truth to power," turning his Ph.D. thesis at the University of North Carolina into 1997's bestselling *Dereliction of Duty*, an indictment of the Joint Chiefs of Staff and national leadership for the lies that led to Vietnam—a historical account studied in the late 1990s by a generation of American officers, including me.

By then McMaster had already earned a solid combat reputation by leading an armor troop during the Gulf War in the Battle of 73 Easting (named for a map reference), where his small unit (nine Abrams tanks and twelve Bradley Fighting Vehicles) destroyed some seventy-five Iraqi armored vehicles in just over twenty minutes.[2] He later added to that reputation with a successful counterinsurgency effort in and around Tal Afar in western Iraq after the Iraq War.

McMaster was a powerful intellect in the Army and so true to his beliefs that he irritated some and, as the story goes, occasionally needed the intervention of appreciative seniors to advance in rank. I had not met him often; in late 2008 he visited me in my CIA office for an extended discussion on a fact-finding effort for Dave Petraeus, who was then taking over Central Command (Iraq and Afghanistan and a lot more). Years later, H.R. and I were actually onstage together for a security conference in New York City the day before President Trump's inauguration. I thought he was an impressive intellect, knowledgeable and thoughtful.

He would have to be . . . and strong, too. The president still had a great deal of affection for the now departed Flynn, with whom he had obviously bonded during the campaign. Flynn at the podium during the Republican convention in July joining in the chant to "lock her up" sent a massive shock wave through the active and retired officer corps, but only endeared him to Trump. The president ultimately fired Flynn for misleading Vice President Pence, but he did so reluctantly. He sat on that information for two weeks and moved on it only after the *Washington Post* made it public.[3]

So McMaster would have to build his own relationship with a president for whom he was not the first choice. Indeed, he wasn't even the second choice, as former Navy SEAL Admiral Bob Harward (who was close to Defense Secretary Mattis) had turned down the position. Still, it would be up to McMaster to build the bridge between the (broadly international) national security departments and agencies and the (America First) circle of family and friends around the president.

He would also have to deal with an NSC staff that he had not selected, that had some residual loyalties to his predecessor, and that he soon discovered he did not have a totally free hand to change. It wasn't until August that he was able to move his too junior/too inexperienced/too disruptive senior director for intelligence programs, Ezra Cohen-Watnick, who had successfully blunted earlier attempts by McMaster by appealing to Bannon, Jared Kushner, and, through them, to the president himself.[4]

At the same time, McMaster had to clean up after one of the weirdest memos in the history of the NSC, a thirty-five-hundred-word screed titled "POTUS and Political Warfare," written by Flynn holdover and Trump campaign loyalist Rich Higgins in the NSC's strategic planning office. The informal memo condemned the warfare against the president's agenda by an unholy alliance of "deep state actors, globalists, bankers, Islamists, and establishment Republicans" and then described "hate speech narratives [as] non-random, coordinated, and fully interoperable escalations of cultural Marxist memes" that were being spread by players that "include the European Union, the UN, and the OSCE [Organization for Security and Co-operation in Europe], the OIC [Organisation of Islamic Cooperation] and the International Muslim Brotherhood." Higgins also reminded his readers that for the United States, "As a Judaeo-Christian Culture, forced inclusion of post-modern notions of tolerance is designed to induce nihilistic contradictions that reduce all thought, all faith, all loyalties to meaninglessness."

The memo seemed crazy and is hard to follow for anyone not

steeped in the patois of alt-right nationalist conspiracy theories. Indeed, there were reports that Higgins's manifesto seemed to echo right-wing blogger Mike Cernovich, a bitter critic of McMaster and his alleged globalism. There were even suggestions in the press that McMaster may have discovered Higgins's memo in a search for whoever was leaking inside NSC information to Cernovich.[5] Higgins was finally shoved out, but his presence on the NSC for half a year (and *Foreign Policy* suggested that the president and Donald Jr. supported his being there) indicated how big a challenge McMaster faced.

The NSC historically has had its share of eccentrics, but Bannon, Cohen-Watnick, Higgins, and this memo suggested a level of weirdness rarely seen before, with predictable results on the smooth flow of information, including intelligence. Until Cohen-Watnick was finally axed, the NSC's senior director for intelligence programs had a fully reciprocated hate-hate relationship with the nation's premier intelligence service. And some powerful people in the White House didn't seem to mind!

And while he was getting his staff up to functioning normally, McMaster would have to impose a disciplined process on a president who was notoriously spontaneous and more trusting of personal relationships than finished staff work. Of all the members of what the press came to call the "axis of adults," McMaster was the most junior, and not sitting atop a powerful bureaucracy like Jim Mattis across the river at the Pentagon. Lacking the personal gravitas of previous occupants of his West Wing corner office like Kissinger, Brzezinski, Powell, Scowcroft, and Jones, McMaster was dependent on the goodwill of a mercurial president. Hence a tendency to describe his task as one of complete service to his boss: "There's nobody there to control the President" or "keep him on the reservation. We're there to . . . help him advance his agenda."[6]

That turned the normal policymaking process a bit on its head. Clearly the personality and preferences of any president matter, but in this administration the NSC process seemed more harnessed to simply implementing the axioms and even mythologies of the president rather than teeing up truly strategic choices.

Beyond his relationship with the president, McMaster would also have to synchronize, harmonize, deconflict, and occasionally direct the powerful personalities heading the national security departments and agencies. The most powerful personality was retired Marine general Jim Mattis, "Mad Dog" Mattis to the president, but better described by those who knew him as "the warrior monk." Mattis was unmarried, thoughtful, well read, steeped in history, and more akin to General George C. Marshall than to the president's frequently invoked George S. Patton, the cartoon image of an aggressive combat commander.

Like Marshall, Mattis was all about the prudent use of American military power *only* when necessary and then *only in concert* with the other tools of American power and influence. Mattis had displayed his internationalist instincts during his confirmation hearings. While on active duty as commander of Central Command, he famously complained to a congressional committee that if the State Department budget were to be cut, he would "need to buy more ammunition."[7]

Respectful of diplomacy (as well as talent and experience), Mattis wanted former ambassador Anne Patterson to be his under secretary for policy. Anne had been ambassador in some of the world's toughest spots: El Salvador, Colombia, Pakistan, Egypt. I knew her best from her time in Pakistan, where we routinely huddled on the secure phone on how to deal with al-Qaeda in the region. She was knowledgeable and tough and seemed to be doing well in the vetting process until the "religious warriors" in the White House and some conservatives in the Senate nixed the choice for her work while in Cairo with the Muslim Brotherhood—which headed up the duly elected government of Egypt at the time.[8]

Mattis used and appreciated intelligence. Shortly after his retirement in 2013 our paths crossed at the Marine Corps Exchange just outside of Washington. He walked across the near-empty store to reintroduce himself and to thank me for the work the Agency had done supporting him even though by then I had been out of government for over four years.

At the Department of State, Rex Tillerson, chief executive officer of energy giant ExxonMobil, seemed an equally substantive choice. Few in Washington policy circles knew him personally, but he came with the public endorsement of former secretaries of state James Baker and Condoleezza Rice and former secretary of defense Bob Gates (the consulting firm of Gates, Rice, and former national security adviser Steve Hadley had also been an adviser to Exxon).[9]

I said at the time that those endorsements were good enough for me because I feared (perhaps like Gates, Rice, Hadley, and Baker) that the summer's "never Trump" letter-writing campaign had severely depleted the available Republican foreign policy bench.

I may have been too hasty in accepting the endorsements of even such a prestigious quartet. Within the year Tillerson seems to have alienated both the White House and his own department. It appears that he actually did call the president a "fucking moron" following a meeting on Afghanistan and then had to endure a public challenge about his and the president's IQs.[10] In the State Department, important posts are unfilled, veteran foreign service officers are departing in record numbers, applications are down nearly 40 percent, and the secretary seems willing to accept losing a quarter of his budget.

It was always a given that Tillerson would need help navigating his sprawling C Street empire, and he selected Elliott Abrams to be his deputy. I knew, liked, and respected Elliott from the George W. Bush administration, where he handled the NSC portfolio for the Middle East and later for global democratization. He was a tough neocon, a staunch supporter of Israel, and a solid Washington hand.

Abrams managed his way through the process to what was described as a positive interview with the president only to be rejected afterward because of an article he had written on Trump the previous May. Elliott had not signed any of the "never Trump" letters, and his piece in the conservative *Weekly Standard,* "When You Can't Stand Your Candidate," was less harsh on Trump than most of the genre. No matter. The thin-skinned new president crossed him from the list.[11] It was yet another sign of how the White House's obsession with loyalty would complicate already difficult questions.

Marine general John Kelly was widely applauded as an excellent choice to head up the Department of Homeland Security. A towering combat leader, he had completed his active service as head of Southern Command, responsible for the Western Hemisphere south of Mexico. I had known John from attending mass with him on Sundays at the small chapel of the Washington Navy Yard and serving on the board of a D.C.-based investment firm with him. On a train ride to visit one of our subsidiaries in New Jersey after his announcement but before his confirmation, I congratulated John on his appointment and said that his record in SOUTHCOM suggested that he understood that real border security for America was best premised on improving the quality of life in Central America rather than on building a wall along the Rio Grande. He didn't actually respond to the observation, and as time went on I came to believe that John was more sympathetic to the president, especially on immigration and border security, than I first believed. He also seemed to share the president's disdain for Congress.

If John was softening any presidential positions, it was hard to detect and was clearly being done in private. When he attempted as much in public—as when he told Democrats that candidate Trump's views on border security were "uninformed," and then told Fox News that the president's views had "evolved"—the president was reported as "fuming" and shot back with, "The Wall is the Wall, it has never changed or evolved from the first day I conceived of it."[12]

The president's choice for homeland security adviser was Tom Bossert, a highly regarded veteran of the George W. Bush administration, and Tom in turn selected Rob Joyce as his right-hand man for cyber security. Joyce had been my pick to run TAO—Tailored Access Operations, NSA's elite hackers—when I was director there, and it was hard for me now to think of a more qualified individual by background, skill, or personality to be the White House cyber security coordinator. A career NSAer, Joyce would know how to get accurate cyber intelligence as the White House charted a cyber way forward.

All in all, this looked like a very impressive team. And

although several of these officers went out of their way to say they were there only to serve the president, most people around town were of the belief that these folks were there not only to correct some of the shortcomings of the previous administration but also to put some clear restraints on the new one. There would be opportunities to demonstrate that.

First was Syria and ISIS, where the choice was pretty clear: accelerate the three-year-old Obama effort to defeat ISIS militarily. This truly was "Obama plus," so it was more than a little unfair and historically inaccurate for Trump to claim after the fall of Raqqa that ISIS hadn't been on the run before because "you didn't have Trump as your president."[13]

But as president, Mr. Trump did push operational decision making down to tactical commanders, did make complex rules of engagement more straightforward, and did commit necessary resources. The result was the accelerated destruction of the physical Islamic caliphate. But there seemed to be considerably less effort and intellectual energy on the "what then?," although that would seem to be one of the core intelligence and policy questions of the conflict.

Secretary of Defense Mattis threw a tantalizing one-liner into one of his press availabilities when he talked about the "stabilization phase" of the counter-ISIS campaign. That's the part where you stick around to change the facts on the ground so that you don't have to go back and kill people again later.

A critic might call that nation building. It doesn't have to be, but by any name it is hardly consistent with candidate Trump's hit-them-hard-and-fast-and-leave gospel on the campaign trail.

Only half-jokingly did I refer to the secretary's press intervention as the first televised NSC meeting ever. I think he was trying to stimulate a necessary conversation, but nothing came of his remark, at least not publicly. A few months later, Homeland Security Adviser Tom Bossert was asked about the future of Syria, and he reemphasized that it was not important that Assad go first, that ISIS was still job one, and that broader conversations were not useful now.

One of the broader conversations would eventually have to be what to do about Syrian/Iranian/Hezbollah forces supported by Russian airpower "drafting" on allied military success to move eastward in Syria and down the Euphrates River valley to build what looks suspiciously like an Iranian-Shia land bridge from Tehran to Beirut. It also means that the rump Syria we all expected to come out of this conflict, the future Alawistan (so named for Assad's sect), is going to be a lot bigger than we previously calculated.

There may be serious NSC discussions about all of this, but there has been nil heard publicly, and, frankly, these are not the kinds of questions that naturally engage the president or about which he does much talking (or thinking).

During the campaign the president had said, "I don't want to broadcast to the enemy exactly what my plan is,"[14] and he repeatedly complained about the effort to retake Mosul as being too public. "Why don't we just go in quietly, right? They used to call it a sneak attack."[15]

Frankly, I always took those kinds of statements as suggesting that the candidate/president didn't understand strategy (no one who did would actually propose a *sneak* attack on a heavily garrisoned/heavily mined city in the middle of a desert), or didn't actually have a strategy, or feared saying much about his strategy for of fear opening it up to comment and criticism. Just like it's easier to just say you're rich than to open up your tax returns and answer questions.

It's also easier for the administration to talk about an operational success in Syria, the retaliatory Tomahawk Land Attack Missile (TLAM) strike in response to Assad's use (again) of chemical weapons. Good marks for doing what should have been done more than three years ago.

And the administration deserves extra credit for its indirect slap at the Russians in doing so. Despite all the rhetoric praising Putin and highlighting the goal of better relations with Russia, ten weeks into his administration President Trump punched Moscow's closest Arab client in the mouth. And his secretary of state hammered Russia, the supposed guarantor of Syria's chemical disarmament in 2013, as "complicit or simply incompetent in preventing Syria's chemical gas attack."[16] At least the United States warned Russian forces at the airfield about the deadly American incoming.

The airfield attack hit a sweet spot in the president's approach to the world and his own decision making. He took Assad's affront personally, and his public reaction to the atrocity was genuine. He's also not inclined to admire problems very long before acting, and an American response (sea-launched cruise missiles) was at the ready and battle proven.

And quick, decisive action would powerfully differentiate him from his predecessor, a goal never far from the president's mind. One cannot avoid the thought that there was more than a little about the Trump "brand" at work here.

CIA director Mike Pompeo has talked about the intelligence

back story to the president's decision. He recounts that he got an afternoon call from the president[17] about the disturbing post-attack images coming out of Syria and a direction to "find out what happened." Pompeo immediately assembled his own Agency team and experts from across the intelligence community to piece together the evidence, which, given the intelligence empha-sis on Syria for the last six years, was likely abundant.

By the time of a scheduled cabinet meeting the next day, Pom-peo could tell the president that the attack had indeed taken place and that the Syrian government had done it. And then the presi-dent turned to him to ask the question that sends a chill down the spine of any CIA director: "Are you sure?" A tough question al-ways, and especially tough here since Pompeo would have known that a yes would prompt immediate and decisive American action.

Pompeo reports that he responded, "Mr. President, we have high confidence in our assessment."

That was the same level of confidence that was in the Intelli-gence Community Assessment that the Russians had interfered in the American electoral process (see chapter 4). Good enough here to bomb, but not good enough there to convince the president of Russian malevolence.

Then again, the Syrian information was welcome, backing up an already preferred course of action. The Russian data was not welcome as it cut across a preferred narrative. All in all, a really bad sign for intelligence.

Director Pompeo outlined the Syrian sequence of events in front of the Intelligence and National Security Alliance, an IC-friendly nonpartisan collection of public, business, private, and academic experts, and it was appropriately applauded by the group. It was an unarguable intelligence success. But there is nothing in the public record or later discussions about any larger questions being raised by the president or answered by the IC. Questions like: "Why do you think Assad did this? Is he cocky or desperate?" or "Where are the Russians on all this? What does it say about how far they'll go with Assad?" or "How will the Iranians read this? Will they dismiss our strike as a one-off or see it as something more important?"

That *may* have been discussed. I certainly hope so. And although it wasn't exactly an intelligence question, there was a broader issue. How did this fit into the president's overall foreign policy?

Candidate Trump had run on a platform of "America First," an explicit and forceful rejection of the internationalism that had governed American policy for much of the past seventy-five years, a world where America often acted "for the good of the order" rather than narrowly defined national interests, and the candidate had been contemptuous of those he said allowed us to be played by an ungrateful global community. But the president himself did exactly that with the Syria strike (to the chagrin of some of his supporters), responding to Syria's violation of an important international norm on chemical weapons.

It wasn't a change in policy toward Assad or even the civilian deaths. There have been far more deaths inflicted by more conventional means, and the administration had already made it clear that Assad's leaving was not job one. No, it wasn't any of that. It was America, alone and uncompensated, without any formal international sanction or authorization or help, acting on behalf of broader principles.

Go figure.

I've talked to a lot of folks about decision making and the role of intelligence in the Trump administration. And although I don't have access to NSC minutes or intelligence notes, the broader pattern has become pretty clear.

Discussion of a topic usually starts with a presidential statement or belief, firmly held if not especially well informed. Then follows a large-scale and long-term effort to better inform the president, to impress upon him the complexity of the issue, to review the relevant history, to surface more of the factors bearing on the problem, to raise second- and third-order consequences, and to explore the feasibility of subsequent moves down the board.

It's not easy. The president is not a patient man. One press account quoted a Trump confidant as saying, "I call the President a two-minute man. The President has patience for a half page."[18]

National Security Adviser McMaster (kind of) admitted as much. "The President," he told an audience at the highly regarded Institute for the Study of War, "is not a policy wonk, at all. He's a business person and what he demands is results. And what that has done is, it's changed the way that we do things." And one of the things changed was creating "succinct" summaries, five-page briefs, rather than sixty-page tomes.[19]

There is something inherently discomfiting in that. There are some problems that cannot be simplified. They are inherently complex.

Still, sometimes the magic works. The president began his August speech announcing his policy for Afghanistan by

confessing, "My original instinct was to pull out—and, historically, I like following my instincts."

And he really tried to. According to NBC News, in a July SIT-
ROOM meeting Trump showed his frustration by complaining
about NATO allies, asking how the United States could tap into
Afghanistan's mineral wealth, and repeatedly saying the top
U.S. general there should be fired.[20] He even allowed his staff
to solicit a plan from security company Blackwater's founder,
Erik Prince, and financier Stephen Feinberg to outsource the war
to private contractors under overall CIA control.[21] I suspect
that concept was a tar baby for which the Agency showed little
enthusiasm.

In the end Mr. Trump admitted that "all my life I've heard that
decisions are much different when . . . you're President of the
United States. So I studied Afghanistan in great detail and from
every conceivable angle. After many meetings, over many months."

Which was how he introduced a speech I thought was worth
listening to.

First of all, it was the product of "regular order," the outcome
of the traditional deliberative process of the American security
establishment. Intelligence got to level-set the picture based on
the best available information, and then the departments and
agencies weighed in with their views, which were then adjudicated in various meetings within the National Security Council
structure. Options were developed, debated, and held up against
the intelligence. They were discussed with the president. He gave
guidance. The options were sharpened. He made a decision. And
then he announced that decision in a twenty-five-minute speech
rather than in 140 characters.

That was a first for the Trump administration and a far cry

from his more routine outbursts like the presidential bomblet at a press op where he suggested there were U.S. military options in Venezuela. That one had the Pentagon redirecting all follow-up questions back to the White House since they had no idea what the president was talking about.

That episode also had me wondering how this administration vetted what its senior officials were saying. In the Bush administration, CIA certainly vetted all formal speeches very carefully, especially after the president was allowed to misspeak about Iraq's pursuit in Africa of yellowcake, a precursor for uranium fuel for reactors. The charge was contained in sixteen words in Mr. Bush's 2003 State of the Union address, and forever after we referred to reviewing major speeches in sixteen-word batches. And we took the review *very* seriously. Fundamentally we were saying that if we objected, we couldn't back up this or that passage.

From the outside looking in, there doesn't appear to be a whole lot of that going on with much of what President Trump says. But the Afghanistan speech was different: deliberate, thoughtful, more comprehensive. With regard to substance, the president announced that he was staying the course in Afghanistan and suggested that troop levels would be increased. That's the path the Obama administration was on and almost certainly would have followed had it not decided to defer this decision (appropriately in my view) to the incoming administration.

Both Trump and Obama had gone to school on the ill-advised decision to leave Iraq in 2011, but President Trump went one better, announcing that future steps would be based on conditions on the ground rather than on an arbitrary timetable, a perennial issue with the Obama administration.

The speech would also have been the path recommended by most of those folks (internationalists, like me) who signed those letters in the summer of 2016 saying that populist, isolationist Donald Trump would be a danger to American security if elected. His decision cut against his campaign rhetoric and the policy preferences of economic nationalists like his just-exiled strategic adviser Steve Bannon. More credit to the president.

Still, to critics, this was less a strategy than it was more of the same, a decision to hang on and hope. The president made multiple references to "winning" in Afghanistan, but never quite described what that would look like. Here we might have to accept the reality that "success" is simply an Afghanistan that has not deteriorated to the point where it constitutes a significant danger to the region and the United States—and that might require a continuous American effort as far forward as the eye could see despite the president's downplaying efforts to construct democracy or change the way other people choose to live.

The most interesting parts of the president's speech had to do with the broader region. He quite correctly criticized Pakistan for the duplicitous role it has been playing, supporting some American efforts while also working its own relationships with the Taliban and the notorious Haqqani network. That's why many in the intelligence community tend to refer to Pakistan as the ally from hell and would happily have confirmed the pattern of Pakistani duplicity to the president.

The president threatened an immediate reduction in U.S. assistance if Pakistan did not move against terrorist safe havens on its territory. He also seemed to leave a big "watch this space" when it comes to his willingness to authorize unilateral American operations across the border if Pakistan did not act.

Equally interesting were the president's comments about the positive role that India plays in Afghanistan and his invitation to India to do even more for Kabul. Pakistan views *any* Indian presence in Afghanistan as strategic encirclement by their longtime rival and have used that presence to justify their relationship with the Taliban. So if it sticks to these positions, the administration could be setting in motion a strategic realignment not just in the region but in America's relationships with countries there.

One thing is certain, though. Whatever complaints the president wanted to make about the mess he inherited, this one was now *his* war.

ran policy followed pretty much the same arc, but to a somewhat different conclusion.

As a candidate, Mr. Trump had called the Joint Comprehensive Plan of Action (JCPOA, i.e., the Iran nuclear deal) "the stupidest deal of all time" and "one of the great dumb deals of our time."[22] In March, before AIPAC (the American Israel Public Affairs Committee), he promised, "My number-one priority is to dismantle the disastrous deal with Iran."[23]

I hadn't been a fan of the JCPOA; I thought we could have driven a harder bargain since the deal should have been more important to Tehran than it was to us. They were the ones desperate for sanctions relief. I also thought that the Obama administration had done a bit of a bait-and-switch when it came to selling Americans on how the deal handled Iranian missile testing, suspect weapon site inspections, and uncovering previous nuclear activities.

Still, Iran was considerably further away from a weapon *with*

the deal than they had been *without* it. The number of centri-
fuges and the stockpile of enriched materials had been capped
and some facilities disabled. Which was why I was more worried
about Iran's nuclear capacity *after* this deal when its various provisions aged off in about a decade.

And then there was everything else that Iran was doing in the
region, like in Iraq (where Iranian-sponsored militias terrorized
Sunnis), or in Syria (where Iran and its proxies were the ground
force complement to Russian airpower), or in Yemen (where Iran
arms and advises Houthi rebels), all contributing to a "Shia arc"
running from Tehran through Iraq and Assad-controlled Syria on
to Hezbollah-controlled Lebanon. That ascendency—along with
ballistic missile tests, unlawful detention of Americans, arms
shipments, the creation of a regional "Shia liberation" force, and
provocative naval strutting in the Persian Gulf—constituted
grounds for great American concern.

The Obama administration had too often stayed its hand on
these questions, apparently for fear of jeopardizing the nuclear
agreement that was the crowning achievement of Obama administration diplomacy. The Obama team also believed it was playing
the long game. They did what they had to do to get the nuclear file
off the table since no movement with Iran was possible with that
unresolved. Then they planned to reintegrate Iran into the global
community and allow American-Iranian relations to "normalize." And all of that was to enable the ultimate goal, the administration's much-desired retrenchment from the region.

Of course, that meant accepting growing Iranian influence.
Late in the administration, President Obama told Tom Friedman
of the *New York Times* that "the truth of the matter is that Iran
will be and should be a regional power."[24] He later told Jeffrey

Goldberg of the *Atlantic,* "The Saudis need to find an effective way to share the neighborhood."[25]

I had my concerns, but all that did echo American policy pre-1979, before the Iranian revolution, when we relied on the twin pillars of a friendly Iran and a friendly Saudi Arabia to stabilize the Gulf region. It also reflected the reality that at the level of people and culture, Iran was inherently more pro-Western and inclusive than was the kingdom. But betting that Iranian *evolution* would trump the Iranian revolution, at least in the short term, felt a lot more like the triumph of hope than the product of experience.

Donald Trump would have none of it, of course—too historic, too nuanced, too strategic, too long-term—and made sure that his first overseas travel (in May) was to Saudi Arabia, Iran's arch-enemy, where he fully embraced his Saudi hosts and comforted them and the fifty other Islamic states that had gathered with the promise that "America will not seek to impose our way of life on others. . . . We are not here to lecture—we are not here to tell other people how to live. . . . We must seek partners, not perfection." The president also referred to Islam as on "one of the world's great faiths," a far cry from his campaign rhetoric about blocking that faith's adherents from entering his country.[26]

And then, after enlisting Muslim-majority countries to take "the lead in combatting radicalization," the president set out to paint the Iranians as the unmitigated forces of darkness in the region. "For decades, Iran has fueled the fires of sectarian conflict and terror . . . [giving terrorists] safe harbor, financial backing and the social standing needed for recruitment." He called for "all nations of conscience . . . to isolate Iran, deny it funding for terrorism, and [in a thinly veiled call for regime change] pray for the day when the Iranian people have the just and righteous government they deserve."

Sunni Arabs, especially in the Gulf states, were delighted to have America realigning itself squarely against Tehran. Some were so emboldened that in early June, two weeks after Trump left, they moved to aggressively isolate—diplomatically and physically—one of their own, Qatar, for being too accommodating to Iran; for condoning funding for Islamic fundamentalists (hardly unique among the Sunnis); for having a sometimes irritating television network (Al Jazeera); and (left unsaid) for being a little too competitive for influence in the region.

The president tweeted his immediate support and claimed that his desert visit was "already paying off. They said they would take a hard line on funding extremism, and all reference was pointing to Qatar. Perhaps this will be the beginning of the end to the horror of terrorism!"[27]

His secretaries of state and defense were more cautious, perhaps because they were more aware of the complexities of Gulf politics or maybe just more aware that the center of American combat power in the Gulf was Al Udeid Air Base just outside the Qatari capital of Doha. The base had been built by the emir of Qatar twenty years ago and now hosted some ten thousand Americans.

Tillerson broke formation with the president by offering to act as peacemaker: "We certainly would encourage the parties to sit down together and address these differences, and we—if there's any role that we can play in terms of helping them address those, we think it is important that the GCC [Gulf Cooperation Council] remain unified."[28]

Two weeks later Tillerson's State Department piled on: "The

more that time goes by, the more doubt is raised about the actions taken by Saudi Arabia and the UAE." And then came this hammer: "At this point, we are left with one simple question: were the actions really about their concerns regarding Qatar's alleged support for terrorism? Or were they about the long-simmering grievances between and among the GCC countries?"[29]

Wow. Compare that with the president's original, spontaneous Qatar tweet. And from the same government, no less.

There were other challenges reconciling presidential rhetoric with complex regional realities. Every three months Mr. Trump had to decide to certify the Iranian nuclear deal, a hook given the president when Bob Corker, chairman of the Senate Foreign Relations Committee, inserted that provision into law in 2015.

In a stormy meeting in July, Trump reluctantly agreed to his second certification, but angrily demanded that Secretary of State Tillerson and the rest of the national security team build the case for decertification next time it came due, in October.[30]

He was done signing off on his predecessor's signature diplomatic achievement. Indeed, that may have been what so energized him about the issue. In that "taking Trump seriously but not literally" meme, the president intended to deal with the Iranian nuclear deal literally. He actually intended to dismantle it.

And that even though few on his national security team thought it was a good idea. Like ripping up the Trans-Pacific Partnership and the Paris Agreement on climate change and pushing what for all the world looked like a Muslim immigration ban, this looked like coming up with a solution to a problem we didn't have. Everyone wanted to push back on Iran's hegemonic reach and no one was enthused about aspects of the nuclear deal sunsetting, but the deal in place was capping Iran's *current* nuclear ambitions. Why mess with that? Mattis and Chairman of the Joint Chiefs General Joe Dunford said as much to the Senate Armed Services Committee, noting that remaining in the nuclear deal was in the national security interests of the United States.[31] Secretary Tillerson conceded that he and the president "have differences of views on things like JCPOA and how we should use it."[32]

National Security Adviser McMaster was publicly very supportive of the president's hard line, but CNN reported one meeting with Democratic senators where McMaster hinted that he didn't think decertifying [was] the right way to go and seemed to be searching for alternative paths.[33]

Oddly, the cabinet member most vocal in his public condemnation of Iran was Mike Pompeo, the director of CIA, who complained in July (at the time of Trump's second certification) about Iran's compliance with the JCPOA. "How many of you have had a bad tenant?" he asked a crowd in Aspen. "You know they don't pay the rent, you call them and then they send a check, and it doesn't clear and they send another one. . . . This is Iranian compliance today. Grudging, minimalist, temporary with no intention of really [doing] what the agreement was designed to do." Pompeo condemned "continued appeasement" and predicted "a fundamental shift" when the administration got its strategy in place.[34]

It would be Pompeo's folks at CIA who would make the intelligence judgments about the status and effects of the JCPOA. There was no doubt that they would document and condemn Tehran's aggressive expansionism, and they would not hesitate to point out the issues that would ultimately emerge when elements of the deal aged off in the next decade.

But on the core issue of Iranian compliance today, bad tenant or not, their view would be that Iran had committed no "material breach" of the agreement; there had been no violation of a provision essential to achieving the purpose of the treaty—the slowing of Iran's march to a weapon.

CIA analysts were in a curious position. They had really been integral to the Obama administration's negotiations with Tehran. Senior negotiators turned to them for the status of the Iranian program; an understanding of Iran's negotiating positions; a description of the critical paths on which Iran would have to depend to achieve weapons status; and what would be essential in the way of inspections and intelligence to ensure compliance. Now these same people were being asked to give a grade not just to the agreement and Iranian compliance, but, in a way, to their own work in terms of the baseline they had set and the standards on which they had insisted. It wasn't quite circular or incestuous, but it was going to require real evidence and not just anger or attitude to get them to move off their position. And since there wasn't evidence of any violations that met the standards of material breach, I feared for a while there would be a real crisis between the White House and Langley if the president insisted there had been such a violation.

In the event, he didn't. The president refused to certify the deal, but not because the Iranians materially breached the JCPOA. He simply declared that the agreement was no longer in the strategic interests of the United States (which Senator Corker's 2015 bill allowed him to do), dutifully bashed the Iranians, and then, despite the tough rhetoric, declined to do much more, other than effectively putting the Iranians on notice that the nuclear deal would not inhibit him in responding to Tehran's aggression elsewhere. In effect, he was telling the Iranians, "If you want to break the deal, go ahead and break the deal. The deal's not that important to me."

That had the effect of freeing the United States to go after all the other things the Iranians were doing, but for now, little would change. The president did not actually impose additional sanctions on Iran (which he had authority to do), but merely tossed the question to Capitol Hill, where it was already agreed there would be no immediate action.

My sense was that the president had gotten to make his speech, fulfill a campaign promise, and publicly dissociate himself (à la Obamacare, the Trans-Pacific Partnership, and the Paris Agreement) from another key element of his predecessor's legacy.

But from the outside looking in, it appears that a lot of folks in government—in Defense, in State, in the intelligence agencies—weren't fans of blowing up the nuclear agreement. So knowing that the president wanted to make a tough speech that clearly painted him as being different from his predecessor, they spent several months devising a way for him to do that, but also to essentially leave the deal intact. It fit the overall pattern of an a priori presidential position followed by departments and agencies raising questions of complexities, linkages, history, follow-on effects, and the like. And it seems to have worked, at least for the moment.

But decertification set in motion processes beyond the White House's control in which Congress; the Europeans, Russians, or Chinese, who are also parties to the deal; or the Iranians can make moves that break the near-term nuclear contract (which, again, was working and promised to be effective for at least several more years). It looks as if the Iranian street gets a vote, too, as deadly demonstrations against the regime erupted at the end of December.

For my nickel this was a move and a danger that we didn't need.

President Trump is fond of saying that he inherited a mess. I usually slough that off to whining and transference. But in the case of North Korea, he has a point.

Within our traditional definition of acceptable risk, by the late Obama years, North Korea was on an arc to have a nuclear-tipped missile capable of reaching the United States within just a few years, a problem recognized and addressed, but not resolved, by the last three administrations. It wasn't illogical, then, for the Trump administration to change the definition of acceptable risk. It just had to do so carefully.

I have a personal history with Korea, having served there twice, the last time in 1997–99, when I negotiated with the Korean People's Army at the truce village of Panmunjom. Our side wasn't trying to do much then, just some increased transparency and some confidence-building measures to prevent or contain incidents along the demilitarized zone between the two Koreas, the most heavily fortified patch of land on the planet. We didn't make much progress. The best we could do was to arrange the dignified return of the remains of some North Korean commandos who had intentionally blown themselves up in a midget submarine that had become disabled during an infiltration of the South.

At the time I marveled at the cognitive dissonance that my North Korean counterparts had to tolerate in order to say and believe the things they told me. In retrospect, though, I think I had my own hang-ups; I really underestimated how much they genuinely believed that I represented a society of undying enmity and abject perfidy. It wasn't performance art on their part. They inhabited a system that took meaning, even existence, from that perception of enmity and perfidy.

So credit to team Trump for trying to deal with something everyone agrees is a pathetic, pathological, and truly irritating little gangster state.

The Trump team has certainly been focused, but even with all the energy of the past year—charged rhetoric, bashing the Obama administration's "strategic patience," multiple naval deployments, and multiple B-1 fly-bys, alternately leaning on and incentivizing China to do more—Kim Jong-un remains undeterred.

Even with an occasional presidential shout-out—Kim's a "pretty smart cookie" and "I would be honored" to meet him—or signals of restraint like Pacific commander Harry Harris characterizing this as about changing minds, not regimes; or Secretary Tillerson working to convince the North Koreans that our goals are not maximalist; or Secretary Mattis's very tough words being focused on actual threats from the North rather than on theoretical capabilities, Kim has been unresponsive.

All of which tends to confirm my belief and that of many intelligence veterans that North Korea is not about to give up its nuclear status. It might be possible to cap, slow, or even roll back some things or perhaps make a residual program more transparent and less prone to proliferation. No doubt Pyongyang would use the occasion to extort more assistance from the global community, and such an arrangement would be as fragile as it would be distasteful. There would always be the danger of the North Koreans cheating. On the other hand, there are no guarantees that the North Korea of Kim Jong-un survives forever, either. And despite charges that this is an irrational regime, *this* North Korea would truly *be* irrational to give up its current weapons entirely. They have seen what happened to Saddam Hussein's Iraq and Muammar Gaddafi's Libya when these weapons were not within reach.

Getting really granular information on Pyongyang has always been hard. During my time at CIA we rated it the toughest intelligence target on earth. Director Pompeo quickly launched a Korea mission center to sharpen focus and improve coordination (much like I had done with Iran and George Tenet had done to fight terrorism), but that didn't diminish North Korea's ruthlessly efficient state security services nor increase the limited number of technical targets in the country nor create an American diplomatic presence there.

So the North Koreans continue their inexorable march to strategic reach and the ability to threaten the United States with a nuclear weapon. In fact, the only thing that has changed much in the last year is that the North has more and longer-range missiles and more and more powerful bombs. In July 2017, North Korea successfully launched an intercontinental ballistic missile. It only went about six hundred miles, but its exaggeratedly high arc showed enough inherent energy for it to travel about four thousand miles with a normal trajectory, enough to reach targets in Alaska, but not (yet) the Lower 48. In September the country detonated what it claimed was a hydrogen bomb. It certainly was big. Estimates ranged up to 280 kilotons. And in November, Pyongyang demonstrated a missile with enough energy to range as far as the East Coast of the United States.

Despite Beijing's embarrassment at Kim Jong-un's flouting

the wishes of the Middle Kingdom, China has continued to abide his behavior rather than inflicting decisive diplomatic and economic pressure on the North. All of which reinforced the Trump administration's instinct to amp up the pressure, particularly via presidential rhetoric, so we were treated to "Rocket Man," "fire and fury," and "totally destroy North Korea"—the last two in front of the UN General Assembly.[35]

Which alarmed a lot of folks like me who couldn't remember any earlier period when we were counting on the leader of North Korea to have enough emotional maturity and geopolitical wisdom to ignore the taunts of an American president. And this North Korean leader was an isolated, ruthless thirty-something steeped in the national mythology created by his grandfather that the United States was one day going to come after him and his country.

The president's secretaries of state and defense were consistently more measured in their words, often making the distinction between Kim's having a nuclear arsenal and his threatening to use it. Here is Mattis coming out of the White House after the September nuclear test: "[W]e have the ability to defend ourselves and our allies, South Korea and Japan, from any attack, and . . . any threat to the United States or its territories, including Guam or our allies, will be met with a massive military response."[36]

And both Mattis and Tillerson wanted to let diplomacy play out as long and as far as possible. Within a week of the president's promise of "fire and fury like the world has never seen," Tillerson signaled the North Koreans, "We continue to be interested in finding a way to get to a dialogue."[37]

But by October the president was publicly dismissing diplomacy, negotiations, agreements, and financial assistance as foolish, failed experiments with Pyongyang, and announced that "only one thing will work" in dealing with North Korea.[38] He didn't further identify the "one thing," but he didn't have to.

Earlier that week, in front of all of the nation's four-star combatant commanders and their spouses during a White House photo op, the president told reporters that the formal scene was the "calm before the storm." Pressed for the meaning of his words, Mr. Trump cryptically replied, "You'll find out." With all the dueling hyperbole between Washington and Pyongyang, there seemed to be an ever-diminishing space for error between the two capitals. Even more concerning was the president's not-so-veiled critique of his own military leadership: "Moving forward, I also expect you to provide me with a broad range of military options, when needed, at a much faster pace."[39]

This was nowhere near the savage campaign taunting of "Lil' Marco" or "Lyin' Ted," the treatment of Sean Spicer or the harsh commentary on Attorney General Jeff Sessions, but it was more important and more ominous. It was the president signaling that he was losing patience with the normal and healthy caution that people who are actually responsible for military action always have. This was his way of trying to pressure them to give him what he thinks he wants. One NSC veteran described it to me as what happens when workable military options cannot be made to fit fixed policy preferences.

For most of the summer and early fall, I had worried that the president could blunder us into war with his language. Now I was afraid he would order us to start one. And I didn't take any comfort in late October when National Security Adviser McMaster told a Washington audience that the president "is not going to accept this regime threatening the United States with a nuclear weapon. He won't accept it. So there are those who have said well what about accept and deter? Well accept and deter is unacceptable. And so this puts us in a situation where we are in a race to resolve this short of military action. . . . The only acceptable objective is denuclearization."[40] McMaster had already told Fox News that when it came to North Korea threatening America with nuclear weapons, the president "is willing to do *anything* necessary to prevent that from happening" (my italics).[41]

Senator Lindsey Graham made it even more stark, characterizing his conversation with the president this way: "If thousands die, they're going to die over there. They're not going to die here—and he's told me that to my face."[42]

I wasn't the only one growing more nervous. Around this time, former CIA director John Brennan put the odds of war in Korea at 20 to 25 percent; Joel Wit, Korean expert and founder of the highly regarded website 38 North handicapped it at 40 percent; the head of the Council on Foreign Relations and former State Department and NSC senior Richard Haass came in at a disquieting 50/50.[43]

Even allowing for administration hyperbole and diplomatic posturing, even conceding that some of this could have been theater to press the Chinese to be more active against the North, I think the general fear, which I shared, was that the guardrails within the White House might not hold this time.

I wondered about the role of intelligence in all of this. Did the traditional assessment about the North's determination still hold? At Aspen, DNI Coats had repeated the calm, sober assessment of North Korean motivation: "[A]nd there is some rationale backing his actions which are survival, survival for his regime, survival for his country." He added that "the nuclear card in your pocket results in a lot of deterrence capability" and then listed Libya and Ukraine as examples of countries that had given up weapons programs and suffered for it.[44]

How was that communicated to the president? And how did he respond? What was said about the prospects for success? The consequences of failure? The dangers of overreach? What questions were being asked of intelligence? Did intelligence weigh in to shape the broad contours of strategy and perhaps bound expectations, or was it merely referred to as an enabler of specific actions already determined, CIA as action arm versus CIA the intelligence service creating the boundaries of logical policy?

CIA takes great pains to construct leadership profiles, personality studies of officials like Kim Jong-un. What did the profile say about the thirty-three-year-old and did that govern the president's aggressive tweet storm against him ("Rocket Man," "short and fat"), or was that more about "Trump being Trump," or perhaps the president's own intuition about how to make this particular deal?

And if the profile and the president's approach were incompatible (even dangerously so), does anyone tell him? Perhaps not. The national security adviser and the president's chief of staff go out of their way to remind us that they are not tweet minders.

The president's instinct toward action, his impatience with process, his lack of interest in history, his focus on "winning," his obsession with protecting the Trump brand (in this case toughness)—all that could conspire to create a very bad decision. Even "kinetic action light"—like shooting at a missile in flight or on the launchpad—could prompt North Korean action, endangering the twenty-five million inhabitants of greater Seoul (along with a couple hundred thousand Americans there), and it would certainly harden North Korean resolve to preserve their nuclear arsenal at any cost.

When I was in government, we used to refer to North Korea as a wicked problem. It's not surprising the issue has been handed off from one administration to another. There simply aren't any good answers here.

There are some problems in life for which there aren't any solutions. And that seems to be an unacceptable formulation for this president.

Afghanistan, Iran, Syria, North Korea, Russia, China. There was no want of issues for the new administration, and there certainly was a great deal of visible activity as it worked to deal with them.

A friend of mine, a security veteran like myself, told me that the administration reminded him of an upside-down duck. Rather than a visible calm above the surface while paddling like hell beneath it, the administration is visibly frenetic (often stimulated by the president's tweets), but there has been less evidence of much going on beneath the surface in terms of developing an overarching, coherent strategy.

He thought that he had identified some themes: an ethnonationalism suspicious of multilateral institutions and agreements; an "America First" attitude that measured success in win-lose short-term deals; economic mercantilism obsessed with balance-of-trade statistics, especially in manufactured goods; and a nearly all-encompassing narcissism that was vulnerable to parades, banquets, and sword dances. To that list I would add a "values-light" approach to the world and human rights, but in all of this we are imputing strategy based on specific actions, words, and tweets rather than the administration laying out a singular vision.

In a notional hundred-day evaluation of administration foreign and security policy, I would give an "incomplete." The administration failed to turn in a term paper, as it were—a coherent, global strategy.

There had been *some* efforts at completing the assignment. The president's speech before the UN General Assembly in September was billed by the White House as "outlining an America First foreign policy," a policy labeled by the press office with the marketable but hardly explanatory phrase "principled realism."

But the UN speech raised more questions than it answered. The president used one or another form of the word "sovereignty" more than twenty times in the speech and identified the concept as the linchpin of a functioning international system. Then, after promising not to impose our way of life on anyone, Mr. Trump skewered five theoretically sovereign nations for what they were doing internally and called for international action against a "depraved" North Korea, a "murderous" Iran, a "criminal" Syria, a "destabilizing" Cuba, and a "corrupt" Venezuela.[45] It was hard to create parallax to a set of common, unifying principles from the points in the speech other than that sovereignty was a permanent condition for us, but a transient one for anyone we so designated.

I suspect that National Security Adviser McMaster understood that the administration was still coming up short on "the vision thing." Early on he hired highly regarded defense expert Nadia Schadlow to write the administration's National Security Strategy. The NSS is an obscure requirement from the

Goldwater-Nichols Department of Defense Reorganization Act of 1986. It is intended precisely for this purpose: to force the executive to articulate his "big picture." Most years it is more of a bureaucratic burden and is often left undone, but occasionally the document breaks new ground. I wrote two for President George H. W. Bush while serving on his NSC staff in the early 1990s, and the drafting prompted a spirited debate over the reversibility of changes then under way in the Soviet Union. Later, the 2002 edition codified the George W. Bush administration's doctrine of preemption.

Now Schadlow had to describe what an "America First" National Security Strategy really looked like, not in 140- or 280-character bursts, but in dozens of coherent, consistent pages. Then she would have to shepherd her draft through an administration that had not really demonstrated strategic consistency or even message discipline. And then this road map had to be approved by a president who cherishes unpredictability and does not seem to be comfortable with the long form of anything.

Administratively, all that is challenging. Substantively, as Schadlow aligned the draft strategy with the president's tweets and statements, it would mark a dramatic break from America's past, shaped since 1950 by the Truman-era policy document NSC-68, the road map for Cold War opposition to the Soviet Union and then, even after the fall of communism, for American engagement in the world.

I dusted off a copy and reread the nearly seventy-year-old document and was struck by its deep sense of history, the scope of its vision, its reverence for American values, and the toughness of the actions it was willing to countenance (like developing a hydrogen bomb). It even had a section devoted to describing the fundamental purpose of the United States: "to assure the integrity and vitality of our free society, which is founded upon the dignity and worth of the individual."

Elaborating on the underlying conflict in the realm of ideas and values, the document gave a full-throated defense of "the marvelous diversity, the deep tolerance, the lawfulness of the free society," and added for emphasis that "the free society does not fear, it welcomes, diversity," Then, describing U.S. intentions, NSC-68 promised to "foster a world environment in which the American system can survive and flourish" while rejecting "the concept of isolation" and affirming "our positive participation in the world community." For emphasis, once again, it repeated its core course of action: ours would be "a policy of attempting to develop a healthy international community."

In late May, National Security Adviser McMaster coauthored a piece in the *Wall Street Journal* with Gary Cohn, director of the National Economic Council. Mixed in with the usual reverence for American values and the promise that "America First" did not mean America alone, McMaster (a career military officer with years of service abroad) and Cohn (a former president and CEO of Goldman Sachs)—the kind of American internationalists you would order from central casting—penned the following startling line: "The world is not a 'global community' but an arena where nations, non-governmental actors, and businesses engage and compete for advantage." NSC-68 this was not.

Nor was the National Security Strategy that was issued in mid-December, the only such document actually accomplished in the first year of an administration and the first rolled out in a speech by the president himself. The NSS continued the theme that the world was a competitive place—politically, economically, militarily, and informationally—and differentiated itself from previous documents by organizing all of its elements around this principle of constant, sustained competition. (One could not help but recall Hobbes's formulation of "all against all.")

Unlike NSC-68, which had been a Department of State and Department of Defense response to Truman's tasking, the NSS self-consciously mirrored President Trump's language in his previous speeches and executive orders. The speechwriters were actively consulted in the drafting process. Thus there was a lot of talk of sovereignty and reciprocity and competition and economic success while downplaying traditional themes like engagement. Sam Greene, director of the Russia Institute at King's College in London, toted up 151 mentions of the economy in the NSS, while there were 17 of Russia, 14 of Europe, and 2 of NATO.

The drafters of the NSS could not afford to ignore the president's tweets, which carried the stamp of policy. That was a tall order. The spontaneity and inconsistency of the tweets—along with the president's wrath at being contradicted—prompted one keen observer, David Ignatius of the *Washington Post,* to refer to the "iron whim" of the Oval Office.[46]

Built into the strategy document was an underlying fear that world events were not moving in our direction and "America First" was designed to get ahead of those trends, to put America on a winning track, and mute the instinct to turn first to international organizations for solutions. Historian Walter Russell Mead wrote that "strategists in the Trump national-security team believe that it is American power, not multilateral institutions, that keeps the West afloat."[47]

Sometimes the language was overtly aggressive: "energy security" was now "energy dominance," for example, not quite the vocabulary of an interdependent world. The text set the stage for the Department of Defense to announce the following month, "We will continue to prosecute the campaign against terrorists, but great power competition—not terrorism—is now the primary focus of U.S. national security."[48] There was also a clear subtext challenging the relevance of the post–World War II institutions spawned by NSC-68. The burden was now on those institutions to show they were still fulfilling their purpose.

Schadlow's work got deservedly good marks for "normalizing" the language of an often rambling, inconsistent, and overly dramatic president. Relying on the talents of a solid staff and the expertise of career professionals, she crafted a document about which serious people could argue rather than simply dismiss out of hand.

And argue they will. Despite the president's electoral win, it is not at all clear that Americans are ready to fully embrace the policies of what Richard Haass has called "the first post–World War II American president to view the burdens of world leadership as outweighing the benefits."[49] A Chicago Council of Global Affairs national opinion survey in the summer of 2017 found that popular support for the United States taking an active role in world affairs was about the same that it was in 1974 (63 percent now, 66 percent then). The percentage saying that maintaining alliances was a very effective way to achieve foreign policy goals actually went up from 38 percent in 2014 to 49 percent today. A record number of Americans now say that international trade is good for American consumers (78 percent), for the economy overall (72 percent), and even for U.S. job creation (57 percent). And the percentage who believe immigrants represent a critical threat to the United States dropped from 55 percent overall in 1998 to only

37 percent today (even though the number of Republicans who believe that they are a threat has remained stable at about 60 percent).[50]

Then there were questions about how much the relatively moderate language of the document actually represented the president, rather than what one observer called a cri de coeur from inside the deep state signaling that some of traditional America endures.[51]

In tone, the administration said that the NSS was all about championing America, but I wondered what America that was: the national/nativist state defined by blood, soil, and shared history? Or America the creedal nation, the Madisonian embodiment of Enlightenment ideals? I suspected that it was the former, since the champion, Donald Trump, had already alleged that American elections were "rigged," three million people had voted illegally (all against him), the seat of government was a "swamp," the free press was the "enemy of the people," crime was at record rates, and the American judicial system was a "joke."

In all that, he sounded a lot like an Internet troll on a botnet controlled from Saint Petersburg. Or like Vladimir Putin.

Whom he never could quite admit had worked to get him elected.

But Putin had. And then some.

SEVEN

TRUMP, RUSSIA, AND TRUTH

Late in the summer of 2017 a detailed story in *Wired* magazine on how Russia was subverting U.S. democracy cited a European study that found that, rather than trying to change minds, the Russian goal was simply "to destroy and undermine confidence in Western media."[1]

Conservative talk radio host and never-Trumper Charlie Sykes echoed the theme: "The essence of propaganda is . . . to overwhelm your critical sensibilities. It's to make you doubt the existence of a knowable truth."[2]

The Russians found a surprising but powerful ally in candidate and later President Trump, who attacked American institutions with much the same ferocity as did Russian propaganda, as when he identified the press as the "enemy of the American people." The attack on the media was essential to the campaign, but it was rarely about arguing the facts. James Poniewozik, TV critic for the *New York Times*, reflected in a June 2017 tweet that Trump didn't try to argue the facts of a case—"just that there is no truth, so you should just follow your gut & your tribe."

Wired also pointed out a remarkable convergence between the themes of the Russian media/web blitz and the Trump campaign: Clinton's emails, Clinton's health, rigged elections, Bernie Sanders's raw deal, and so on.

And then there was the echo chamber between Russian news and American right-wing outlets, epitomized by the sight of Sean Hannity on Fox News shilling his fantasy that the tragic murder of DNC staffer Seth Rich was somehow related to the theft of DNC emails and the dumping of them to WikiLeaks—that it was an inside job and not connected to Russia at all.

There is a lot of American responsibility and even guilt to go around here. Trump seemed the perfect candidate for the Russians' purpose, and that was ultimately our choice and not theirs. But the central fact to be faced and understood here is that the Russians have gotten very good indeed at invading and often dominating the American information space.

For me, that story goes back twenty years.

I arrived in San Antonio, Texas, in January 1996 to take command of what was then called the Air Intelligence Agency. As I've written elsewhere,[3] Air Force intelligence was on the cutting edge of thinking about the new cyber domain, and I owed special thanks to my staff there for teaching me so much about this new battle space.

There was a question in Texas that we debated with all the intensity of Jesuits arguing an issue of theology at a medieval university: Were we in the cyber business or were we in the information dominance business? Did we want to master cyber networks as a tool of war or influence or were we more ambitious, with an intent to shape how adversaries or even societies received and processed all information? Since the United States now has a Cyber Command (and not an Information Dominance Command), you can probably figure how this all turned out. But the debate was lively.

Cyber was complicated enough as we worked through the legal, policy, operational, and oversight considerations of new and untested concepts like computer network operations (CNO), computer network defense (CND), computer network attack (CNA, i.e., destroying networks or information), and computer network exploitation (CNE, i.e., spying).

It was all so complicated that taking on information dominance looked like a bridge too far. Not only would we have had to deal with all the challenges of computer network operations, but we would have to fold in such esoteric topics as deception, public affairs, public diplomacy, perception management, and psychological operations and still keep a handle on the more traditional tasks of electronic countermeasures, jamming, and defense suppression. That, and more, would be what information dominance would demand.

Besides, we knew we could not get very far along in the information dominance space without creating serious First Amendment implications. In a globalized, interconnected world, how does one affect, say, Belorussian perceptions without also affecting the perceptions of Americans (which is clearly prohibited)?

So we stuck with door number one: *cyber dominance.*

Russia, we now know, opted for door number two: *information dominance.*

It was a logical choice for a weak but proud nation, one that could not match the West in the traditional forms of economic or military power. And it was less about matching the West than it was about bringing the West (especially the United States) down to Russia's level by challenging its confidence in itself and its institutions.

And the enabler for all of this was the World Wide Web and social media, the ability to "publish" without credentials, without the need to offer proof (at least in the traditional sense) or even to identify yourself. The demise of a respected media as an arbiter of fact or at least as a curator of data let loose impulses that were at once leveling, coarsening, and misleading. A. C. Grayling, the British philosopher, says that this explosion of information overwhelmed us and happened so quickly that education did not keep up, leaving us, he laments, with regularly reading the biggest washroom wall in history.

In a way, it is surprising that the Russians would be the first to so ruthlessly exploit all this since in 1991, at the fall of the Soviet Union, Russia inherited a dysfunctional communications system with limited global connectivity.[4] But by 2017 three-fourths of the country had access to the Internet; some Russian firms, like Kaspersky Lab, were global leaders; and Russian organized crime groups had adopted cyber tools as a significant engine of profit. The weak rule of law, economic uncompetitiveness elsewhere, and the technical skills of the Russian people combined to create a capacity that soon attracted the attention of the Russian state.

And the Russian most interested in that capacity was General Valery Gerasimov, an armor officer of some talent who, after combat time in the Second Chechen War, served as commander of the Leningrad and then Moscow military districts. Writing in

2013, Gerasimov pointed to the "blurring [of] the lines between the state of war and the state of peace" and—after noting the Arab Awakening—observed that "a perfectly thriving state can, in a matter of months and even days, be transformed into an arena of fierce armed conflict . . . and sink into a web of chaos."

He continued, "The role of nonmilitary means of achieving political and strategic goals has grown," and the trend now was "the broad use of political, economic, informational, humanitarian, and other nonmilitary measures—*applied in coordination with the protest potential of the population*" (my emphasis).

Seeing large clashes of men and metal as "a thing of the past," Gerasimov called for "long-distance, contactless actions against the enemy" and included in his arsenal "informational actions, devices, and means." He concluded, "The information space opens wide asymmetrical possibilities for reducing the fighting potential of the enemy," and so new "models of operations and military conduct" were needed.[5]

It was, of course, taken as a given that Russia was already in a state of conflict with the West.

Putin had appointed Gerasimov chief of the general staff in late 2012. Fifteen months later there was evidence of his doctrine in action with the Russian annexation of Crimea and occupation of parts of the Donbas in eastern Ukraine. Now called "hybrid war" by the West, Russia's approach limited the overt use of force, focused extraordinary attention on the population, and combined surprise, ambiguity, and plausible deniability in a way that seemed to freeze any opposition. Gerasimov's notorious "little green men"—special operations forces with modern Russian weaponry but no insignia and balaclava masks covering their faces—effected a bloodless takeover of the Crimean peninsula.

In eastern Ukraine, Russia promoted the fiction of a spontaneous rebellion by local Russian speakers against a neofascist regime in Kiev, aided only by Russian volunteers, a story line played out in clever, high-quality broadcasts from news services like RT and Sputnik coupled with relentless trolling on social media.

With no bands, banners, or insignia, Russia had altered borders within Europe—by force—but with an informational canopy so dense as to make the aggression opaque, responsibility unclear, and responses uncertain.

One incident illustrates the extent of the Russian informational and population-centric effort: the downing by Russian advisers and Ukrainian separatists in July 2014 of a *scheduled and on-course* Malaysian airliner over Ukraine with 298 innocents on board. Western intelligence knows a lot about the weapon used, the Buk or SA-11/13 system. It's widely deployed, it's big, and it consists of multiple tracked vehicles. It has unique radar signals to acquire and identify targets and to launch, track, and control its missiles.

Overhead satellites would routinely gather electronic intelligence that locates the radar. Imagery satellites would be tasked with imaging the areas where it operates. There is also a branch of intelligence that measures physical phenomena. Measurement and signature intelligence surely would have recorded the heat from the airliner's explosion and likely would have detected the heat plume of the missile itself.

Admittedly, *some* of the data may not have been collected in this specific instance and *not all* of the information would have been releasable to the public. But in a fact-based world, the evidence of what the Russians/separatists did would have been compelling.

Little matter. This world was not fact-based.

Shortly after the shootdown, the Russian information machine created an alternative universe and manufactured a Ukrainian fighter in the vicinity of the airliner and even spiced up the narrative by claiming Vladimir Putin's plane was in the area returning from Brazil at about the same time.[6] With all the obfuscation, within two weeks of the shootdown, 82 percent of Russians were convinced that the Malaysian jet had been downed by the Ukrainian government. One percent admitted Russian culpability.

Beleaguered Russians were a ready-made audience for this kind of thing, of course, but how different is this from the many "beleaguered" Americans—subjected to the same kind of information barrage—who now believe that Hillary Clinton actually arranged for American uranium to be shipped to Russia even though she didn't and they haven't received any?

All the Russian story lines in the shootdown case were quite inventive, fine examples of Gerasimov's use of the "information space." They finally settled on the shot being taken by a Buk, but one under Ukrainian government rather than Russian separatist control. Various other explanations had been floated and changed quickly. Those false starts, rather than undercutting Moscow's credibility, seemed to merely erode confidence that anyone could ever know for sure.

To me all the "explanations" were predictable and easy to dismiss. But they were *not* dismissed. It all seemed a version of a DC Comics plotline where Superman visits Bizarro World and all is reversed: up is down, in is out, good is bad. Peter Pomerantsev, in his recent book on Russia, *Nothing Is True and Everything Is Possible*, attributes that to strident media nationalism and propaganda appealing to the pride of a traumatized people. But the techniques used were transferable. Now these same Russian information operations have been used to undercut democratic processes in the United States and Europe, and to erode confidence in institutions like NATO and the European Union.

Indeed, Garry Kasparov, Soviet chess champion turned Russian dissident, outlined the progression for me. Putin's attacks were "developed and honed first in Russia and then the Russian-speaking near abroad before expanding to Europe and the U.S." Unable to play for parity, Russia—an inherently weaker power—now just tries to bring its opponents down to its level.

America in general and U.S. intelligence in particular were slow to recognize and appreciate this new Russian approach. In retirement, former DNI Jim Clapper admitted, "We had a general awareness . . . of Russian use of social media—Facebook ads, use of Twitter, fake news implants . . . but now, as time has elapsed . . . I've certainly learned a lot more about the depth and breadth of what the Russians were about."[7] Jim's intelligence community was often consumed by the more immediate tasks of counterterrorism and counterproliferation, and policymakers in the Obama administration tended to view the Russians as an irritant rather than a strategic danger.

And then there was the question of the lens we were using to understand all of this. Committed to a path of *cyber* dominance for ourselves, we seemed to lack the doctrinal vision to fully understand what the Russians were up to with their more full-spectrum *information* dominance. Even now, many commentators refer to what the Russians did to the American electoral process as a cyber attack, but the actual cyber portion of that was fairly straightforward.

American intelligence eventually detected that and some other aspects of the Russian effort and dutifully tried to alert its political masters. But there was so much more involved, and our understanding of the story evolved only slowly over time.

There was one man, however, who more than any other was trying to ring the alarm more than two years before the 2016 elections.

I sat with Clint Watts on an overcast November 2017 afternoon in an office in midtown Manhattan that had been made available by one of Clint's former West Point classmates. I had recently been on a panel with Clint discussing Russian active measures against the West and was aware of his extraordinary testimony on that topic to the U.S. Congress.

Clint is an FBI veteran and has done work at West Point's Combating Terrorism Center and as a contractor for the intelligence and special operations communities, in addition to his scholarly work at George Washington University and the Foreign Policy Research Institute.

In early 2014, Watts and two colleagues, J. M. Berger and Andrew Weisburd, were studying the use of social media by ISIS to recruit and proselytize its members when he came across unexpected connections between a Syrian/Iranian troll[8] network and Russian social media accounts. This looked like a common effort to support Assad, but Clint saw more. The longer he looked into the Western-looking accounts, the more he was convinced that Russia was reigniting its old active measures campaign, defined years ago by the U.S. Information Agency as the "manipulative use of slogans, arguments, disinformation and carefully selected true information . . . to try to influence the attitudes and actions of foreign publics and governments." But this time the Russians were taking full advantage of easily accessible, low-cost social media platforms.

As the Malaysian airliner story above suggests, the Russians had already succeeded in what Clint calls "bubbling" their own population, that is, isolating and controlling their news flow. But the accounts he thought were backed by the Russians had ties to both the United States and Europe. The longer he watched, the more he was convinced that this was an organized effort against the West. To Clint, it looked like the Russians were taking what had worked for them domestically and exploring how well these techniques would work with a foreign audience.

Evidence mounted. The faux personae created at the Russian bot farm—the Saint Petersburg–based Internet Research Agency— were routinely represented by stock photos taken from the Internet, and the themes they pushed were consistently pro-Russian. There was occasional truth to their postings, but clear manipulation as well, and they all seemed to push in unison.

The Russians knew their demographic. The most common English words in their faux Twitter user profiles were "God," "military," "Trump," "family," "country," "conservative," "Christian," "America," and "Constitution." The most commonly used hashtags were #nuclear, #media, #Trump, and #Benghazi . . . all surefire dog whistles certain to create trending.

It was straightforward science for Clint, J.M., and Andrew to use smart algorithms to determine whether something was trending because of genuine human interaction or simply because it was being pushed by the Russian botnet.[9] And Clint could see that the bots ebbed and flowed based upon the needs of the moment. He tried to call attention to what he was discovering, but found American intelligence fixated on his original ISIS mission, with little energy left over to explore or even be much interested in his Russia discovery.

Clint characterized 2014 to me as a year of capability development for the Russians and pointed to a bot-generated petition movement calling for the return of Alaska to Russia that got more than forty thousand supporters while helping the Russians build their cadre and perfect their tactics. In 2015, with that success in hand, the Russians started a real push toward the American audience, by grabbing any divisive social issue they could identify. They were particularly attracted to issues generated from organic American content, issues that had their origin in American commentary. Almost by definition, issues with a U.S. provenance could be portrayed as genuine concerns to Americans, and they were already preloaded in the patois of the American political dialogue (and often U.S.-based conspiracy theorists).

"Jade Helm 15" was an American military exercise conducted across several southern and western states in the summer of 2015 that Russian-based but Western-looking social media accounts portrayed as the impending imposition of martial law, a characterization echoed in American alt-right media outlets. The *New York Times* reported that Infowars, a website operated by Alex Jones, a Texas-based libertarian talk radio host, ominously suggested that the name "Helm" was an acronym for "Homeland Eradication of Local Militants."[10]

Jones fed the conspiracy plotline—one that eventually included trains with shackles transiting Texas, an exercise map labeling Texas and Utah as hostile territory, and abandoned Walmarts being used as prison camps—by broadcasting, "This is just a cover for deploying the military on the streets. I've hardly ever heard of something joint like this unless they're planning an invasion."[11]

In this and similar episodes, Twitter was the most powerful tool. Watts pointed out to me that Twitter makes falsehoods seem more believable through sheer repetition and volume. He labeled it a kind of "computational propaganda." Twitter in turn drives mainstream media, and it also inspires subsequent, more detailed content posts and pulls on Facebook.

And Twitter as a gateway is easier to manipulate than other platforms since in the twitterverse we voluntarily break down into like-minded tribes, easily identified by our likes and by whom we follow. Watts says that the Russians don't have to "bubble" us—that is, create a monolithic information space friendly for their messaging. We have already done that to ourselves since, he says, social media is as gerrymandered as any set of state electoral districts in the country. Targeting can become so precise that he considers social media "a smart bomb delivery system." In Senate testimony, Watts noted that with tailored news feeds, a feature rather than a bug for those getting their news online, voters see "only stories and opinions suiting their preferences and biases—ripe condition for Russian disinformation campaigns."[12]

Charlie Sykes, the "never Trump" conservative, believes "many Trump voters get virtually all their information from inside the bubble. . . . [C]onservative media has become a safe space for people who want to be told they don't have to believe anything that's uncomfortable or negative. . . . The details are less important than the fact that you're being persecuted, you're being victimized by people you loathe." Thomas Rid, a German-born, London-based, America-knowledgeable expert on cyber conflict, stressed the point in front of the U.S. Congress: "The more polarized a society, the more vulnerable it is."[13]

There were so many tweets and YouTube videos "proving" that Jade Helm was an attempt to impose martial law on hostile states that President Obama later jokingly identified it as his favorite conspiracy theory while in office.[14] It was no laughing matter at the time, though, as Governor Greg Abbott was forced to deploy observers from the Texas National Guard to calm public concerns.

It didn't offer much humor for the future, either, with the Russians pocketing a success achieved by amplifying and manipulating themes all too native to America.

And now there was the specter of the leading Republican presidential candidate reinforcing the belief that the Obama administration was indeed capable of such things. He also went out of his way to personally validate conspiracy-mongers like Jones. Before 2015 was out, Donald Trump gushed, "Your reputation is amazing. I will not let you down." Jones responded that 90 percent of his audience supported the candidate.[15]

And this is the same Alex Jones who is a 9/11 truther and who broadcasts that the Sandy Hook murder of twenty little children and six staffers never happened. It was all a hoax.

By the summer of 2015, in light of Russia's successful experiments with broad American audiences, Watts was convinced the Russians would go after the American election. He told me that clear patterns in Russian trolling and messaging soon emerged: suppress Democratic turnout by discouraging voters; push Trump via a sympathetic echo chamber; support Green Party candidate Jill Stein to bleed votes away from Hillary Clinton; sow overall discontent among Democrats by saying Bernie Sanders had gotten a raw deal; discredit Clinton on a host of issues.

All of this was also useful in supporting the core goal: to broadcast the dysfunction and corruption of American democracy. Watts explains that Russia's actual hacking of voter databases was likely more to erode American confidence than to change or even to exploit any American information. And, he added, the Russians probably feared the U.S. response if they actually tried to affect the vote.

It wasn't surprising that in October 2016 the overarching theme of the Russian campaign had become the rigging of the election and voter fraud. We now know WikiLeaks' Julian Assange was already suggesting this theme in messages to Donald Trump, Jr. Even with a Clinton win, the Russians could still achieve many of their objectives if Trump simply called foul.

There were certainly sympathetic echoes from Trump himself. In October he was routinely telling campaign crowds, "Remember, we are competing in a rigged election. They even want to try and rig the election at the polling booths, where so many cities are corrupt and voter fraud is all too common."[16]

The candidate frequently tweeted on the topic.

> **Donald J. Trump** ✔
> @realDonaldTrump
>
> The election is absolutely being rigged by the dishonest and distorted media pushing Crooked Hillary - but also at many polling places - SAD
>
> 12:01 PM - Oct 16, 2016
>
> 💬 16,264   ↻ 20,904   ♡ 53,946

Beyond the candidate's sympathetic ear and voice, the Russians were abetted in all these endeavors by their theft of emails from the Democratic National Committee and from Clinton campaign chairman John Podesta. The embarrassing correspondence was pushed through platforms like WikiLeaks and DCLeaks where it was scooped up, interpreted, and amplified by (sometimes) unwitting but (always) enthusiastic bloggers, tweeters, and even the mainstream media.

Russian public news outlets—flashy, high-tech Sputnik and RT—would also pick up the stories, and although they had few actual viewers in the United States, they would add to the buzz and create high-quality English-language news hits that were then posted to YouTube and other social media sites where they enjoyed a wide following (even if the sourcing was often murky and unattributed).

One former reporter from Sputnik news says that he was told to "push narratives that the US government is hypocritical, corrupt and lacks the moral standing to confront Putin's dictatorship on human rights."[17] He was specifically encouraged to push the conspiracy theory about the killing of DNC staffer Seth Rich.

Despite the seemingly elegant synchronization, Watts was quick to tell me that the Russian effort wasn't always tightly orchestrated. His explanation seemed to me to echo the differences between American football and what the rest of the world calls football: soccer. Both are choreographed, but the former is characterized by a strategic planning conference every thirty-five seconds (a huddle) to assign specific tasks and detailed duties to every player, whereas the latter assigns general roles to be followed as the game demands and players respond.

The Russian effort was clearly the latter, but their efforts were always alert to sympathetic vibrations within the American information universe when American news outlets, such as Fox

News, picked up on their themes. Max Boot, a "never Trump" Republican neocon, points out how Sean Hannity, Fox Business Network's Lou Dobbs, and even Fox commentator and former Speaker of the House Newt Gingrich all seemingly bought into the Rich conspiracy, a dynamic that allowed the Russians to reinforce and reenergize their narrative. Boot railed against the Fox network as "Trump TV," Trump's "own version of RT," and its prime-time ratings czar Sean Hannity as "the president's de facto minister of information."[18] Boot later added that Trump often repaid the debt by retweeting their work favorably to his vast Twitter following.

My own sample set of Fox News these days is fairly limited. That's the product of my own (regrettable) self-filtering, I suppose, but I do recall a day in August 2017 as CNN and MSNBC were in high pitch about North Korea, but at the moment in commercial break, when I tuned my car's satellite radio to Fox only to hear a rather detailed story about gun rights being under assault in the process of adopting children. It seemed a perfect metaphor for the broader trend.

There are some genuine heroes on the Fox network like Shepard Smith, Chris Wallace, Charles Krauthammer, Bret Baier, Dana Perino, and Steve Hayes (the last three, personal friends), but for the most part I agree with Boot. Hannity, for example, enthusiastically gave a platform to WikiLeaks' Julian Assange shortly before Trump's inauguration, traveling to London to interview him at the Ecuadorian embassy, where Assange had taken refuge from authorities following a Swedish rape allegation.

When Hannity asked how he had obtained the DNC emails, Assange responded that "our source is not the Russian government and it is not a state party."[19] Hannity later told Fox News, "I believe everything [Assange] said," and lavished praise on the

Internet activist.[20] He also seconded the Assange/Russia/Trump themes about corrupt America and fake news: "What we learned in this election is how deeply corrupt . . . the level of our politics is, and collusion between media outlets and campaigns. There is not objective journalism in America. And of course, the media doesn't want to cover that story."[21]

President-Elect Trump—a Fox News junkie and Hannity fan—picked up on the exchange to quickly tweet, "Julian Assange said . . . Russians did not give him the info!"

That comment, of course, was like mother's milk to a president-elect jealous of his electoral legitimacy and only two days away from an American intelligence briefing (the January 6 briefing at Trump Tower described in chapter 4) that would tell him quite the opposite.

It all worked, at least for some. In that Pittsburgh back room I visited, one participant noted Assange's denial that he got the DNC emails from the Russians. His word (and the Trump tweet) seemed enough for her, and my observation that Assange was a known liar and unlikely to even know the ultimate provenance of the emails didn't seem to matter. "Truth" was what was trending, a classic case of a Russian acolyte (Assange), a Trump acolyte (Hannity), the Russian media machine, twitterverse trends, and Trump tweets aligning to create an unbreakable narrative.

The Fox/Trump/RT alliance resurfaced in the fall of 2017, this time pivoting off the TV testimony of Bill Binney, an NSA technician who quit the agency in protest in late 2001. Binney had taken a technical difference within NSA and turned it into a moral crusade against alleged criminal surveillance by the agency, a story told in some detail in my book *Playing to the Edge*.

Not surprisingly, Binney has become something of a regular

on Fox as the network traded its traditional conservative, national security credentials for a brand of Trump populism. Binney was on air ten times in the twelve months after September 2016, largely pushing his theory of indiscriminate surveillance, including, conveniently enough, the surveillance of Trump Tower.

In March 2017, he began to push the theory that the DNC hack could well have been a CIA "false flag" operation with American intelligence using its technological wizardry to masquerade as the Russians. It was the deepest of deep state plots, a renegade IC mucking with an American election and blaming it on a foreign power, a theme also pushed by conservative talk radio host Rush Limbaugh and Russian news outlet Sputnik.[22]

Then in August, Binney made the unfounded claim to Fox News' Tucker Carlson in a nonchallenging, uninterrupted, obediently nodding, near-cheerleading interview that the download speed of the DNC hack would not have permitted it to be done remotely. It had to have been an inside job (a variation of the Seth Rich plot).

President Trump watches Fox and consults with Hannity, and it wasn't long before he was leaning on CIA chief Mike Pompeo to check out Binney and his theory. The theory, after all, aligned nicely with his own views on what the Russians did (or, more accurately, did not do).

Pompeo, understandably, demurred. Approaching Binney would have given status to someone whom most in the IC thought was a wack-a-doodle. And of course, there was always the option of simply asking NSA if Binney's published technical theory was even feasible. Even several members of Binney's own circle, the conspiracy-minded and usually united Veteran Intelligence Professionals for Sanity, believed this one to be a crackpot theory.

Pompeo meeting with Binney would give his views gravitas beyond their merits and stoke the fires of conspiracy theorists nationally, which is perhaps what the president wanted, since he insisted, and Pompeo finally heard out Binney at CIA headquarters for an hour in late October. By early November the entire affair was public, with Binney being interviewed at length by RT.

RT!

In *that* interview Binney said he believed his audience with Pompeo had been driven by his Fox News hits and the president's desire "to get some facts" because, in Binney's view, the intelligence agencies weren't telling the president the truth, as usual changing their "story to fit their agenda." He also condemned the "emotionally generated, agenda-driven dribble" that characterized the Russia story in the press. RT quickly posted the interview on YouTube.[23]

Binney continued his accusations in a second interview on RT America with Ed Schultz, former MSNBC talk show host, praising the president and Pompeo but again railing against the continued dishonesty of the press and the intelligence community.[24]

Pompeo could not have welcomed any of this. It threatened to compromise him with his workforce, who had their own views of Binney and, as far as the president's attitude toward the Russians was concerned, had their own views of him, too. The agency press office dutifully repeated its support for the original intelligence community assessment: the Russians did it.

Within a few days, Pompeo would again have to pledge his commitment to the assessment, this time following a Trump-Putin pull-aside on the margins of the Asia-Pacific Economic Cooperation (APEC) summit in Vietnam. Trump came out of that meeting saying that Putin really believed his own denials, and Trump seemed to agree when he condemned Obama-era intelligence leaders responsible for the Russian report as "political hacks" and then added, "I mean, give me a break. So you look at it, I mean, you have Brennan, you have Clapper, and you have Comey. Comey is proven now to be a liar and he is proven now to be a leaker."

The president's charge of "political hacks" at the head of the American intelligence community was part of a broader pattern. When the institutions of the American government refuse to kowtow to the president's transient whim, he sets out to devalue and delegitimize them in a way rarely, if ever, seen before in our history. A free (but admittedly imperfect) press is "fake news," unless, of course, it is Fox; the FBI is in "tatters," led by a "nut job" director and conducting a "witch hunt"; the Department of Justice, and particularly the attorney general, is weak; the intelligence community, in addition to being led by political hacks, is "Nazi"-like; the courts are manned by "so called" judges. Even the National Football League and the Boy Scouts of America have had to defend their integrity against presidential attacks designed solely to protect the president's brand.

In this case, the president had to walk back a bit the next day, saying, "As to whether I believe it or not, I'm with our agencies, *especially as currently constituted. As currently led, by fine people,* I believe very much in our intelligence agencies."[25]

But that did more harm than good, since it assesses the reliability of the intelligence community based on the personal political loyalty of its leadership. That dynamic, which shows every sign of continuing, is horribly destructive. If that takes hold, it will take a generation for these institutions to claw back their reputations for objective, fact-based analysis in some future administration.

I often wonder if the president is aware of the dynamic, or even cares. And has anyone in or near his inner circle, more aware of the consequences, tried to explain it to him?

I do not envy the IC leadership. The jobs are inherently tough without the added burden of working in a minefield of politics and ego. And when the IC leadership speaks publicly, it is sometimes hard to craft language accurate enough to please the workforce but tuned politically enough not to anger the White House.

DCIA Pompeo had to dig out of such a hole when he told a D.C. think tank audience that "the Russian meddling that took place *did not affect the outcome of the election*," a line that mirrored the Trump line since the fateful January 6 meeting at Trump Tower, but which the intelligence community never said or supported. "Too tough to call" had always been their view.[26]

The full context of the interview makes Pompeo's quote less stark than reported, and the Agency was quick to issue the standard clarification: "The intelligence assessment with regard to Russian election meddling has not changed, and the director did not intend to suggest that it had."

And in a later interview the CIA chief warned, "This threat is not going to go away. The Russians have been at this a long time, and I fully expect they'll continue to be at it."[27]

But all this highlights the challenge of publicly sustaining analytic precision in the face of presidential language that was far from precise and language that has often been echoed by Moscow via the Twitter accounts of Kremlin-linked groups. #ReleaseTheMemo—supporting a Republican effort to discredit the FBI—was the top-trending hashtag for those groups in January until it was overtaken by #SchumerShutdown, a reference to the president's description of that month's three-day government stoppage. #ReleaseTheMemo came back to the top of the charts after the government shutdown ended. So rather than the president condemning the Russians for what they have done, we have the strange phenomenon of Russia often amplifying what the president says.[28]

With that kind of dynamic and a president who has imposed an overpowering cult of loyalty on his administration, the ghost of politicization is always lingering close by for sincere but conflicted senior officials.

It has also become the habit of President Trump, drained of his moral authority by repeated untruths, to rely on that of his key subordinates. And in so doing, he adds the erosion of personal reputation to the damage he is doing to the institutions of government. Thus we saw highly regarded Chief of Staff John Kelly, retired Marine general and Gold Star father, defend the president's behavior during a bereavement call to the widow of a soldier killed in Niger.

I understand Kelly's motivation. No one who has ever been required to make this most difficult of calls would criticize a president who has. I was also offended that Congresswoman Frederica Wilson—who was not an intended recipient of the call, but overheard it—decided to talk about it publicly. And General Kelly in his White House press room remarks gave a soaring account of how the remains of American service members are honorably handled.

But, sadly, he then conducted a Trumplike, blistering, unnecessary, and (it turns out) inaccurate ad hominem assault on the congresswoman for her alleged behavior during the dedication of an FBI building in Miami in 2015. Of course, nowhere in his remarks could he refer to the president lying about the contents of the call since, despite Trump's denials, there was now agreement that he had actually said, "He knew what he signed up for," when he referred to Sergeant Johnson.[29]

To round things out, White House press secretary Sarah Huckabee Sanders pushed back against later criticism by saying it would be "highly inappropriate" to get into a debate with a four-star general. It was as if Kelly's rook had just been used to neatly castle Trump's king.

Former chairman of the Joint Chiefs of Staff Mike Mullen noticed, later telling ABC News that "John's politicizing the death of his own son . . . is indicative of the fact that he clearly is very supportive of the president no matter what. And that, that was really a sad moment for me."[30]

Very strong words, but I've heard similar concerns from other former senior officers with whom I have spoken, and I had my own example of General Kelly being "very supportive" of the president. Two days after the president tweeted his infamous "Obama wiretapped me" charges, Kelly (then secretary of homeland security) was asked by Wolf Blitzer about it and responded with what seemed to me to be both true and a perfect safe haven: "I don't know anything about it."

Case closed. Or at least it should have been.

But General Kelly then volunteered his reputation to protect the president: "If the President of the United States said that, he's got his reasons to say it. He must have some convincing evidence that took place." And then for good measure he issued a slammer against Barack Obama: "I don't pretend to even guess as to what the motivation may have been for the previous administration to do something like that."[31] Protection of the president? Protection of the office? Perhaps, but none of it borne out by any facts.

National Security Adviser H. R. McMaster is junior to Kelly in rank, age, and experience. No one questions his intelligence or courage, but little in his career prepared him for this task. He is probably the best exemplar of Mullen's caution that this is "a foreign environment to all of them and so they're trying to get their job done while operating in a political environment that they're adjusting to."

With his years of experience in the SITROOM, Mullen cautioned that the role of the national security adviser was "to really just present options," not pitch policy internally or externally, and feared that McMaster "got out a little early on policy."

In one infamous example, McMaster found himself where no national security adviser would ever want to be: uncomfortably (and from all appearances reluctantly) providing political top cover to the president, in this case trying to rebut charges that the president had shared sensitive intelligence given to the United States by a third party with Russian foreign minister Sergei Lavrov. McMaster claimed that the sharing was routine and appropriate and available from open-source reporting while also maintaining that the president "wasn't aware of where this came from. He wasn't briefed on the source of the information."

His explanations were undercut the next day when the president cited his "absolute right" to release "facts pertaining to terrorism and airline flight safety" and the White House declined to push back on stories that the administration had actually asked for a damage assessment from the intelligence community on the president's revelations to the Russians.[32]

McMaster later found himself forced to defend/endorse/

validate the president's comments on Charlottesville ("bigotry and violence on many sides, on many sides"),[33] the president's apparent criticism of British security forces in the midst of a terrorist attack (the terrorists "were in the sights of Scotland Yard . . . must be proactive and nasty"),[34] and his incendiary words on North Korea at the United Nations ("totally destroy . . . Rocket Man . . . suicide mission").[35]

In early December, McMaster was again called on to defend the president, this time over his retweeting of three videos purporting to show gruesome Muslim violence against innocents that had been originally produced and captioned by a fringe anti-immigrant British group whose leader had been convicted of a Muslim hate crime. The Dutch embassy in Washington said that one of the videos showing its citizens was patently false, and British prime minister Theresa May condemned all of them, at the same time rebuking Trump for endorsing them.

The tweets really smacked of the red-meat anti-Muslim language of the campaign. It was Trump after dark at his most vile and thoughtless. It looked the product of an ungoverned id emitting vindictive thoughts to stoke an undiscerning base into fear and thus support.

Chris Wallace asked McMaster on national TV, "General, why did President Trump send out those videos?"

McMaster at first deferred: "Well, President Trump is the best judge of why he did that."

That was a good and true answer and the general should have left it there. But the White House would have anticipated the question on this Sunday and would have prepared talking points that paralleled Sarah Huckabee Sanders's earlier in the week. And would have expected the national security adviser to use them. So McMaster continued: "But I know it was his intention to highlight the importance of creating safe and secure environments for our citizens—to make sure that we have the right laws in place, enforcement mechanisms in place, to ensure that, at this critical time, when ISIS is being defeated in the Middle East, that there is no return of terrorists and extremists who can pose a risk to the American people, or to our allies and partners."

All that seemed a remarkable task for three little violent videos without any recommendations, proposals, or programs attached. So Wallace continued by asking why inaccurate fringe videos would be useful for those purposes.

McMaster repeated that the videos highlighted a real risk (a doubtful proposition given their provenance) and that they could be used to fight the false narrative that this was really a war of religion, a statement unhinged from the actual videos and their impact. Indeed, one of the videos showed a statue of the Virgin Mary being destroyed. Then, in the moments that followed, McMaster talked about the need to break the cycle of "ignorance, hatred, and violence," a cycle to which the three unprovoked videos had almost certainly just contributed.

That prompted Wallace to immediately and forcefully ask, "But his tweets were all about anti-Muslim—about Muslim violence, he was making it . . ."

McMaster sidestepped that in favor of some unrelated points on attacking terrorist governance and ideology and working with allies and partners across the world.

There simply was no real defense for the president retweeting the vile videos, and McMaster had to know that. In 2006, then-colonel McMaster had conquered and pacified the Iraqi town of Tal Afar through innovative tactics, hard fighting, and "developing relationships, by action, by dialogue with people and by addressing local grievances."[36] It would have required a brain and personality transplant for H.R. to judge the president's actions as warranted, useful, or even worthy of the office or the nation. And yet here he was on a Sunday morning feeling obliged to apply his considerable talents and reputation to defending the indefensible.

John McLaughlin—the iconic former head of CIA analysis, deputy director, and then acting director of the Agency—had earlier told me of his fear that "[t]he lie will become the truth and people who normally tell the truth will end up explaining the lie."

Michael Gerson was even more harsh: "Trump has made a practice of forcing people around him to lower their standards and abandon their ideals before turning against them when their usefulness ends."[37]

Tom Bossert, the administration's highly regarded homeland security adviser and Bush administration veteran, was another regular on Sunday talk shows, especially as a series of hurricanes hammered the U.S. mainland and Puerto Rico. Seemingly without fail Bossert would be called on to explain or defend a presidential tweet when all he wanted to talk about was wind speed, rainfall, and recovery efforts. He did his best.

In July he was ambushed with a video the president had just tweeted of Trump taking down CNN à la a WWE brawl. The Sunday hosts pressed him about the president encouraging violence against the press.

Bossert rejected the thesis: "No, I certainly don't. I don't think so." Fair enough, although the point is debatable, but then Bossert went on to stress the White House's *political* theme of the president as victim: "There's a lot of cable news shows that reach directly into hundreds of thousands of viewers, and they're really not always very fair to the president." And then to give him a character reference: "He's a genuine president expressing himself genuinely."[38]

CNN's Ana Navarro, never one to shade her views, characterized the video as an incitement to violence and then reflected on Bossert: "You could see that he is ceding his principles. . . . You can't stand here and say the difference between right and wrong? He is surrounded by enablers that do nothing, but shake their heads and nod their heads in agreement."[39]

That was harsh, but an intelligence community veteran emailed me the same day, "I saw the clip this morning and just put my head in my hands. This is how decent people are ruined."

Bossert was put into pretty much the same position a month later after Charlottesville and the president's ambiguous condemnation of the actors there. He cited the president's general comments about the level of violence and hatred in the country and finally, pressed by CNN's Jake Tapper, offered a personal view: "I think you've belabored it, so let me say I condemn white supremacists, and Nazis, and groups that favor this type of exclusion."[40]

Two weeks later Bossert was on ABC and this time was forced to defend the president's preemptive pardoning of Arizona sheriff Joe Arpaio, the face of harsh crackdowns against illegal immigrants, although some would say all immigrants and others would simply say Hispanic-looking people. The pardon was an unadulterated sop to the president's political base.

Bossert simply commented that all presidents end up with some controversial pardons, and he didn't think it was fair to the president "to characterize him as not caring about the rule of law." He also repeated the White House talking points about Arpaio's veteran status and "lifetime of service."[41]

It was probably the least he could do and still be in good standing in the West Wing on Monday morning. The president was doing more than just harming institutions. He was harming people, good people, American heroes, who deserve our gratitude.

That was clear in February when Republicans on the House Intelligence Committee approved a memo written for and signed by their chairman, Devin Nunes, charging the FBI and the Department of Justice with malpractice and politicization for using the notorious Steele dossier to get a FISA warrant on former Trump campaign adviser Carter Page. Most folks like me condemned the memo's thin four pages, especially its injection of hyperpartisanship into what has historically been a matter between career intelligence or law enforcement professionals and the federal courts. The memo was also misleadingly silent with regard to other evidence presented to the FISA judge beyond the Steele dossier and was almost immediately contradicted by press reports that the judge had indeed been aware of the political motivation behind those bankrolling Steele.

Not surprisingly, the memo was met with enthusiasm by a president anxious to undercut the Russia probe as a "hoax" and the Special Counsel's investigation as a "witch hunt." The president tweeted: "The top Leadership and Investigators of the FBI and the Justice Department have politicized the sacred investigative process in favor of Democrats and against Republicans." And then, "A lot of people should be ashamed of themselves." Casting aside concerns from within his own government about real damage to dedicated people and important institutions and processes, the president opted for what best served his personal legal and political needs of the moment.

Full credit to FBI director Christopher Wray and Deputy Attorney General Rod Rosenstein for pushing back against the House intel committee Republicans and the White House. Fighting release of the memo, the FBI warned about "material omissions of fact that fundamentally impact the memo's accuracy" and afterward Director Wray reminded his workforce that "talk is cheap" and they still needed to "tackle hard."

But it was a little surprising and even more disappointing that other voices in the executive branch were not heard in support of Wray, even via "informed sources" or "people familiar with the thinking of . . ." After all, there should be no reason to think they or their people would be immune from arbitrary presidential shaming in the future, and this was especially true of the intelligence community, since information from other agencies like CIA and NSA is routinely included in FISA applications and this particular FISA was part of a counterintelligence investigation that comes under the broad responsibilities of the director of national intelligence.

There was reporting that DNI Coats did push back privately in the West Wing against the memo, and as a former member of both the House and Senate, he must have been appalled at this example of "oversight." But whatever objections he had were not heeded by either branch of government.

Which gives greater urgency to the question: At what point do even good people stop being buffers and guard rails and simply became enablers and legitimizers? And at what point do they have to leave or suffer permanent damage to their character and reputation?

EIGHT

THE FUTURE OF TRUTH

The Future of Truth." That was the title of the 2017 Nobel Week Dialogue. I was as surprised as anyone that the organizers invited me, a former director of the Central Intelligence Agency, to participate in the daylong event at the modern conference center in Gothenburg, Sweden, the day before the Nobel presentations in Stockholm. It was a broad topic and the format was fast-paced: short keynotes sprinkled among formal panels in a large conference hall and then simultaneously running breakout sessions.

Everything was organized around the meaning and practice of truth: political truth, art and truth, artistic truth, the fragility of truth, documenting the truth, truth and democracy, truth and social media, truth and the scientific method. The list went on, but despite the universality of the themes, most of the conversations quickly became discussions about the status of truth in the

United States and how much the American president did or did not embrace it.

The focus on America was so great that late in the afternoon, when Iranian dissident and 2003 Nobel Peace Prize winner Shirin Ebadi complained about the fixation, there was more than scattered applause from the audience. But neither she nor they should have been surprised at the focus. There were concerns, serious concerns.

A summer 2017 Pew poll found that confidence in the U.S. president to do the "right thing" in world affairs had sunk an amazing 83 percent in Sweden, from 93 percent to a mere 10 percent. That was the worst globally in a poll conducted in more than thirty-seven nations that had median confidence in the American presidency sinking from 64 percent to 22 percent. The view of the presidency improved only in Israel (+7 percent) and Russia (+42 percent).[1]

America itself hadn't fared quite as badly as its presidency; in the global poll, 49 percent still had a favorable attitude toward the country, down from a recent 64 percent, but still better than the 39 percent now unfavorable.

In the green room, Nobel laureates and others—in between questions and comments about Washington's politics and Washington's president—seemed to reflect a sad but still affectionate "We miss America."

I wasn't surprised to hear that attitude. My friend and former acting director of CIA John McLaughlin tweets often with this international audience in mind. After the Virginia statewide elections in November 2017, he posted, "Int'l friends: the diversity, welcome and tolerance u see in Virginia tonite transcend politics. Means the America you knew is reviving." After the Alabama

Senate race in December, he observed, "Internat'l friends: our great state of Alabama tonite transcends politics, winners and losers: the America you knew continues to revive."

I shared John's feelings and concerns, so I felt a special responsibility in Gothenburg as I gave an eleven-minute TED-style talk on "The Role of Intelligence in a Post-Truth World." I was in the large conference hall in front of the fifteen hundred gathered there, and that was followed by my appearing on two other panels. If you have gotten this far in this book, the things I spoke about would be pretty familiar: the task of intelligence to represent the world as it is and to set the left- and right-hand boundaries of legitimate policy discussion; the natural tensions between intelligence professionals and policymakers (inductive versus deductive reasoning, pessimistic versus optimistic personalities, and so forth); the peculiar challenges associated with a president as spontaneous, instinctive, ahistorical, and transactional as Donald Trump.

I went out of my way to make the point that intelligence as practiced in Western democracies was as much a child of the Enlightenment as any of the other disciplines represented in the hall: respect for data, empiricism, humility in the face of complexity, and so on.

But I had gone to Sweden more to listen and learn than to transmit, and it was worth the trip. Early sessions asked what is required for truth to be known, and talked about the relationship between facts and truth and how they correspond but are different, facts leading to coherent theories (truth), which justify action, whose results in turn test belief.

A healthy skepticism teaches that theories (i.e., current truths) are only temporary tools, subject to inquiry and observation, but this is the only path to knowledge, which is—in the Nobel tradition—the only course to betterment. Hence the alarm was sounded at the beginning of the day by Lars Heikensten, executive director of the Nobel Foundation, that "knowledge and pure facts are being questioned." Ebadi, the Iranian activist, later warned that "cruelty to man begins with cruelty to words"; she cited "Islam" as a code word for misogyny, "nationalism" for xenophobia, "globalization" for closed factories, but there could have been many other examples.

Zeynep Tufekci, a Turkish-born writer on the social impact of technology who is currently at the University of North Carolina, pulled the philosophical discourse into the raw reality of today's social media, where, she said, like-minded people can now find one another. Good news if you are talking about democratic activists in a totalitarian state. Not so good if you are linking up and empowering white supremacists, racists, and religious fanatics who previously were isolated and weak.

Tufekci blamed the coarseness of modern dialogue on the loss of control by old mediators who, whatever their faults and prejudices, operated with an ethos of public service. Replacing them were algorithms designed to keep people on a site, the process driven by a business model where profit was measured by the number of clicks and time spent on a platform.

She compared it to junk food feeding us salt, fat, and sugar to keep us coming back. Except now Google, Facebook, and YouTube were feeding us parallel thoughts and like-minded people based on our cataloged likes, preferences, and browsing history— building ever more homogeneous media ghettos. And as junk food creates a craving for even more salt and fat, we want to be dished up even stronger versions of our particular worldview (and there are no warning labels here as to their calorie count or salt content).

Roger McNamee, a Facebook investor and mentor to founder Mark Zuckerberg, confessed as much in a remarkable January 2018 article. There he pointed out that "filter bubbles," i.e., Facebook algorithms, give consumers "what they want" with "an unending stream of posts that confirm each user's existing beliefs. . . . [E]veryone sees a different version of the internet tailored to create the illusion that everyone else agrees with them . . . while also making them more extreme and resistant to contrary facts."[2]

McNamee also offered this remarkable observation: "Algorithms that maximize attention give an advantage to negative messages. People tend to react more to inputs that land low on the brainstem. Fear and anger produce a lot more engagement and sharing than joy. The result is that the algorithms favor sensational content over substance."

Which, coincidentally, all seemed ideally suited to a candidate whose message was anchored on the apocalyptic message of "American carnage."

Back in Sweden, Tufekci went further, pointing out that the purpose of free speech was to enable intelligent action, the marketplace of ideas animating and helping to guide prudent choice. That is becoming more difficult not only because of polarization and coarsening, but also because a growing volume of noise, inattention, deception, and distraction is breaking the link between truth and action.

Information is still there; free speech is not necessarily suppressed, but its desired effects are. The modern information glut is perversely a form of censorship, Tufekci says, overwhelming and freezing us into inaction, a condition made worse when evidence-based enterprises are intentionally devalued or when distractions are purposefully magnified.

Because of the seven-hour time difference, Tufekci was speaking just a few hours after Donald Trump had left a stage in Pensacola, Florida, from where he was messaging the south Alabama TV market to vote for alleged child predator Roy Moore for the Senate. Trump seemed to be acting out Tufekci's scenario. With multiple charges raging against Moore, Trump focused on other themes, especially the always reliable "fake news." He invited folks to get a lawyer and sue ABC News, referred to a Pew poll showing him at 32 percent as "such a fake," and claimed that CNN should have been continually apologizing for the last two years.

The president had taken on CNN barely two weeks before when he tweeted, "@FoxNews is MUCH more important in the United States than CNN, but outside of the U.S., CNN International is still a major source of (Fake) news, and they represent our Nation to the WORLD very poorly. The outside world does not see the truth from them!"

The network responded that it never intended to be an organ of the U.S. government, that Trump's words put correspondents even more at risk, and that the president of the United States had just legitimated attacks on the free press by autocrats globally. Indeed, the governments of Egypt and Libya quickly pivoted off of the president's remarks to condemn recent CNN stories, and *Politico* cataloged another dozen countries, mostly authoritarian, that had picked up the president's wording (and the latent moral authority of his office) to condemn coverage that conflicted with *their* preferred view of reality.[3]

I read the president's CNN tweet shortly after it was posted, feeling anger and even greater (and genuine) fear that an institution so important to global freedom had been attacked with such indifference. I also had a fleeting (nonpositive) thought about how Fox News might feel about being effectively labeled state TV. I drafted a response, suppressed a momentary hesitation, and then tweeted, "If this is who we are or who we are becoming, I have wasted 40 years of my life. Until now it was not possible for me to conceive of an American President capable of such an outrageous assault on truth, a free press or the First Amendment."

I did make it conditional: "*If* this is who we are . . ." But the concern over a vital institution and a vital concept was real, and I truly never expected to hear such sentiments from an American president. It wasn't a difficult tweet to compose. When the dust settled, it had been seen by five and a half a million other accounts, 10 percent interacting with it, with fifty thousand retweets and over one hundred thousand likes. I wasn't the only one concerned or offended.

Clearly there were many others who disagreed with the president. In Pensacola he had a name for all of us: "These are very, very bad and evil people. They know who they are." He also claimed that American governance was "a rigged system . . . a sick system."

Then the president pulled out his old campaign staple of attacking alleged deadbeat allies, thereby trashing ten months of work by his secretaries of state and defense to reassure friends about America's treaty commitments. He inexplicably complained about some NATO country getting "frisky" with Russia (no mention of the other way around), and, sounding every bit the landlord, excited the crowd with, "You gotta pay, you gotta pay . . . You don't pay, we're outta there, right?"[4]

And then, once again without evidence and in the face of his own administration saying otherwise, the president trotted out his familiar wiretapping canard: "Oh, surveillance? That sounds familiar. That sounds familiar. Remember when I suggested something like that—everyone said, Trump, why is he saying? Well, it turned out I was right about that one, wasn't I?"[5]

He wasn't, of course. But that and the other tropes met the campaign needs of the moment and perfectly fit Tufekci's formula, to obfuscate and delegitimize to break the link between data (the accusations against Moore) and action (Tuesday's vote).

The *New York Times* White House correspondent Maggie Haberman was another prominent commentator in Gothenburg. With her current position and the president's long-term love-hate relationship with the *Times* (or at least his apparent need for its approval) and her earlier years as a political reporter with the *New York Post*, *New York Daily News*, and *Politico*, Haberman has as much insight into Donald Trump as anyone.

She pointed to "a lifelong thread of wanting to be taken seriously," a Queens real estate developer desperate for recognition in Manhattan, and even now obsessed with protecting his own legitimacy as he indulged a cable news passion that was reflected almost daily in what and when he tweeted.

Haberman told the audience about Trump's habit of dominating lives and situations, sucking up all the oxygen in a room. She admitted that his comments came with a level of vitriol she had never seen before and that for her it was much like cyber bullying, with the president's followers continuing to come after her long after he had moved on from a particular issue. She also conceded that there was not much of a bottom on what the president chooses to do or say. Much of his language (like the attacks on "a rigged system") neither reflects nor seems much affected by the fact that he is, after all, *the president.*

All of which, I suppose, could feed the narrative favored by the president's supporters that the press and especially Haberman and her newspaper were just anti-Trump—less a free press than the opposition or even the resistance. Haberman seemed to consciously preempt that line by arguing that to cover Trump accurately was to cover him unfairly from his point of view: "He is always selling," and selling "the picture of what he wants reality to be, . . . never treating life as if it is filled with objective truth."

That theme and the apparent bottomlessness of presidential behavior were borne out two weeks later when, as much of the country was embarking for holiday destinations and the president was landing at Mar-a-Lago, Trump pressed the narrative that the FBI was in "tatters," the Russia plot was a "hoax," and Bob Mueller's investigation was a "witch hunt."

He did it through a pair of tweets (no surprise there) that would have drawn flags for taunting in the NFL. In the first, he exulted that FBI deputy director Andrew McCabe (who served under Jim Comey) was "racing the clock to retire with full benefits. 90 days to go?!!!" And then on Christmas Eve he expressed faux surprise with, "Wow, 'FBI lawyer James Baker reassigned' . . ."[6]

Baker wasn't just any lawyer. He was Jim Comey's top lawyer and now the target of anonymous Hill Republicans who were pushing the theory that Baker and others at the Bureau were working to take down the White House.[7] Specifically, they were pointing to Baker as *Mother Jones* reporter David Corn's source for Christopher Steele's dodgy dossier, a connection that Corn himself denied.

In Sweden, Haberman had confessed to a certain numbness to Trump's attacks, language, and behavior. I and several folks like me had informally resolved to work against that natural response: to never be numbed, to never normalize presidential behavior that should not be considered normal, to reject the moral bankruptcy inherent in dismissing the brutally bizarre with "that's just Trump being Trump."

John McLaughlin had reflected this kind of fear earlier: "If you . . . are not dismayed . . . you may now be *numb* and no longer capable of outrage. Scary if that's our new normal."

I also recalled Eliot Cohen's earlier tweet from the first days of the administration: "This isn't normal. Its not humane, its not thought through, its not necessary, its not wise, its not decent and above all, its not American." Eliot spoke specifically to the ill-fated and ill-considered immigration ban, but he meant it to apply broadly.

Using the power of the presidency to trash the reputations of dedicated career officers for political advantage, or to distract the public, or to delegitimize potential indictments, or just for triumphalist spite seemed a similar assault on appropriate norms of governance (and decency).

I knew McCabe only by reputation, which was impeccable. His core sins seem to have been working for Comey and having a wife who ran for delegate to the Virginia House of Burgesses as a Democrat with her party's support.

I knew Jim Baker beyond reputation. I worked with him after 9/11 when he was head of DOJ's Office of Intelligence Policy and

Review. We were all trying to respond to new challenges and those of us in the intelligence community found him tough, knowledgeable, fair, patriotic, and dedicated to the rule of law. In 2006 he was recognized for his efforts by CIA, in 2007 by NSA.

I readily joined a string of former security officials who decried the scene. John McLaughlin seemed to be shaking his head on Twitter: "I've served in both Republican and Democratic administrations and have seen some unusual things . . . but this is some really strange stuff." *Lawfare*'s Ben Wittes listed ten (very positive) things about Baker and then started a string of donations to the FBI Agents Association in Baker's and McCabe's names that went sufficiently viral to temporarily crash the association's site. Ben was uncharacteristically direct about Trump: "The President of the United States is a profoundly bad person."

Wittes's partner in starting the *Lawfare* blog, Jack Goldsmith (now at Harvard Law but once head of DOJ's Office of Legal Counsel in the George W. Bush administration), quickly joined in: "The real target of the President's just-made despicable attacks on McCabe, Baker, and FBI, is Mueller, Wray and Rosenstein." That thought, of course, concerned the fate of the independent counsel looking into potential collusion with Russia.

Not surprisingly, that and the thought of the president more generally was never far from any of the conversations in Gothenburg. The day there had actually ended on an upbeat note, with seven Nobel laureates on the main stage being asked about their personal views on the future of truth. Most were scientists. All were optimistic. The nature of truth is that it builds, it accumulates, said one; errors fall away. Another added that reality cannot be denied. Truth will prevail, added a third, because "what else is there." Ebadi, the Iranian activist who earlier had complained about the day's focus on America, even supported her belief that the future of civilization moves toward progress by citing the movement from African enslavement to an African American president in the United States. Steven Chu, an American laureate in physics, said that scientists have to be optimistic because they fail most of the time and, reflecting the undercurrent of the day's events, predicted that ultimately "truth will trump Trump."

But there were cautions. It was pointed out that humanity has seen epochs of decline in the past. Joseph Stiglitz, an American economist, worried about prevailing in the battle over the immediate future, cautioning against just betting on the long run since, as Keynes pointed out, "in the long run we are all dead." Peter Doherty, an Australian Nobel winner for physiology or medicine, worried aloud about getting political masters and broader societies to accept truths. Which, of course, was the issue of the day.

I would have been hard pressed to find a forum, panel, or audience more elite, global, empirical, scientific, confident, or successful than this one. But they and I are living in a world that is increasingly populist, nativist, instinctive, mythological, uncertain, and beleaguered.

There are political leaders around the world and in the United States who are both creating and riding that wave. That their efforts are abetted by the active measures of an autocratic and ambitious Russia barely rated mention in Sweden. This was a day for philosophy, introspection, and reflection—not accusation or condemnation. And there was obvious merit in focusing for a day on what made us vulnerable rather than on which foreign actors were exploiting those vulnerabilities.

But that does not change the reality or the effect of Russian actions.

These actions continue to this day, not at the moment to affect a particular election, but to provoke, coarsen, divide, and weaken American civil polity, driving political discourse to the edges and emptying the center.

Russia's ongoing efforts have excited much of the American think tank community, where, on a given afternoon, one can attend a session in which representatives of prestigious bodies— mostly the center and center-left of that community—are discussing the topic. Conspicuously underrepresented (actually not represented at all) is the U.S. government, where what the Russians did and are still doing is not a priority of the president.

In mid-December the *Washington Post* ran a lengthy story about how the President's Daily Brief was affected by the Russia question. "To raise the issue is to affirm its validity" was how one of the *Post*'s sources framed the problem, so talking about Russia, meddling, or interference always threatened to take the morning briefing "off the rails."

I was no longer in that room for the morning briefing, but I am willing to cut the intelligence folks some slack with regard to *how* to present an item. Each president learns in his own way, and all have their sensitivities. So deciding to put an item early or late; written or verbal; in a large group or a small group—all that is normal. Even if *this* president's hypersensitivity on *this* issue is not.

I was quoted early in the *Post* article (my *only* contribution, I quietly assured CIA), saying that the Russian effort exposed a previously unimagined American vulnerability and required a unified American response. I was doubtful that there would be such a response unless the president clearly said something like, "We know the Russians did it, they know they did it, I know they did it, and we will not rest until we learn everything there is to know about how [they did it] and do everything possible to prevent it from happening again." And I sadly concluded that Trump "has never said anything close to that and will never say anything close to that."[8]

In fact, a leader of one group that had organized individuals from political campaigns, Internet companies, and cyber security firms along with former government officials to prevent actual vote tampering told me that it was hard to brief their findings to Congress, where members "feared a tweet," or to officials in the executive branch, where folks were "nervous to be seen as acting on this."

When asked where these private efforts did or should hook into the formal government, no one in the room had an answer. One participant—a former senior security official—said that he feared that "there is no one defending the country."

Concerns went beyond just the apparent inaction. A late November report from the Council on Foreign Relations agreed that "the Trump administration has shown little interest in confronting Russian cyber operations." But it was even worse than that since "the president himself is actively engaged in the divisive use of social media."[9]

Laura Rosenberger, former Obama state department and NSC staffer and campaign adviser to Hillary Clinton, is now director of the Alliance for Securing Democracy, a project of the German

Marshall Fund of the United States, whose Hamilton 68[10] dash-board tracks Russian influence operations on Twitter in near real time. In a mid-December 2017 presentation, she cataloged trending themes like attacks on Morgan Freeman, Hollywood actor and spokesman for director Rob Reiner's Committee to Investigate Russia; on Senator John McCain, who had voted against a Trump-favored health care bill; on Hillary Clinton for her alleged collusion with Russia on the sale of a uranium company while she was secretary of state.

But Rosenberger showed some special passion when she talked about the Russian role in the controversy over the NFL anthem protests. Turned out that she, like me, is a Pittsburgh Steeler fan (her Twitter profile says she bleeds black and gold), and the Steelers were especially victimized by the national anthem affair.

All this began on a Friday evening in late September when President Trump, before a red-hot Alabama crowd of his political base, decided to treat the SOBs who wouldn't stand for the anthem the way he has previously treated other groups like Mexicans (murderers and rapists), intelligence professionals (Nazis), immigrants (deeply unfair), refugees (dangerous), and Muslims (they hate us).

"Wouldn't you love to see one of these NFL owners, when somebody disrespects our flag, to say, 'Get that son of a bitch off the field right now. Out. He's fired. He's fired!' You know, some owner is going . . . to say, 'That guy that disrespects our flag, he's fired.' . . . When people like yourselves turn on television and you see those people taking the knee when they are playing our great national anthem. The only thing you could do better is if you see it, even if it's one player, leave the stadium, I guarantee things will stop. Things will stop. Just pick up and leave. Pick up and leave."

For extra measure, the president claimed the NFL was ruining the game with rule changes to reduce player injury: "Today, if you hit too hard, fifteen yards, throw him out of the game!"

To paraphrase Abraham Lincoln, Donald Trump does not appeal to "the better angels of our nature."

The NFL—players, coaches, owners, and league officials—had to make decisions quickly. Sunday's kickoffs were less than forty hours away when the president walked off that stage in Huntsville. Nearly half the league would be getting on planes in less than twelve hours.

There were tough choices to make: respect for the flag, respect for the anthem, respect for teammates, respect for justice, respect for fans, respect for free speech. The president had created what logicians call a false dilemma, that support for free speech or for teammates equated to disrespect for flag, anthem, and country. And he did it for raw political advantage.

My hometown team, the Steelers, rejected the false dilemma. Head coach Mike Tomlin said, "We're not going to play politics. We're football players, we're football coaches. We're not participating in the anthem today, not to be disrespectful to the anthem, but to remove ourselves from the circumstance."

So the team did not go out onto the field for "The Star-Spangled Banner," although Alejandro Villanueva—starting left tackle, West Point graduate, decorated Army Ranger—broke consensus slightly to appear at the mouth of the tunnel with his hand over his heart, but several players said they understood Villanueva's unique circumstance.

Pittsburgh is a patriotic town. There was a lot of anger about the Steelers not showing up. But they had been dealt a bad hand and played it as best they could. Or, more accurately, they tried not to play.

And the dealer here was Donald Trump. The week before, six NFL players protested social injustice and police brutality by sitting or taking a knee during the pregame anthem. *Six*. This was *not* a national issue. Two days after Trump's speech, though, three teams did not go out for the anthem, almost all the other players and coaches locked arms, and more than two hundred in the NFL knelt, sat, or otherwise demonstrated their displeasure.

And, to be specific, their displeasure was largely with the president and what he had said about them, their teammates, and their rights. Forced again to defend the indefensible, White House press secretary Sarah Huckabee Sanders said the president's Huntsville stand was about "honoring the men and women who fought to defend" the flag.

I disagreed. I wrote in an op-ed that, as a thirty-nine-year military veteran, I thought I knew something about the flag, the anthem, and patriotism, and I also thought I know why we fight. And it wasn't to allow the president to divide us by wrapping himself in the national banner. His words smacked of what historian Timothy Snyder has called "the treacherous use of patriotic vocabulary."

Because of my op-ed, my military experience, and my Pittsburgh and Steeler background, I was asked to sit in for a conversation with team leadership, the heads of Pittsburgh veterans' organizations, and Rocky Bleier—Steeler icon, Vietnam veteran, and Purple Heart winner. My wife and Air Force veteran daughter sat in as well.

It was actually a calm and constructive conversation.

Everyone in the room knew that successful NFL franchises—the ones that play a lot in January—benefit from a special bond between players, coaches, organizations, and the city they represent. Pittsburgh has had that for at least forty years, and all of us knew it had been put at risk by events launched and nurtured by the president of the United States.

It was a chance for me to see that costs were real, not theoretical. And it wasn't just Trump pushing the conversation to the edges. Even as the president continued his incendiary tweets, the Russians were all over the issue.

Based on Hamilton 68's dashboard of Russian-linked influence on Twitter, in the forty-eight hours after the Huntsville speech, #TakeAKnee was used as a hashtag nearly eight hundred times, with other NFL-related hashtags used on nearly six hundred other occasions. This was from a standing start by the Russian trolls and bots. The usage of #DumpNFL increased nearly 14,000 percent in those forty-eight hours; #TakeAKnee was up nearly 2,000 percent. And, typically, the Russians were playing both sides of the issue, pushing America to the extremes to both distract and weaken it.

The Russians' job was made easier by simply drafting on the president's remarks. His indifference had literally set this up for them. Not much skill was required, as one experienced intelligence officer pointed out to me.

Julia Ioffe, the Russian-born American journalist, agreed that this isn't really rocket science: "Putin is not a super villain. He is not invincible, or unstoppable. He pushes only to the moment he meets resistance."[11]

I asked Garry Kasparov the same questions. "He's a poker player, not a chess player," the chess champion replied, "a good reader of people and bluffer, not a strategist. Unfortunately, Putin's potential rivals have been drawn into his poker game instead of a strategic response."

He added, "Putin has also been genuinely lucky. . . . [He] is an opportunist and . . . his active measures exploit existing weaknesses instead of creating new ones." He also said that "these initiatives . . . would never have succeeded against Western recognition of Putin's threat and a consistent policy of deterrence." As an example, he offered that "Trump openly criticizing NATO is Putin's dream," to which I could have added divisive issues like the NFL.

Two days into the new year, National Security Adviser McMaster talked to the Voice of America about Russian interference, including in the 2016 election, a position he claimed the president was on public record as supporting. Actually, I think that was quite a reach given all the presidential to-ing and fro-ing on the question, but McMaster then went on to highlight the Russians' purpose. It was to "really polarize societies and pit communities against each other, to weaken their resolve and their commitment." He then said we needed to "confront their destabilization [*sic*] behavior."[12]

One way to do that, of course, would be to walk the fifty paces from his corner office in the West Wing to the Oval Office and remind the occupant there about the destructive effects of his own behavior.

In the real world, though, what happened was that the Russian-linked network actively promoted stories in the pro-Trump alt-right media that was exploiting the divisive NFL issue as aggressively as had the president.

Truthfeed—a mysterious pro-Trump, alternative-facts news

site with a massive Facebook following—fed the racial undercurrents of the NFL dispute with a piece on African American Steelers head coach Mike Tomlin hosting a "lavish" 2016 fund-raiser for Hillary Clinton. "Well, well, well, the NFL's REAL reason for 'taking the knee' is becoming much clearer," the article began.[13] Not surprisingly, personalities like Mike Cernovich and Sarah Palin piled on the Tomlin-Clinton theme.

Breitbart used Villanueva's unique circumstances to drive another wedge, once again invoking Tomlin. "In what might just be the most 2017 NFL story ever, Steelers coach Mike Tomlin ripped one of his players, an Afghan war veteran, for coming out of the locker room for the national anthem."[14]

That was not what Tomlin said before, during, or after the game, and indeed, Villanueva later gave a heartfelt press conference highlighting the anguish the issue had created for the team and his personal discomfort at being singled out as different from his teammates.

Hard right Gateway Pundit—a Trumpist, conspiracy-minded site with a trail of debunked stories but now with a White House–accredited correspondent—struck a theme that grew steadily as time wore on: the failing NFL. The headline blared, "NFL HELL: Several Stadiums Nearly Empty as Anthem Protest Backlash Rolls into Week 7." And the blame was easy to fix: "If the NFL thought Americans would ease the backlash against the league—they were sadly mistaken. Photos of empty stadiums from around the league show how dire a situation kneelers have spurred." The site gleefully praised Trump "for driving this hot button issue, waging a culture war against the NFL that has been damaging to both their players and owners."[15]

It was a remarkable cycle. A presidential taunt. Russian bots.

Alt-right press. And a fire stoked hot enough to stir argument in my personal extended family, and I am sure many others.

Little wonder the Russians continue to play. No real costs. Ready-made issues. A divided society to target. Americans seemingly working in parallel. A frozen U.S. government response.

Something perverse tells me to begin this last section by reprising the title of Lenin's early-twentieth-century political pamphlet *Chto Delat?* (*What Is to Be Done?*).

First, of course, is defining the problem.

There are, it should be obvious by now, really two issues, although they are intimately intertwined: the declining relevance of truth as traditionally understood (i.e., the evidence-based patterns developed during the Enlightenment), and Russia both exploiting and exacerbating that phenomenon.

The former has its own dynamic driven by personalities, politics, economics, and technology. It would exist without the latter, which is clearly dependent on it.

So, fix the first and the second largely goes away. The Russians have been less successful manipulating less fractured societies like Norway or even Germany and France. The long-term cure has more to do with core principles and basic political health than it does with technology.

In the meantime, though, societies like America need to defend themselves as best they can from external exploitation and manipulation. A major portion of *that* task falls squarely to American intelligence—but so does a not unimportant role in addressing the first and larger question.

The two—the state of truth and the state of Russian

meddling—actually intersected in a July 2017 NPR/*PBS News-Hour*/Marist poll that found that 73 percent of Democrats thought Russia was a major threat to U.S. elections, while only 17 percent of Republicans thought so. A quarter of Republicans rejected the concept that Russia was ever involved in the first place.[16]

Which meant that a unanimous, high-confidence judgment of the American intelligence community was more of a national Rorschach test than a warning of danger, a guide to policy, or a stimulus to action.

The president and a sufficient number of members of his party in Congress are comfortable enough with the no-big-deal thesis that the consensus view of American intelligence (expressed privately by those still in government and publicly by those retired and more free to speak) is that we will remain well short of the sustained, comprehensive, energized response that we need.

The Trump administration gets generally good marks for cyber security, but cyber security is just a subset of the broader Russian interference question. There is little evidence that the president or his government has identified the protection of American democratic processes as a national security challenge. And although the president's commission to investigate the alleged three million illegal Clinton voters tried to bully the states for voter information (before shutting down), there is far less federal effort to cut through the thicket of American federalism to improve the security of state voter rolls and actual election tallies. The permanent institutions of American intelligence have shared their lessons-learned with European allies, but there has been little action at the political level and nary a word from the president about the importance of preserving American and allied democracy.

With the right government assistance, pressure, incentives, or just interest, there are practical steps that the private sector could take to better protect the critical underpinning of democracy in today's technical environment. We are not unarmed in this conflict. After all, the unarguable global centers for technology (Silicon Valley) and image creation (Hollywood) are only about three hundred miles apart in California.

It is within technological reach, for example, to identify when an item is trending on social media because of the actions of individuals or machines (e.g., botnets). Filtering out the latter won't completely purify our discourse, but it will help defend it from inauthentic stimulation.

McNamee, the disillusioned Facebook investor/mentor, has come up with his own recommendations, which are less about just monitoring content and botnets and more about changing Facebook's core business model, its ownership of data and its monopoly status. After months of rejecting such messages, the company now seems resigned that it will have to do *something*.[17]

No one wants the government (or anyone else for that matter) filtering the flow of news through social media, but there are ways to help consumers make better choices. The crowdsourced movie reviews of the website Rotten Tomatoes help people make informed decisions before they invest their time and money. *The Interview*, the coarse 2014 "comedy" about assassinating North Korean dictator Kim Jong-un that provoked the destructive cyber attack on Sony Pictures, is generously rated at 51 percent (a "rotten" score), whereas 1998's *Saving Private Ryan* still earns a well-deserved 92 percent (a solid "fresh" score). I've seen both movies, but I knew what I was getting into going in; the scores were quite predictive.

News sites could be similarly rated along lines of transparency (who are they?), accuracy (how big a Pinocchio inventory?), history (how long online?), alignment (apparent or announced affiliations?), originality (writing fresh stories or spinning existing ones?), and similar characteristics. It wouldn't be perfect and the ratings themselves would no doubt be a source of controversy, but this would be a step above embracing news sources simply because they seem to agree with us.

And any such system should be part of an overall educational project to teach one how to consume news in an uncurated tsunami of information. We should also extend to online political advertising the kinds of reporting and transparency requirements we already apply to traditional print and broadcast media.

But all this requires leadership from a government seized of the issue—and *this* government is not.

The IC is a big place with lots of talented people and there is no doubt significant work going on. But the intelligence community ultimately responds to the president's priorities. Since it is not *this* president's priority, there have been no extraordinary structures set up (like the Counterterrorism Center and the Iran Operations Division under Bush 43), no structure with the first pick of talent and resources and the challenge to create new processes to solve new problems.

A truly effective response would require a heavy organizational and policy lift, since the Russian effort strikes at historical seams between the public and private sectors, between questions of politics and policy, between federal and state jurisdictions, and between law enforcement and intelligence equities, organizations, and authorities. Absent presidential interest and

sustained NSC focus, there is little likelihood that the needed organizational and policy adjustments can be made.

Put another way, even if intelligence is developed, where does
it go? To whom is it to be presented to translate it into action?
What interagency body has been charged by the president to get
to the bottom of this? What senior official, like the vice president
(who *was* the chairman of the now defunct commission on alleged voter fraud), is the go-to person for guidance and direction?

On some days the intelligence community must feel as if
trapped in a rerun of the classic British comedy *Fawlty Towers*,
specifically the 1975 episode where Basil, about to host some
German tourists, warns his staff, "Don't mention the war!" The
phrase has since achieved memelike status to warn against
speaking about things that could cause an argument or tension.

Which returns us to the larger question, the status of truth
today and what that larger question means for intelligence.

I have no doubt that officers and offices, within the resource
constraints set by the president's determination of priorities,
will continue their professional duty to collect and analyze intelligence. I am actually more concerned about the presentation of
intelligence, and not only on the Russia question.

It is always a difficult question of how, when, where, and to
what degree to push back against preferred policy narratives when
they slip the bonds of what the IC believes to be objective reality.

This is more than a question of simple honesty. There are real
issues of effectiveness involved as well. Push too hard on one issue and you likely lose access and relevance for others. Push not
enough and you concede a course of action that is unproductive at
best and sometimes a lot worse.

This is a complicated relationship. Mark Lowenthal was the chief of analysis for the entire intelligence community for several years under DCI George Tenet. Mark is a smart and thoughtful man (1988 *Jeopardy!* grand champion, no less), author of several books on intelligence and analysis. A few years ago he wrote, "Policymakers do more than receive intelligence; they shape it. Without a constant reference to policy, intelligence is rendered meaningless." Policymakers can exist without the intelligence community, Lowenthal adds, but the intelligence community cannot exist without them.[18]

Which isn't to say that policymakers get to *shape* their intelligence in terms of what its conclusions might be, but rather that in addition to being competent and honest, intelligence needs to be relevant and useful—and relevance and utility *are* largely in the hands of the policymaker and especially of the president.

And this president at various times has signaled his distrust, questioned the credibility, risked the capabilities, and downplayed the value of his intelligence community and, after ten months in office, when asked about vacancies in various foreign policy positions that historically have advised the White House, famously responded that this shouldn't be a concern because "I'm the only one that matters."

So when do you push? When do you concede? And when do you walk?

This is hard, and although the nation should be grateful to those who have not, it might be right for some people to take a pass.

About two or three months into the administration I received a phone call from an old colleague who said he might be on a very short list for a very senior position. He asked my opinion. I told him that three months earlier I would have talked to him about his duty; six weeks ago I would have told him to follow his conscience; now I'm telling him, "Say no."

He breathed an audible sigh of relief and said, "Thank you." That was where his head and heart had been, but he feared he was just being selfish.

I told him that I didn't think that he was, that I doubted he could make any fundamental difference, that he would be frustrated and then tarred by the other activities of the administration, and that he wouldn't finish out the term. "You're a young man," I said. "Don't put yourself at risk for the future. You have a lot to offer . . . someday."

Months later I talked with a recently retired case officer, something of an Agency legend, who told me something similar. He was glad to be out, he said, after establishing his apolitical credentials by telling me that he hadn't voted since homeroom. He said he was very happy not to be at the office coffee pot after one tweet or another and being asked by a junior officer, "Hey, Chief, what do you think?"

He didn't speculate on how he would answer, but repeated to me what he thought was the important question: "How will I be judged?" And again, for emphasis: "How will history judge me?"

Which applies to institutions at least as much as it applies to individuals, especially since institutions don't have the freedom to opt out, and that judgment of history might be the most important question that American intelligence as an enterprise faces today.

Preserving relevance and utility is indeed important, but there have to be limits. History—and the next president—will judge American intelligence, and if it is found to have been too accommodating to this or any president, it will be disastrous for the community.[19]

When asked for counsel these days by serving officers, I usually respond with something like, "Do your duty," and then remind them of their responsibility to help the duly elected president succeed. Elections matter. I then add, "Protect yourself. Take notes and save them. And, above all, protect the institution. America still needs it."

A lot of the noises from Washington these days are (thankfully) the sounds of American institutions pushing back against a president who routinely sounds authoritarian, but whose office lacks the wherewithal—at least for now—to actually be so. That was the not-so-hidden context of Donald Trump Jr.'s complaint to a group of young conservative activists in late December that "there are people at the highest levels of government that don't want to let America be America."[20]

I was thrown that quote by Don Lemon on CNN a few minutes after getting off a train in Washington that same evening and instinctively responded that I thought that it was "an appeal to the heart of autocracy."

It was. And I'm glad I said it, because the current line of confrontation in Washington over presidential power is not the one designed by the founders—the one that should exist between the executive and Congress, which has been surprisingly compliant—but between the executive and the other institutions of government and civil society.

But Lemon's question and my answer highlighted an important issue. I feel that *my* credentials to comment on air are based on my intelligence experience. I am (or at least try to be) the "fact witness." Given the president's routine distance from the facts,

I often appear to be in opposition. The *Washington Post* recorded nearly two thousand false or misleading statements by the president in just his first year.[21] Two thousand!

But I am *not* the opposition. And I am certainly not the *resistance*. I actually look for things positive to say about the administration (for instance, the decision to stay the course in Afghanistan or pushing battlefield decision making down to the tactical level).

There are now quite a few former intelligence officials on the 24/7 news networks: Phil Mudd, former counterterrorism analyst at both CIA and FBI; Michael Morell, former acting director of CIA; Jeremy Bash, Leon Panetta's former chief of staff; Leon Panetta himself; John McLaughlin, former deputy director and acting director of CIA; Jim Clapper, former director of national intelligence; occasionally John Brennan, former DCIA; the list goes on. Current CIA leadership is (at least publicly) less than thrilled with the phenomenon. In October 2017, Mike Pompeo complained, "There are an awful lot of former CIA talking heads on TV," adding that their obligation to remain quiet about their work "far extends beyond the day you turn in your badge."[22]

I suspect that Director Pompeo's legitimate concerns about security might have been reinforced by the morning-after comments of a cable-news-fixated president. Michael Morell, after echoing Pompeo's caution against leaking, appropriately added, "But, to be clear, critiquing policy is not leaking."

Still, there is no doubt that the comments of people like me, Clapper, McLaughlin, Brennan, Morell, and others have created the impression in the minds of some (many?) that we are merely the public voice of a deep state intelligence community opposed to Donald Trump.

If we are, we aren't very efficient. We don't coordinate on commentary. What you see on air is what you get. If there is broad consistency, it is the product of a common worldview and shared life experiences, not an orchestrated theme of the week.

Mike Morell seems to have a bit of buyer's remorse, suggesting that his criticism of Trump and endorsement of Clinton during the campaign may have helped accelerate the estrangement between Trump and the IC, and that he (Morell) should have thought more about the potential downsides to the intelligence community from that. Michael included my criticism of the candidate's campaign language and policies (I did not endorse Clinton) as a contributing cause as well.[23]

Perhaps it was. But I was telling the truth as I believed it to be. Both of us had been commenting on the networks for years, and although neither of us signed on just to oppose Trump, pointing out things that weren't true just seemed the right thing to do. And there was no escaping the IC findings about the Russian intervention.

Since the inauguration, the two most senior leaders of the community under Barack Obama, DNI Jim Clapper and DCIA John Brennan, joined in with somewhat more basic challenges to the president's character and competence. One of Clapper's early TV appearances raised questions about Trump's fitness for office, a comment that excited some emails from more traditional senior intelligence alumni about staying above politics.

But there is what diplomats call "a range of views" on that subject. I live a short distance from the Agency and have frequent chance encounters with currently serving officers. What I hear from them is "thank you" and "keep it up." Some of that is certainly just politeness; some of it perhaps gratitude for some earlier TV appearances defending them and their work. But I suspect at least part of it is about what is being said now.

Still, the longer we are on air, the more the questions trend toward a value judgment of the president himself and not just the president's actions, as it becomes increasingly clear that he will not change, that the office will not shape the man, and that, in fact, it has been and will be the other way around.

So how do individuals and institutions hold their ground without being destructive and judged as reflexively negative, as being the opposition, or part of the resistance?

Tough work. And it may get tougher.

The president has already tweeted that the entire Department of Justice is the deep state and has called for the jailing of a political opponent (Huma Abedin). And that was largely without any proximate provocation. He also told a *New York Times* reporter, "I have [an] absolute right to do what I want to do with the Justice Department."[24]

Adam Schiff, the senior Democrat on the House Intelligence Committee, is a smart man, but he is also a political animal. So I am not sure what to make of his December tweet: "Here is what we know: The Russians offered help. The Campaign accepted help. The Russians gave help. The President made full use of that help."

Remember John McLaughlin's four stages of the Trump-intelligence relationship (chapter 4). We have traversed three: ignorance, hostility, unavoidability. Sometime in 2018 we will reach John's fourth stage: what happens after Special Counsel Bob Mueller reports out. It is not impossible to imagine even more difficult circumstances post-Mueller.

Or what if the talented people around the president—the "axis

of adults" as described in the press, the "benign junta" as someone else described it to me—cannot contain the president's worst
impulses with regard to Korea or Iran or some other trouble spot?

I began this book with a stroll through wartime Sarajevo, an
observation about the fragility of civilization, and a caution that
I was not predicting civil war or societal collapse here. I am still
not making such a prediction. But these are truly uncharted waters for the Republic—and I am saying that with full knowledge
of other crises we have (successfully) faced. But there most often
we argued over the values to be applied to objective reality, or
occasionally over what constituted objective reality, not the existence or the relevance of objective reality itself.

Timothy Snyder keeps coming back to the importance of
reality and truth in his magnificent pamphlet-length book *On
Tyranny*. "To abandon facts," he writes, "is to abandon freedom.
If nothing is true, then no one can criticize power because there
is no basis to do so." He then chillingly observes, "Post-truth is
pre-fascism."[25]

Nothing is free or guaranteed in this world.

On a recent visit to CIA, as I was standing near the iconic shield
in the grand lobby, I was approached by a young officer who
was anxious to introduce himself and tell me his story.

He was a master of several Arabic dialects. He had been born
in Iraq and first became associated with America as a translator
for U.S. forces during the heavy fighting in Anbar province. He
later made his way to this country, had an opportunity to attend
an Ivy League college, but opted to serve in the Army instead. He
became a cryptologic linguist, working for several years for NSA,

helping non–native-Arabic-speaking fellow soldiers master the intricacies of the language. He then applied for and was accepted by CIA, where he was, with obvious enthusiasm, putting his skills to good use.

(He would not, I should note, have been allowed to enter the United States had the administration's first immigration ban been in place at the time.)

I was at the Agency that day to attend the retirement ceremony of a Chinese American officer who had supported me in my overseas travel while director, and I got to meet her still very Chinese parents and, of course, a bunch of other officers. I left the headquarters building that day with a little more hope than when I entered. For me, that morning felt more like America and its promise than I was routinely seeing elsewhere.

Still, I wondered if the officers I saw at the ceremony realized how much we are now counting on them. If there are those who do not, this book intends to remind them that we're looking to them to guard their own integrity, look to the long-term health of their institution, stand tall in the bunker, and continue to tell the truth.

We are accustomed to relying on their truth telling to protect us from foreign enemies. Now we may need their truth telling to save us from ourselves.

AFTERWORD

arly in the afternoon of February 16, 2018, getaway Friday of Presidents' Day weekend for the federal workforce, Deputy Attorney General Rod Rosenstein entered a Department of Justice auditorium to announce to the press, to the world, and to Vladimir Putin that the United States was indicting thirteen Russian nationals and three Russian companies "for committing federal crimes while seeking to interfere in the United States political system, including the 2016 presidential election."

Let that sink in. Crimes. Real crimes. No "phony," no "hoax," no "witch hunt," no "fake news."

Rosenstein's comments and the accompanying indictment followed the familiar arc of what the intelligence community had been saying for more than a year, and beneath the bland charges of "identity theft, bank fraud, wire fraud, and conspiracy to defraud the United States," the indictment cataloged stunning operational details. The defendants had conducted what they themselves called information warfare "through fictitious U.S. personas on social media platforms and other Internet-based media" with a goal to "sow discord" and spread distrust "towards the candidates and the political system in general . . . [by] supporting the presidential campaign of then-candidate Donald J. Trump and disparaging Hillary Clinton. . . . They engaged in operations primarily intended to communicate derogatory information about Hillary Clinton, to denigrate other candidates such as Ted Cruz and Marco Rubio, and to support Bernie Sanders and then-candidate Donald Trump."[1] President Trump had been alerted to the indictments shortly before Rosenstein stepped to the podium and by midafternoon had tweeted: "Russia started their anti-US campaign in 2014, long before I announced that I would run for President. The results of the election were not impacted. The Trump campaign did nothing wrong - no collusion!"

Rosenstein had been careful to emphasize that *this* indictment made no claim about witting American collusion with the Russians, nor whether the Russians had any effect on the election. But with the indictment and Rosenstein's carefully crafted statement, the president, the intelligence community, and America had entered what John McLaughlin had said would be phase four of the IC–Trump relationship. Recall that John had cataloged the sequence of that relationship as first ignorance (the candidate and his team knew little about the intelligence business); followed by hostility (charges of Nazis, political hacks, and such); and developing into inevitability (jettisoning "I'm, like, a smart person. I don't have to be told the same thing" in favor of regular briefings). Phase four, John had predicted, would start when Mueller began to report his findings.

And so he has, and the former FBI director appears far from

being done. Washington is alive with stories of his interest in Trump Tower meetings, Trump finances, Russian money, campaign communications, and a proposed Moscow hotel and his possibly interviewing the president.

The president, for his part, has lashed out against practically everyone except Russia and Putin since the indictment. He didn't just contradict but publicly humiliated his national security adviser after H. R. McMaster told a security conference in Munich that evidence of Russian interference was now "incontrovertible." The president quickly and angrily tweeted a critique: "General McMaster forgot to say that the results of the 2016 election were not impacted or changed by the Russians and that the only Collusion was between Russia and Crooked H, the DNC and the Dems. Remember the Dirty Dossier, Uranium, Speeches, Emails and the Podesta Company!"

The tweet was a melange of inaccuracies, vagaries, conspiracy theories, and shopworn accusations, and it must have made for a long flight back to Washington for H.R. Trying to project closure as well as alert the Europeans, he had succeeded only in provoking his boss, undercutting his own status, and laying bare America's post-truth divisions for all to see.

Still, McMaster's view was supported by American intelligence in two remarkable appearances that bookended Rosenstein's press conference. The first was the worldwide threat briefing in front of the Senate Intelligence Committee, an annual event designed to give both the Senate and the public an appreciation of global circumstances, but an event that has just as often been diverted by the news or crisis of the day.

On the Tuesday before Rosenstein's blockbuster, Director of National Intelligence Dan Coats was joined by the heads of

three-letter agencies like CIA, NSA, and the FBI to give his assessment. He kept the emphasis on cyber dangers that have marked
such testimony for several years now. Proliferation of weapons of
mass destruction followed, with terrorism third on his list. Coats
added a new entry, emerging threats in space, and concluded
with transnational crime.

That was solid, if unremarkable, fare, but I was struck that—
apocalyptic campaign rhetoric to the contrary—terrorism no longer enjoyed its once dominant focus, and in the fine print of the
DNI's statement there were other observations that deviated from
administration orthodoxy. I wondered, for example, how Coats's
comment that North Korea sees nuclear weapons as essential to
regime survival would affect any American negotiating position
with Pyongyang. So, too, with the observation that the Iranian
nuclear deal puts Tehran further away from a weapon than it
would otherwise be and continues to contribute to our visibility
into that program.

One didn't need to read the fine print to see the unwavering
intelligence community consensus that the Russians interfered
in the 2016 election and planned to do the same in 2018. In his
opening remarks, Coats predicted that Russian operations "will
continue against the United States and our European allies, using
elections as opportunities to undermine democracy, sow discord,
and undermine our values," and then added, "There should be no
doubt that Russia perceived its past efforts as successful, and
views the 2018 U.S. midterm elections as a potential target for Russian influence operations."[2]

Later, one by one, the five intelligence chiefs at the witness
table with Coats publicly confirmed that the president, despite

their obvious concern, had not tasked them to focus on this issue or do much about it.

Mike Rogers, the director of NSA, easily joined consensus that Tuesday. Two weeks later (and ten days *after* the Russia indictments), he was alone in front of the Senate Armed Services Committee in his dual-hatted role as commander of U.S. Cyber Command, and he was answering some of the same questions. There Rogers predicted that "if we don't change the dynamic here, this is going to continue and 2016 won't be viewed as isolated. This is something that will be sustained over time." And then he offered this judgement: ". . . we're probably not doing enough . . . it hasn't changed the calculus. . . . It certainly hasn't generated the change in behavior that I think we all know we need."[3]

That's a pretty clear warning. And a pretty good sign that American intelligence remains steadfast on this issue and, one hopes, more broadly in its commitment to objective truth.

It's also a pretty good sign that phase four in the relationship between the IC and the president will be lengthy, contentious, divisive, and unpredictable. Stand by.

ACKNOWLEDGMENTS

My thanks to all those individuals—active and retired intelligence veterans; interested observers and contractors; foreign officials and intelligence partners; academics, philosophers, and scientists; journalists and historians; friends, relatives, and neighbors; politicians and statesmen; never Trumpers and Trump diehards; strangers on a train, in an airport, or on Twitter accounts—who were willing to share their unvarnished views with me. Most of you will remain nameless here, but you functioned as a needed compass in unexplored terrain, and I have worked hard to give a fair account of the depth, honesty, and legitimacy of your thoughts and feelings.

Thanks, too, to the folks at Penguin Press, especially Scott Moyers and Elisabeth Calamari, and agent Andrew Wylie, who would hazard a second book on my part with none of the inherent buzz of a CIA memoir. Thanks, too, to other editors at *The Hill*, CNN, and the *Washington Post*, who urged me to write on these subjects as they were happening and helped me put thoughts to paper.

And I've also got to thank the Sisters of Mercy, Marianists and Spiritans who, over fourteen years of liberal education, gave me an appreciation for history and philosophy that became even more important as I grew older. They also added a love of country, a love of America as a creedal nation, one that was always more revolutionary idea than territory, population, or blood.

And, of course, to my wife, Jeanine, who—in addition to all the love and support—patiently endured draft after draft as first reader and unsparing critic.

NOTES

Chapter One: Why This? Why Now?

1 "Oxford Dictionaries Word of the Year 2016 Is . . . Post-Truth," Oxford Dictionaries, Oxford University Press, November 16, 2016, https://www.oxforddictionaries.com/press/news/2016/12/11/WOTY-16.

2 Jack Goldsmith, "Will Donald Trump Destroy the Presidency?," *Atlantic*, October 2017, https://www.theatlantic.com/magazine/archive/2017/10/will-donald-trump-destroy-the-presidency/537921/.

3 John Nichols, "'The Economist' Just Downgraded the US from a 'Full Democracy' to a 'Flawed Democracy,'" *Nation*, January 26, 2017, https://www.thenation.com/article/the-economist-just-downgraded-the-us-from-a-full-democracy-to-a-flawed-democracy/; and Elena Holodny, "The US Has Been Downgraded to a 'Flawed Democracy,'" *Business Insider*, January 27, 2017, http://www.businessinsider.com/economist-intelligence-unit-downgrades-united-states-to-flawed-democracy-2017-1.

Chapter Two: Whither America . . . and Everyone Else?

1 "A World in Transformation" (article) by Brent Scowcroft published by the Atlantic Council, April 26, 2012.

2 Graham Allison, *Destined for War* (New York: Houghton Mifflin Harcourt, 2017), and Graham Allison, "The Thucydides Trap," *Foreign Policy*, June 9, 2017.

3 Julia Ioffe, "What Putin Really Wants," *Atlantic*, January–February 2018, https://www.theatlantic.com/magazine/archive/2018/01/putins-game/546548/.

4 "Nuclear Weapons: Who Has What at a Glance," Arms Control Association, January 18, 2018, https://www.armscontrol.org/factsheets/Nuclearweaponswhohaswhat; and Sajid Farid Shapoo, "The Dangers of Pakistan's Tactical Nuclear Weapons," *The Diplomat*, February 1, 2017, http://thediplomat.com/2017/02/the-dangers-of-pakistans-tactical-nuclear-weapons/.

5 Edward Luce, *The Retreat of Western Liberalism* (New York: Atlantic Monthly Press, 2017), 47, 68.

6 David Brooks, "When Politics Becomes Your Idol," *New York Times*, October 30, 2017, https://www.nytimes.com/2017/10/30/opinion/when-politics-becomes-your-idol.html.

7 Paul Wehner quoting Christine Herman, "Why We Argue Best with Our Mouths Shut," *Christianity Today,* May 26, 2017, http://www.christianitytoday.com/ct/2017/june/why-we-argue-best-with-our-mouths-shut.html. Dr. Herman is a Ph.D. chemist turned public radio journalist.

8 Luce, *The Retreat of Western Liberalism*, 35.

9 Andrew McGill, "Many of Trump's Supporters Never Left Their Hometowns," *Atlantic,* October 6, 2016, https://www.theatlantic.com/politics/archive/2016/10/trump-supporters-hometowns/503033/.

10 French sociologist-philosopher Raphaël Liogier quoted in A. C. Grayling, *Democracy and Its Crisis* (London: Oneworld, 2017), 115.

11 Jake Bright, "Globalization and the US Election: We Need to Take the Voices of the Discontented More Seriously," World Economic Forum Annual Meeting (Davos, Switzerland, January 17–20, 2017), World Economic Forum, January 9, 2017, https://www.weforum.org/agenda/2017/01/globalization-and-the-us-election-we-need-to-take-the-voices-of-the-discontented-more-seriously/; and a conversation with J. D. Vance, author of *Hillbilly Elegy*, in September 2017.

12 Luce, *The Retreat of Western Liberalism*, 7.

13 Nile Gardiner and Morgan Lorraine Roach, "Barack Obama's Top 10 Apologies: How the President Has Humiliated a Superpower," Heritage Foundation, June 2, 2009, http://www.heritage.org/europe/report/barack-obamas-top-10-apologies-how-the-president-has-humiliated-superpower.

14 Thom Shanker, "Warning Against Wars Like Iraq and Afghanistan," *New York Times*, February 25, 2011, http://www.nytimes.com/2011/02/26/world/26gates.html.

15 David Ignatius, "Talk Boldly with Iran," *Washington Post*, June 23, 2006, http://www.washingtonpost.com/wpdyn/content/article/2006/06/22/AR2006062201469.html.

16 Luce, *The Retreat of Western Liberalism*, 10.

17 Gillian Tett, "Why We No Longer Trust the Experts," *Financial Times*, July 1, 2016, https://www.ft.com/content/24035fc2-3e45-11e6-9f2c-36b487ebd80a.

18 Max Fisher, "What Is Donald Trump's Foreign Policy?," *New York Times,* November 11, 2016, https://www.nytimes.com/2016/11/12/world/what-is-donald-trumps-foreign-policy.html.

Chapter Three: The Candidate and the Campaign

1 Thomas M. Nichols, *The Death of Expertise: The Campaign Against Established Knowledge and Why It Matters* (New York: Oxford University Press, 2017), ix, 3, and 28.

2 Grace Guarnieri, "Trump Questions Climate Change in Piers Morgan Interview," *Newsweek*, January 28, 2018, http://www.newsweek.com/trump-questions -climate-change-piers-morgan-793135.

3 David Badash, "Trump Calls Immigrants 'Vicious Snakes' as He Celebrates 100th Day with 'the Most Divisive Speech Ever,'" The New Civil Rights Movement, April 30, 2017, http://www.thenewcivilrightsmovement.com/davidbadash/trump_cel ebrates_his_100th_day_like_he_did_his_first_delivering_the_most_divisive_ speech_ever.

4 Emily Cadei, "Pope Francis and President Trump: A Brief History of Their War of Words," *Newsweek*, March 23, 2017, http://www.newsweek.com/trump-pope -timeline-war-words-613770.

5 Delia Gallagher, "Catholic Journal Criticizes Trump 'Value Voters,'" CNN, July 25, 2017, http://www.cnn.com/2017/07/14/politics/pope-advisers-trump-supporters /index.html.

6 Charles Collins, "Jesuit Journal Close to Pope says 'Manichean Vision' Behind Trump," Crux, July 13, 2017, https://cruxnow.com/vatican/2017/07/13/jesuit -journal-close-pope-says-manichean-vision-behind-trump/.

7 Jenna Johnson and Abigail Hauslohner, "'I Think Islam Hates Us': A Timeline of Trump's Comments about Islam and Muslims," *Washington Post*, May 20, 2017, https://www.washingtonpost.com/news/post-politics/wp/2017/05/20/i-think -islam-hates-us-a-timeline-of-trumps-comments-about-islam-and-muslims/.

8 J. Lester Feder, "This Is How Steve Bannon Sees the Entire World," BuzzFeed, updated November 16, 2016, https://www.buzzfeed.com/lesterfeder/this-is-how -steve-bannon-sees-the-entire-world.

9 Michael Gerson, "Roy Moore's Deep Devotion to the Gospel of Bannon," *Washington Post*, September 28, 2017, https://www.washingtonpost.com/opinions/roy -moores-deep-devotion-to-the-gospel-of-bannon/2017/09/28/fbe40c48-a479 -11e7-b14f-f41773cd5a14_story.html.

10 Conversations with A. C. Grayling in August and October 2017.

11 David D. Kirkpatrick, "For Evangelicals, Supporting Israel Is 'God's Foreign Policy,'" *New York Times*, November 14, 2006, http://www.nytimes.com/2006/11/14 /washington/14israel.html.

12 Michael Hirsh, "Team Trump's Message: The Clash of Civilizations Is Back," *Politico*, November 20, 2016, http://www.politico.com/magazine/story/2016/11/don ald-trump-team-islam-clash-of-civilizations-214474.

13 Tom LoBianco, "Donald Trump on Terrorists: 'Take Out Their Families,'" CNN, December 3, 2015, http://www.cnn.com/2015/12/02/politics/donald-trump-ter rorists-families/index.html.

14   Tierney McAfee, "Donald Trump Promises to Bring Back Waterboarding and Worse Torture: 'If It Doesn't Work, They Deserve It Anyway,'" *People*, November 24, 2015, http://people.com/celebrity/donald-trump-wants-to-bring-back-water boarding-and-worse-torture/.

15   Demetri Sevastopulo and Geoff Dyer, "US Foreign Policy Experts Round on Donald Trump," *Financial Times*, March 2, 2016, https://www.ft.com/content/c25b7 3b8-e0bb-11e5-9217-6ae3733a2cd1.

16   Warren Strobel, Jonathan Landay, and Matt Spetalnick, "Republican Foreign Policy Veterans Rebuke Trump Worldview," Reuters, March 2, 2016, http://www .reuters.com/article/us-usa-election-trump-foreignpolicy/republican-foreign -policy-veterans-rebuke-trump-worldview-idUSMTZSAPEC33FXD386.

17   Jessica Schulberg, "GOP Foreign Policy Experts Warn a Trump Presidency Would Endanger America," Huffington Post, March 3, 2016, http://www.huffingtonpost .com/entry/foreign-policy-experts-trump_us_56d7c294e4b03a40567779d4.

18   *Morning Joe*, March 16, 2016, MSNBC.

19   *Meet the Press*, August 16, 2015, MSNBC.

20   Jeremy Diamond and Nicole Gaouette, "Donald Trump Unveils Foreign Policy Advisers," CNN, March 21, 2016, http://edition.cnn.com/2016/03/21/politics/donald -trump-foreign-policy-team/index.html.

21   Ryan Teague Beckwith, "Read Hillary Clinton and Donald Trump's Remarks at a Military Forum," *Time*, September 8, 2017, http://time.com/4483355/commander -chief-forum-clinton-trump-intrepid/.

22   FSB: Russia's Federal Security Service, the main successor to the KGB.

23   The intelligence community later publicly concluded (see chapter 4) with high confidence that Russian motivation extended to punishing Hillary Clinton, delegitimizing her expected presidency, and, finally, putting a Russian thumb on the American electoral scale to help Trump win.

24   Michelle Ye Hee Lee, "Every Russia Story Trump Said Was a Hoax by Democrats: A Timeline," *Washington Post,* June 1, 2017, https://www.washingtonpost.com /news/fact-checker/wp/2017/06/01/every-russia-story-trump-said-was-a-hoax -by-democrats-a-timeline/.

25   SVR. Russia's Foreign Intelligence Service.

26   Abigail Tracy, "Trump's 'Coffee Boy' Keeps Sabotaging His Russia Story," *Vanity Fair*, November 17, 2017, https://www.vanityfair.com/news/2017/11/george-papa dopoulos-trump-campaign-russia.

Chapter Four: The Transition

1   Candace Smith, "Jeb Bush on Donald Trump: He's a 'Chaos Candidate' and He'd Be a 'Chaos President,' ABC News, December 15, 2015, http://abcnews.go.com /Politics/jeb-bush-donald-trump-chaos-candidate-hed-chaos/story?id=35788736.

2 Adam Edelman, "Group of 75 Retired Diplomats Pen Letter Blasting Donald Trump as 'Entirely Unqualified,'" *New York Daily News*, September 22, 2016, http://www.nydailynews.com/news/politics/75-retired-diplomats-pen-letter-blasting-trump-unqualified-article-1.2802249.

3 Eli Stokols, Bryan Bender, and Michael Crowley, "The Husband-and-Wife Team Driving Trump's National Security Policy," *Politico*, February 13, 2017, http://www.politico.com/story/2017/02/trump-national-security-gorka-234950.

4 Jon D. Michaels, "Trump and the 'Deep State,'" *Foreign Affairs*, September–October 2017, https://www.foreignaffairs.com/articles/2017-08-15/trump-and-deep-state.

5 "Hannity: Deep State's Massive Effort to Destroy Trump," Fox News, June 17, 2017, http://www.foxnews.com/politics/2017/06/17/hannity-deep-states-massive-effort-to-destroy-trump.html.

6 Ioffe at the Aspen Security Forum, July 2017.

7 Glenn Greenwald, "What's Worse: Trump's Campaign Agenda or Empowering Generals and CIA Operatives to Subvert It?," The Intercept, August 5, 2017, https://theintercept.com/2017/08/05/whats-worse-trumps-campaign-agenda-or-empowering-generals-and-cia-operatives-to-subvert-it/.

8 Michael J. Glennon, *National Security and Double Government* (Harvard National Security Journal 1, January 2014, passim).

9 Glennon, *National Security and Double Government*, 39.

10 For a detailed account, see Michael V. Hayden, See *Playing to the Edge: American Intelligence in the Age of Terror* (New York: Penguin Books, 2016).

11 "5 Faith Facts on Mike Pence: A 'Born-Again, Evangelical Catholic,'" *National Catholic Reporter*, July 15, 2016, https://www.ncronline.org/blogs/ncr-today/5-faith-facts-mike-pence-born-again-evangelical-catholic.

12 James Risen and Matthew Rosenberg, "White House Plans to Have Trump Ally Review Intelligence Agencies," *New York Times*, February 15, 2017, https://www.nytimes.com/2017/02/15/us/politics/trump-intelligence-agencies-stephen-feinberg.html.

13 Matthew Rosenberg and James Risen, "Trump's Intelligence Nominee Gets Early Lesson in Managing White House," *New York Times*, March 9, 2017, https://www.nytimes.com/2017/03/09/us/politics/trump-coats-national-intelligence.html.

14 John Helgerson, *Getting to Know the President: Intelligence Briefings of Presidential Candidates, 1952–2004* (Washington, DC: Center for the Study of Intelligence, 2012), https://www.cia.gov/library/center-for-the-study-of-intelligence/csi-publications/books-and-monographs/getting-to-know-the-president/pdfs/U-%20Book-Getting%20to%20Know%20the%20President.pdf.

15 Marc Fisher, "Donald Trump Doesn't Read Much. Being President Probably Wouldn't Change That," *Washington Post*, July 17, 2016, https://www.washingtonpost.com/politics/donald-trump-doesnt-read-much-being-president-probably

-wouldnt-change-that/2016/07/17/d2ddf2bc-4932-11e6-90a8-fb84201e0645_
story.html.

16   Michael Gerson, "A Huge Question for Trump's North Korea Crisis," *Washington Post*, August 10, 2017, https://www.washingtonpost.com/opinions/a-huge-question-for-trumps-north-korea-crisis/2017/08/10/f2b1ed4e-7df4-11e7-9d08-b79f191668ed_story.html.

17   Grayling, *Democracy and Its Crisis*, 119.

18   Admittedly, much of this description comes from the early days of the administration. One hopes that, as time has passed, sessions have become more normalized, although the unique personality of the president is a constant. CIA director Mike Pompeo, who has become the de facto daily briefer, told a Washington audience in January that the president is "deeply engaged" and asks "hard questions." He cited examples of the president pushing back on analysis related to humanitarian issues in Yemen and finances in Venezuela, but his claim that the president takes the briefing like "a 25-year intelligence professional" might be the DCIA's form of what Mr. Trump calls truthful hyperbole. Marc A. Thiessen, "Rest Easy About Trump's Fitness," *Washington Post*, January 25, 2018, https://www.washingtonpost.com/opinions/rest-easy-about-trumps-fitness/2018/01/25/b9087844-0204-11e8-9d31-d72cf78dbeee_story.html.

19   Kyle Feldscher, "Trump 'Screamed' at National Security Adviser H. R. McMaster over Comments to South Korea: Report," *Washington Examiner*, May 8, 2017, http://www.washingtonexaminer.com/trump-screamed-at-national-security-adviser-hr-mcmaster-over-comments-to-south-korea-report/article/2622437.

20   Julia Zorthian, "President Trump Suddenly Ends Interview When Asked About Obama Wiretapping Claim," *Time*, May 1, 2017, http://time.com/4762517/donald-trump-barack-obama-wiretapping-interview-cbs/.

21   Graham Vyse, "Donald Trump Says It's Okay for Him to Lie Since 'People Agree With Me.'" Minutes, *New Republic*, 2017, https://newrepublic.com/minutes/140136/donald-trump-says-its-okay-lie-since-people-agree-me.

22   Alana Abramson, "Boy Scouts 'Unaware' of Call Trump Said He Received from Organization Praising Jamboree Speech," *Time*, August 1, 2017, http://time.com/4883422/donald-trump-boy-scouts-wall-street-journal-transcript/.

23   Steve Chapman, "The Bottomless Ignorance of Donald Trump," *Chicago Tribune*, October 26, 2016, http://www.chicagotribune.com/news/opinion/chapman/ct-donald-trump-ignorance-trade-perspec-1027-md-20161026-column.html.

24   Matthew Rosenberg, "Trump Misleads on Russian Meddling: Why 17 Intelligence Agencies Don't Need to Agree," *New York Times*, July 6, 2017, https://www.nytimes.com/2017/07/06/us/politics/trump-russia-intelligence-agencies-cia-fbi-nsa.html.

25   Chuck Todd, Mark Murray, and Carrie Dann, "Trump Has Been Strikingly Consistent in Denying Russian Hacking Role," NBC News, January 6, 2017, https://www

.nbcnews.com/politics/first-read/trump-has-been-strikingly-consistent
-denying-russian-hacking-role-n703866.

26 Eugene Kiely, "Trump Misleads on Russia Hacking," FactCheck.org, Annenberg
Public Policy Center, updated July 7, 2017, http://www.factcheck.org/2017/07
/trump-misleads-russia-hacking/.

27 Eileen Sullivan, "Trump Dismisses 'Russia Hoax' as Facebook Turns Over Ads
Tied to Campaign," *New York Times*, September 22, 2017, https://www.nytimes
.com/2017/09/22/us/politics/trump-russia-hoax-facebook-ads.html.

28 Mark Landler, "Trump Under Fire for Invoking Nazis in Criticism of U.S. Intelligence," *New York Times*, January 11, 2017, https://www.nytimes.com/2017/01
/11/us/donald-trump-nazi-comparison.html.

29 Julian Borger, "John McCain Passes Dossier Alleging Secret Trump-Russia Contacts to FBI," *Guardian*, January 11, 2017, https://www.theguardian.com
/us-news/2017/jan/10/fbi-chief-given-dossier-by-john-mccain-alleging-secret
-trump-russia-contacts.

Chapter Five: The First Hundred Days (More or Less)

1 Margaret Vice and Hanyu Chwe, "Mexican Views of the U.S. Turn Sharply Negative," Pew Research Center, September 14, 2017, http://www.pewglobal.org/2017
/09/14/mexican-views-of-the-u-s-turn-sharply-negative/.

2 Eliot A. Cohen, "How Trump Is Ending the American Era," *Atlantic*, October 2017,
https://www.theatlantic.com/magazine/archive/2017/10/is-trump-ending-the
-american-era/537888/0.

3 "Transcript: Donald Trump's Foreign Policy Speech," *New York Times*, April
27, 2016, https://www.nytimes.com/2016/04/28/us/politics/transcript-trump-for
eign-policy.html.

4 Thomas Wright, "Five Things We 'Learned' from Trump's Foreign Policy Speech,"
Brooking Institution, April 27, 2016, https://www.brookings.edu/blog/order
-from-chaos/2016/04/27/five-things-we-learned-from-trumps-foreign-policy
-speech/.

5 Daniel White, "Read Donald Trump's Ohio Speech on Immigration and Terrorism,"
Time, August 15, 2016, http://time.com/4453110/donald-trump-national-secu
rity-immigration-terrorism-speech/.

6 Peter Baker, "In a Shift, Trump Will Move Egypt's Rights Record to the Sidelines,"
New York Times, March 31, 2017, https://www.nytimes.com/2017/03/31/world
/middleeast/in-major-shift-trump-taking-egypts-human-rights-issues-private
.html.

7 Robin Wright, "Why Is Donald Trump Still So Horribly Witless About the World?,"
New Yorker, August 4, 2017, https://www.newyorker.com/news/news-desk/why
-is-donald-trump-still-so-horribly-witless-about-the-world.

8　Missy Ryan and Dan Lamothe, "Placing Russia First Among Threats, Defense Nominee Warns of Kremlin Attempts to 'Break' NATO," *Washington Post*, January 12, 2017, https://www.washingtonpost.com/world/national-security/senate-set-to-question-trumps-pentagon-pick-veteran-marine-gen-james-mattis/2017/01/11/b3c6946a-d816-11e6-9a36-1d296534b31e_story.html.

9　James O. Ellis, Jr., James N. Mattis, and Kori Schake, "Restoring Our National Security," in George Shultz, ed., *Blueprint for America* (Washington, DC: Hoover Institution Press, 2016), https://www.hoover.org/sites/default/files/research/docs/george_shultz_blueprint_for_america_ch10.pdf.

10　Maxwell Tani, "'This Is the Most Unpleasant Call All Day': Trump Bashed the Australian Prime Minister in a Call, Saying 'Putin Was a Pleasant Call,'" Business Insider, August 3, 2017, http://www.businessinsider.com/trump-call-australian-prime-minister-putin-2017-8.

11　Nada Bakos, "This Is What Foreign Spies See When They Read President Trump's Tweets," *Washington Post*, June 23, 2017, https://www.washingtonpost.com/outlook/president-trumps-twitter-feed-is-a-gold-mine-for-foreign-spies/2017/06/23/e3e3b0b0-5764-11e7-a204-ad706461fa4f_story.html.

12　Associated Press, "How Donald Trump's Plan to Ban Muslims Has Evolved," *Fortune*, June 28, 2016, http://fortune.com/2016/06/28/donald-trump-muslim-ban/.

13　Jeffrey Gettleman, "State Dept. Dissent Cable on Trump's Ban Draws 1,000 Signatures," *New York Times*, January 31, 2017, https://www.nytimes.com/2017/01/31/world/americas/state-dept-dissent-cable-trump-immigration-order.html.

14　"'This Week' Transcript 3-5-17: Sarah Huckabee Sanders, Josh Earnest, and Sen. Al Franken," ABC News, March 5, 2017, http://abcnews.go.com/Politics/week-transcript-17-sarah-huckabee-sanders-josh-earnest/story?id=45911284.

15　David Smith, "White House Does Not Know if Alleged Surveillance of Trump Was by Wiretap," *Guardian*, March 6, 2017, https://www.theguardian.com/us-news/2017/mar/06/white-house-trump-surveillance-wiretap-sean-spicer.

16　Elliot Hannon, "What Made Trump So Sure Obama 'Wiretapped' Him? A Fox News Segment the Night Before, He Says," *Slate*, March 15, 2017, http://www.slate.com/blogs/the_slatest/2017/03/15/trump_talks_to_fox_news_tucker_carlson_about_obama_wiretap_claim.html.

17　Jana Heigl, "A Timeline of Donald Trump's False Wiretapping Charge," PolitiFact, March 21, 2017, http://www.politifact.com/truth-o-meter/article/2017/mar/21/timeline-donald-trumps-false-wiretapping-charge/.

18　Michael Hayden, "Michael Hayden: US Intel Agencies Win Big, But Russia Intel Wins Bigger in Comey Hearing," The Hill, March 22, 2017, http://thehill.com/blogs/pundits-blog/the-administration/325250-michael-hayden-us-intel-agencies-win-big-but-russia.

19　Alastair Jamieson, "Britain's GCHQ Denies 'Ridiculous' Claim It Helped Wiretap Trump," March 17, 2017, https://www.nbcnews.com/news/world/britain-s-gchq-denies-ridiculous-claim-it-helped-wiretap-trump-n734756.

20 Brian Barrett, "Devin Nunes: A Running Timeline of His Surveillance Claims and White House Ties," *Wired*, April 12, 2017, https://www.wired.com/2017/04/devin-nunes-white-house-trump-surveillance/.

21 Jessica Taylor, "Report: Trump Asked Intel Heads to Push Back on FBI Russia Probe," NPR, May 22, 2017, http://www.npr.org/2017/05/22/529586885/report-trump-asked-intel-heads-to-push-back-on-fbi-russia-probe.

22 Ben Macintyre, "General Michael Hayden: 'Trump Fired James Comey Because He Was Too Much His Own Man,'" *Times* (London), May 15, 2017, https://www.thetimes.co.uk/article/general-michael-hayden-trump-fired-james-comey-because-he-was-too-much-his-own-man-7b3v67rxq.

23 Mahita Gajanan, "President Trump to Russian Diplomats: Firing 'Nut Job' James Comey Relieved Pressure from Russia Probe," *Time*, May 19, 2017, http://time.com/4786698/president-trump-james-russia-comey-nut-job/.

24 Julie Hirschfeld Davis, "Trump's Cabinet, with a Prod, Extols the 'Blessing' of Serving Him," June 12, 2017, https://www.nytimes.com/2017/06/12/us/politics/trump-boasts-of-record-setting-pace-of-activity.html.

25 Emily Schultheis, "Former Presidential Advisers Discuss: What Makes a Good President?," CBS News, August 14, 2016, https://www.cbsnews.com/news/former-presidential-advisers-discuss-what-makes-a-good-president/.

26 Jamie Tarabay, "CIA Director: The North Koreans Would Love to See Kim Jong Un Go," *Newsweek*, July 20, 2017, http://www.newsweek.com/pompeo-cia-north-korea-kim-639998.

27 David Ignatius, "The CIA Is Entering a Danger Zone. Here's the Map," *Washington Post*, July 25, 2017, https://www.washingtonpost.com/opinions/the-cia-is-entering-a-danger-zone-heres-the-map/2017/07/25/e845890a-717a-11e7-8f39-eeb7d3a2d304_story.html.

28 Matthew Rosenberg, "Trump Likes When C.I.A. Chief Gets Political, but Officers Are Wary," *New York Times*, August 7, 2017, https://www.nytimes.com/2017/08/07/us/politics/mike-pompeo-cia.html; and Greg Miller, "At CIA, a Watchful Eye on Mike Pompeo, the President's Ardent Ally," *Washington Post*, August 25, 2017, https://www.washingtonpost.com/world/national-security/at-cia-a-watchful-eye-on-mike-pompeo-the-presidents-ardent-ally/2017/08/24/18c1d716-7ed0-11e7-9d08-b79f191668ed_story.html.

29 Thomas Gibbons-Neff, Eric Schmitt, and Adam Goldman, "A Newly Assertive C.I.A. Expands Its Taliban Hunt in Afghanistan," *New York Times*, October 22, 2017, https://www.nytimes.com/2017/10/22/world/asia/cia-expanding-taliban-fight-afghanistan.html.

30 Bill Gertz, "Director Pompeo Details How the CIA Is Changing Under President Trump," Washington Free Beacon, July 26, 2017, http://freebeacon.com/national-security/interview-cia-director-pompeo-cia-changing-president-trump/.

Chapter Six: Getting On with It

1 Mark Landler and Richard Pérez-Peña, "Flynn Was Brought Down by Illegal Leaks to News Media, Trump Says," *New York Times*, February 15, 2017, https://www .nytimes.com/2017/02/15/us/politics/trump-condemns-leaks-to-news-media -in-a-twitter-flurry.html.

2 Matthew Cox, "McMaster's Tank Battle in Iraq May Shape Advice in New Role," Military.com, February 23, 2017, http://www.military.com/daily-news/2017/02 /23/mcmasters-tank-battle-in-iraq-may-shape-advice-in-new-role.html.

3 Karen DeYoung and Jenna Johnson, "White House Dismisses Questions over Why It Waited to Fire Michael Flynn," *Washington Post*, May 9, 2017, https://www .washingtonpost.com/world/national-security/white-house-dismisses -questions-over-why-it-waited-to-fire-michael-flynn/2017/05/09/1314d506 -34ee-11e7-b4ee-434b6d506b37_story.html.

4 Greg Jaffe, "McMaster Ousts Second Official on National Security Council," *Washington Post*, August 2, 2017, https://www.washingtonpost.com/world /national-security/mcmaster-ousts-second-senior-official-on-national-security -council/2017/08/02/7ad0ad88-77cd-11e7-8f39-eeb7d3a2d304_story.html.

5 Jana Winter and Elias Groll, "Here's the Memo That Blew Up the NSC," *Foreign Policy*, August 10, 2017, http://foreignpolicy.com/2017/08/10/heres-the-memo -that-blew-up-the-nsc/.

6 Kevin Baron, "McMaster: I'm Here to Serve, Not 'Control the President,'" Defense One, September 26, 2017, http://www.defenseone.com/politics/2017/09/mcmaster -trump-control/141285/.

7 "Mattis Ammunition," C-SPAN, March 5, 2013, https://www.c-span.org/video/? c4658822/mattis-ammunition.

8 Karen DeYoung, "Defense Secretary Mattis Withdraws Patterson as Choice for Undersecretary for Policy," *Washington Post*, March 14, 2017, https://www.wash ingtonpost.com/world/national-security/defense-secretary-mattis-withdraws -patterson-as-choice-for-undersecretary-for-policy/2017/03/14/dd5ec8bc-08b6 -11e7-93dc-00f9bdd74ed1_story.html.

9 Theodore Schleifer, Elise Labott, and Gregory Krieg, "GOP Heavyweights with Ties to Exxon Pushed Tillerson," CNN, December 13, 2016, http://www.cnn.com/2016 /12/13/politics/rex-tillerson-robert-gates-condoleezza-rice/index.html.

10 Maggie Serota, "MSNBC Host: Source Said Tillerson Called Trump 'a Fucking Mo-ron,' Not Just a Regular Moron," Death and Taxes, Billboard-Hollywood Reporter Media Group, October 4, 2017, https://www.deathandtaxesmag.com/347297/ms nbc-host-source-said-tillerson-called-trump-a-fucking-moron-not-just-a -regular-moron/; and Martin Pengelly, Sabrina Siddiqui, and David Smith, "Trump Challenges Tillerson to 'Compare IQ Tests' after Reported 'Moron' Dig," *Guardian*, October 10, 2017, https://www.theguardian.com/us-news/2017 /oct/10/donald-trump-forbes-rex-tillerson-moron.

11 Anne Gearan, "Trump Rejects Veteran GOP Foreign Policy Aide Elliott Abrams for State Dept. Job," *Washington Post*, February 10, 2017, https://www.washington post.com/world/national-security/trump-rejects-veteran-gop-foreign-policy -aide-elliott-abrams-for-state-department-job/2017/02/10/52e53ce6-efbd-11e6 -9973-c5efb7ccfb0d_story.html.

12 John Wagner, Josh Dawsey, and Robert Costa, "Trump Pushes Back on Chief of Staff's Claims That Border Wall Pledges Are 'Uninformed,'" *Washington Post*, January 18, 2018, https://www.washingtonpost.com/politics/trump-pushes-back-on -chief-of-staff-claims-that-border-wall-pledges-uninformed/2018/01/18 /78960980-fc68-11e7-8f66-2df0b94bb98a_story.html.

13 Zachary Cohen and Dan Merica, "Trump Takes Credit for ISIS 'Giving Up,'" CNN, October 17, 2017, http://www.cnn.com/2017/10/17/politics/trump-isis-raqqa/in dex.html.

14 Jacob Pramu, "Trump: I Don't Give a Specific ISIS Plan Because I Don't Want Enemies to Know It," CNBC, September 7, 2016, https://www.cnbc.com/2016/09/07 /trump-i-dont-give-a-specific-isis-plan-because-i-dont-want-enemies -to-know-it.html.

15 Eric Schmitt, "Donald Trump Is Wrong on Mosul Attack, Military Experts Say," *New York Times*, October 20, 2016, https://www.nytimes.com/2016/10/21/us /politics/donald-trump-mosul-iraq.html.

16 Abigail Williams, "Secretary Tillerson on Russia: 'Complicit or Simply Incompetent' on Syrian Chemical Weapons," NBC News, April 7, 2017, https://www .nbcnews.com/news/world/secretary-tillerson-russia-complicit-or-simply -incompetent-syrian-chemical-weapons-n743686.

17 Note: The president called the head of the CIA, *not* the director of national intelligence, but that's another story (see chapter 4 for more background).

18 Greg Jaffe and Philip Rucker, "National Security Adviser Attempts to Reconcile Trump's Competing Impulses on Afghanistan," *Washington Post*, August 4, 2016, https://www.washingtonpost.com/world/national-security/the-fight-over -trumps-afghan-policy-has-become-an-argument-over-the-meaning-of-america -first/2017/08/04/f2790c80-785f-11e7-8f39-eeb7d3a2d304_story.html.

19 Baron, "McMaster: I'm Here to Serve, Not 'Control the President.'"

20 Carol E. Lee and Courtney Kube, "Trump Says U.S. 'Losing' Afghan War in Tense Meeting with Generals," NBC News, August 2, 2017, https://www.nbcnews.com /news/us-news/trump-says-u-s-losing-afghan-war-tense-meeting-generals- n789006.

21 Mark Landler, Eric Schmitt, and Michael R. Gordon, "Trump Aides Recruited Businessmen to Devise Options for Afghanistan," *New York Times*, July 10, 2017, https://www.nytimes.com/2017/07/10/world/asia/trump-afghanistan-policy -erik-prince-stephen-feinberg.html.

22 Ariane Tabatabai, "Trump Said He'd Tear Up the Iran Nuclear Deal. Now What?," *Bulletin of the Atomic Scientists*, November 10, 2016, https://thebulletin.org

/trump-said-hed-tear-iran-nuclear-deal-now-what10148; and Nora Kelly, "Where the 2016 Candidates Stand on the Iran Nuclear Deal," *Atlantic*, September 1, 2015, https://www.theatlantic.com/politics/archive/2015/09/where-the-2016 -candidates-stand-on-the-iran-nuclear-deal/448380/.

23   "Full Text of Donald Trump's Speech to AIPAC," *Times of Israel*, March 22, 2016, http://www.timesofisrael.com/donald-trumps-full-speech-to-aipac/.

24   Thomas L. Friedman, "Obama Makes His Case on Iran Nuclear Deal," *New York Times*, July 14, 2015, https://www.nytimes.com/2015/07/15/opinion/thomas -friedman-obama-makes-his-case-on-iran-nuclear-deal.html.

25   Jeffrey Goldberg, "The Obama Doctrine," *Atlantic*, April 2016, https://www .theatlantic.com/magazine/archive/2016/04/the-obama-doctrine/471525/.

26   Donald Trump, "President Trump's Speech to the Arab Islamic American Summit," May 21, 2017, White House, https://www.whitehouse.gov/the-press-office /2017/05/21/president-trumps-speech-arab-islamic-american-summit.

27   Karl Vick, "President Trump Says Isolating Qatar Could End Terrorism. He's Wrong," *Time*, June 6, 2017, http://time.com/4807216/donald-trump-twitter -qatar-terrorism/.

28   Nahal Toosi and Madeline Conway, "Tillerson: Dispute between Gulf states and Qatar Won't Affect Counterterrorism," *Politico*, June 5, 2017, https://www.polit ico.com/story/2017/06/05/qatar-dispute-saudi-arabia-egypt-bahrain-uae -239134.

29   Julian Borger, "US Rebukes Saudi Arabia over Qatar Embargo in Reversal after Trump," *Guardian*, June 20, 2017, https://www.theguardian.com/world/2017/jun /20/us-saudi-arabia-qatar-embargo-trump.

30   David E. Sanger, "Trump Seeks Way to Declare Iran in Violation of Nuclear Deal," *New York Times*, July 27, 2017, https://www.nytimes.com/2017/07/27/world /middleeast/trump-iran-nuclear-agreement.html.

31   Wesley Morgan, "Mattis: Stick to Iran Deal," *Politico*, October 3, 2017, https:// www.politico.com/story/2017/10/03/jim-mattis-iran-deal-243411.

32   Krishnadev Calamur, "Tillerson Acknowledges 'Differences' With Trump on Iran Deal," *Atlantic*, August 1, 2017, https://www.theatlantic.com/news/archive/2017 /08/tillerson-iran-jcpoa/535602/.

33   Elise Labott, Kevin Liptak, and Zachary Cohen, "President Trump Plans to 'Decertify' Iran Nuclear Deal Next Week," CNN, October 6, 2017, http://www.cnn .com/2017/10/05/politics/trump-iran-deal-deadline-plan/index.html.

34   "CIA's Mike Pompeo on Iran," The Iran Primer, United States Institute of Peace, July 31, 2017, http://iranprimer.usip.org/blog/2017/jul/31/cia's-mike-pompeo -iran.

35   Ali Vitali, "Trump Threatens to 'Totally Destroy' North Korea in First U.N. Speech," CNN, September 21, 2017, https://www.nbcnews.com/news/us-news/trump-un -north-korean-leader-suicide-mission-n802596.

36 Frank Camp, "SecDef Mattis Issues Powerful Statement After North Korea Alleg-
    edly Tests Hydrogen Bomb," Daily Wire, September 3, 2017, http://www.dailywire
    .com/news/20579/secdef-mattis-issues-powerful-statement-after-frank-camp.

37 Bob Fredericks, "Tillerson: US 'Interested' in Negotiating with North Korea," *New
    York Post*, August 15, 2017, http://nypost.com/2017/08/15/tillerson-us-interested
    -in-negotiating-with-north-korea/.

38 Jenna Johnson, "Trump on North Korea: 'Sorry, But Only One Thing Will Work!'"
    Washington Post, October 7, 2017, https://www.washingtonpost.com/news/post
    -politics/wp/2017/10/07/trump-on-north-korea-sorry-but-only-one-thing-will
    -work/.

39 Donald Trump, "Remarks by President Trump Before Meeting with Senior Mili
    tary Leaders," October 6, 2017, White House, https://www.whitehouse.gov/the
    -press-office/2017/10/06/remarks-president-trump-meeting-senior-military
    -leaders.

40 "FDD's National Security Summit," Foundation for the Defense of Democra-
    cies, October 19, 2017, https://www.defenddemocracy.org/content/uploads/docu
    ments/Transcript_FINAL_McMaster.pdf.

41 "Gen. H.R. McMaster on President Trump's New Iran Strategy," Fox News, Octo-
    ber 15, 2017, http://www.foxnews.com/transcript/2017/10/15/gen-h-r-mcmaster
    -on-president-trumps-new-iran-strategy.html.

42 "Lindsey Graham: Trump 'Told Me' He Will Bomb North Korea if It Keeps Testing
    Missiles," Vox, August 1, 2017, https://www.vox.com/world/2017/8/1/16075198
    /trump-lindsey-graham-north-korea-war.

43 Nicholas Kristof, "Slouching Toward War with North Korea," *New York Times*,
    November 4, 2017, https://www.nytimes.com/2017/11/04/opinion/sunday/nuc
    lear-war-north-korea.html.

44 "Aspen Security Forum 2017: At the Helm of the Intelligence Community," Aspen
    Security Forum 2017, Aspen Institute, July 21, 2017, Aspen, Colorado, http://as
    pensecurityforum.org/wp-content/uploads/2017/07/At-the-Helm-of-the
    -Intelligence-Community.pdf.

45 Donald Trump, "Remarks by President Trump to the 72nd Session of the United
    Nations General Assembly," White House, September 19, 2017, https://www
    .whitehouse.gov/the-press-office/2017/09/19/remarks-president-trump-72nd
    -session-united-nations-general-assembly.

46 David Ignatius, "Want a Clue to Trump's Policy? Look at His Schedule," *Washing-
    ton Post*, September 28, 2017, https://www.washingtonpost.com/opinions/want
    -a-clue-to-trumps-policy-look-at-his-schedule/2017/09/28/159cdf30-a483-11e7
    -b14f-f41773cd5a14_story.html.

47 Walter Russell Mead, "Trump's 'Blue Water' Foreign Policy," *Wall Street Journal*,
    December 25, 2017, https://www.wsj.com/articles/trumps-blue-water-foreign-
    policy-1514233158.

48   Kevin Baron, "Mattis: Pentagon Shifting Focus to Great Power Competition—'Not Terrorism,'" Defense One, January 19, 2018, http://www.defenseone.com/politics /2018/01/mattis-declares-pentagon-will-shift-focus-great-power-competition -not-terrorism/145305.

49   Richard Haass, "America and the Great Abdication," Atlantic, December 28, 2017, https://www.theatlantic.com/international/archive/2017/12/america -abidcation-trump-foreign-policy/549296/.

50   Dina Smeltz, Ivo Daalder, Karl Friedhoff, and Craig Kafura, "What Americans Think about America First," 2017 Chicago Council Survey, Chicago Council on Global Affairs, https://www.thechicagocouncil.org/sites/default/files/ccgasur vey2017_what_americans_think_about_america_first.pdf.

51   Max Boot, "Trump Security Strategy a Study in Contrasts," Council on Foreign Relations, December 18, 2017, https://www.cfr.org/expert-brief/trump-security -strategy-study-contrasts.

Chapter Seven: Trump, Russia, and Truth

1   Garrett M. Graff, "A Guide to Russia's High Tech Tool Box for Subverting US Democracy," Wired, August 13, 2017, https://www.wired.com/story/a-guide-to -russias-high-tech-tool-box-for-subverting-us-democracy/.

2   Sean Illing, "'A Giant Fog Machine': How Right-Wing Media Obscures Mueller and Other Inconvenient Stories," Vox, October 31, 2017, https://www.vox.com /2017/10/31/16579820/mueller-clinton-russia-uranium-manafort-charlie-sykes.

3   Hayden, Playing to the Edge.

4   Andrew Soldatov and Irina Borogan, The Red Web: The Struggle Between Russia's Digital Dictators and the New Online Revolutionaries (New York: Hachette Book Group, 2015), x.

5   Valery Gerasimov, "The Value of Science Is in the Foresight: New Challenges Demand Rethinking the Forms and Methods of Carrying out Combat Operations," trans. Robert Coalson (originally published as "Ценность Науки В Предвидении," Military-Industrial Kurier, February 27, 2013), Military Review, January– February 2016, http://usacac.army.mil/CAC2/MilitaryReview/Archives/English /MilitaryReview_20160228_art008.pdf, 27.

6   Robert Coalson, "MH17 Downing: One Tragedy, One Truth, But Many Stories," Radio Free Europe/Radio Liberty, July 16, 2015, https://www.rferl.org/a/russia -ukraine-mh17-conspiracy-theories/27132875.html.

7   Susan B. Glasser, "'The Russians Have Succeeded Beyond Their Wildest Expectations,'" Politico, October 30, 2017, https://www.politico.com/magazine/story /2017/10/30/james-clapper-russia-global-politico-trump-215761.

8   Troll as a noun, a figure you can pretend to be in chat groups, and as a verb, the practice of trying to lure others into sending responses to carefully designed

incorrect statements or similar "bait." Margaret Rouse, "Troll," WhatIs.com, TechTarget, May 2008," http://whatis.techtarget.com/definition/troll.

9 *Botnet:* a network of private computers infected with malicious software and controlled as a group without the owners' knowledge. "Botnet," Oxford Dictionaries, Oxford University Press, https://en.oxforddictionaries.com/definition/botnet.

10 Manny Fernandez, "As Jade Helm 15 Military Exercise Begins, Texans Keep Watch 'Just in Case,'" *New York Times,* July 15, 2015, https://www.nytimes.com/2015 /07/16/us/in-texas-a-military-exercise-is-met-by-some-with-suspicion.html.

11 Adam Gabbatt, "Operation Jade Helm: Why Conspiracy Theorists Fear the US Is Invading Texas," *Guardian,* July 15, 2015, https://www.theguardian.com/us -news/2015/jul/15/jade-helm-texas-conspiracy-theory.

12 Clint Watts, "Clint Watts' Testimony: Russia's Info War on the U.S. Started in 2014," March 30, 2017, Daily Beast, https://www.thedailybeast.com/clint-watts -testimony-russias-info-war-on-the-us-started-in-2014.

13 Kathryn Watson, "Former NSA Director Says Russia Was Involved in 2016 Election," CBS News, March 30, 2017, https://www.cbsnews.com/news/senate-intel -russia-hearing-live-updates/.

14 Matt Levin, "Obama Picks 'Jade Helm' as His Favorite Conspiracy Theory about His Presidency," *San Francisco Chronicle,* November 19, 2015, http://www.sfgate .com/national/article/Obama-picks-Jade-Helm-as-his-favorite-6644618.php.

15 Eric Bradner, "Trump Praises 9/11 Truther's 'Amazing' Reputation," CNN, December 2, 2015, http://www.cnn.com/2015/12/02/politics/donald-trump-praises -9-11-truther-alex-jones/index.html.

16 Stephen Collinson, "Why Trump's Talk of a Rigged Vote Is so Dangerous," CNN, October 19, 2016, http://www.cnn.com/2016/10/18/politics/donald-trump -rigged-election/index.html.

17 Andrew Feinberg, "My Life at a Russian Propaganda Network," *Politico,* August 21, 2017, https://www.politico.com/magazine/story/2017/08/21/russian-propa ganda-sputnik-reporter-215511.

18 Max Boot, "Fox News Has Completed Its Transformation Into Trump TV," *Foreign Policy,* August 8, 2017, http://foreignpolicy.com/2017/08/08/fox-news-has-comp leted-its-transformation-into-trump-tv/.

19 Alex Shephard, "Julian Assange and Sean Hannity Are Giving Donald Trump the Cover He Needs on Russia," *New Republic,* 2017, https://newrepublic.com/min utes/139582/julian-assange-sean-hannity-giving-donald-trump-cover-needs -russia.

20 "Assange: Russian Government Not the Source of WikiLeaks Emails," Fox News, January 3, 2017, http://www.foxnews.com/politics/2017/01/03/assange-russian -government-not-source-wikileaks-emails.html.

21 Tim Hains, "Sean Hannity After Interviewing Julian Assange: 'I Believe Every Word He Says,'" Real Clear Politics, January 3, 2017, https://www.realclearpoli

tics.com/video/2017/01/03/sean_hannity_after_interviewing_julian_assange_
i_believe_every_word_he_says.html.

22 Maxwell Tani, "Conservative Media Figures Are Embracing a Wild WikiLeaks
Conspiracy Theory That the CIA Hacked the DNC, and Then Framed Russia,"
Business Insider, March 9, 2017, http://www.businessinsider.com/sean-hannity
-wikileaks-conspiracy-theory-cia-hacked-2017-3.

23 "'Zero Evidence' for Claims Russia Hacked DNC—NSA Whistleblower," RT, You-
Tube, November 28, 2017, https://m.youtube.com/watch?v=F7J2DdiXM9Q.

24 "'Zero Evidence' That Russia Hacked DNC, Says NSA Whistleblower (VIDEO)," RT,
November 8, 2017, https://www.rt.com/usa/409269-binney-cia-dnc-hack-meeting/.

25 Italics added. Julian Borger and Oliver Holmes, "Trump Believes Putin on Russia
Meddling, but Then Backs US Agencies," Guardian, November 12, 2017, https://
www.theguardian.com/world/2017/nov/11/putin-and-trump-want-political
-solution-to-syria-conflict-kremlin-says.

26 Italics added. Zachary Cohen and Jim Sciutto, "CIA Corrects Director's Russian
Election Meddling Claim," CNN, October 20, 2017, http://www.cnn.com/2017
/10/19/politics/cia-pompeo-russia-meddling-election/index.html.

27 Graham Lanktree, "Russia Will Meddle in 2018 Midterm Elections, Says CIA
Chief Mike Pompeo," Newsweek, January 30, 2018, http://www.newsweek.com
/russia-will-meddle-2018-midterm-elections-says-cia-chief-mike-pompeo-
trump-794863.

28 Christina Zhao, "Russian Bots' Top Hashtag Is Schumer Shutdown as Government Closure Reaches Day Three," Newsweek, January 22, 2018, http://www
.newsweek.com/schumershutdown-top-hashtag-used-russian-government
-shutdown-chuck-schumer-786784.

29 Melissa Chan, "Sgt. La David Johnson's Widow Breaks Silence on Trump's Phone
Call: 'I Was Very Angry,'" Time, October 23, 2017, http://time.com/4993045/my
eshia-johnson-donald-trump-frederica-wilson/.

30 "'This Week' Transcript 11-26-17: Sen. Tim Scott and Adm. Mike Mullen," ABC
News, November 26, 2017, http://abcnews.go.com/Politics/week-transcript-11-26
-17-sen-tim-scott/story?id=51381100.

31 John Nichols, "Meet John Kelly, Donald Trump's New Enabler in Chief," Nation,
July 28, 2017, https://www.thenation.com/article/meet-john-kelly-donald-trumps
-new-enabler-in-chief/.

32 Peter Baker and Julie Hirschfeld Davis, "Trump Defends Sharing Information on
ISIS Threat with Russia," New York Times, May 16, 2017, https://www.nytimes
.com/2017/05/16/us/politics/trump-intelligence-russia-classified.html.

33 Rebecca Savransky, "McMaster Defends Trump's Charlottesville Statement: 'The
President Has Been Very Clear,'" The Hill, August 13, 2017, http://thehill.com
/homenews/administration/346385-mcmaster-defends-trumps-charlottesville
-statement-the-president-has.

34 "McMaster Defends Trump Tweets on UK Attack," The Hill, September 15, 2017, http://thehill.com/homenews/administration/350895-mcmaster-defends -trump-tweets-on-uk-attack.

35 Dan Glunderman, "H.R. McMaster Calls Trump's Comments about North Korea's Leader, Destruction 'Completely Appropriate,'" New York Daily News, September 21, 2017, http://www.nydailynews.com/news/politics/h-mcmaster-defends -trump-u-n-comments-north-korea-article-1.3511249.

36 Jon Finer, "H.R. McMaster Is Hailed as the Hero of Iraq's Tal Afar. Here's What that Operation Looked Like," Washington Post, February 24, 2017, https://www .washingtonpost.com/posteverything/wp/2017/02/24/h-r-mcmaster-is-hailed -for-liberating-iraqs-tal-afar-heres-what-that-looked-like-up-close/.

37 Michael Gerson, "The Cowardice Among Republicans Is Staggering," Washington Post, February 5, 2018, https://www.washingtonpost.com/opinions/the-coward ice-among-republicans-is-staggering/2018/02/05/41852454-0aa9-11e8-8890 -372e2047c935_story.html.

38 Anthony Smith, "Homeland Security Adviser Thomas Bossert Awkwardly Defends Trump's Latest Controversial Tweet," Mic, July 2, 2017, https://mic.com/articles /181311/homeland-security-adviser-thomas-bossert-awkwardly-defends -trumps-latest-controversial-tweet.
For the record, over the 2017 Christmas holidays, Trump retweeted a photo of what looked like a bug splat on his shoe labeled as "CNN" under the Charlie Sheen–esque label "WINNING."

39 "'This Week' Transcript 7-2-17: Gov. John Kasich, Thomas Bossert," ABC News, July 2, 2017, http://abcnews.go.com/Politics/week-transcript-17-gov-john-kasich -thomas-bossert/story?id=48391573.

40 Maxwell Tani, "'I Haven't Heard You Say "I Condemn White Supremacists"': Jake Tapper Confronts White House Adviser over Trump's Refusal to Explicitly Call Out Neo-Nazis," Business Insider, August 13, 2017, http://www.businessinsider.com /jake-tapper-tom-bossert-trump-charlottesville-white-supremacists-nazis -2017-8.

41 Abbey Phillip, "White House Aide Defends Trump's Pardon of Former Arizona Sheriff Joe Arpaio," Washington Post, August 27, 2017, https://www.washington post.com/news/post-politics/wp/2017/08/27/white-house-aide-defends -trumps-pardon-of-former-arizona-sheriff-joe-arpaio/.

Chapter Eight: The Future of Truth

1 Richard Wike, Bruce Stokes, Jacob Poushter, and Janell Fetterolf, "U.S. Image Suffers as Publics Around World Question Trump's Leadership," Pew Research Center, June 26, 2017, http://www.pewglobal.org/2017/06/26/u-s-image-suffers -as-publics-around-world-question-trumps-leadership/.

2   Roger McNamee, "How to Fix Facebook—Before It Fixes Us," *Washington Monthly*, January/February/March 2018, https://washingtonmonthly.com/magazine/jan uary-february-march-2018/how-to-fix-facebook-before-it-fixes-us/.

3   Jason Schwartz, "Trump's 'Fake News' Mantra a Hit with Despots," *Politico*, December 8, 2017, https://www.politico.com/story/2017/12/08/trump-fake-news -despots-287129.

4   Fred Kaplan, "The Free World's Landlord," *Slate*, December 12, 2017, http://www .slate.com/articles/news_and_politics/war_stories/2017/12/trump_went_back_ to_nato_bashing_in_pensacola_speech.html.

5   Chris Cillizza, "Trump's 41 Most Eye-Popping Lines from His Pensacola Speech," CNN, December 9, 2017, http://edition.cnn.com/2017/12/09/politics/trump-pen sacola-speech-analysis/index.html.

6   Maegan Vazquez, Evan Perez, Pamela Brown, and Shimon Prokupecz, "Trump Takes Aim at Top FBI Officials," CNN, December 24, 2017, http://www.cnn.com /2017/12/23/politics/trump-fbi-mccabe-baker-tweets/.

7   "'Trump Fears Them': Former Officials Defend FBI Leaders Swept Up in the Trump -Russia Firestorm," Business Insider, December 24, 2017, http://www.business insider.com/fbi-general-counsel-james-baker-reassigned-amid-trump-russia -firestorm-2017-12.

8   Greg Miller, Greg Jaffe, and Philip Rucker, "Doubting the Intelligence, Trump Pursues Putin and Leaves a Russian Threat Unchecked," *Washington Post,* December 14, 2017, https://www.washingtonpost.com/graphics/2017/world/national -security/donald-trump-pursues-vladimir-putin-russian-election-hacking.

9   Kier Giles, "Countering Russian Information Operations in the Age of Social Media," Council on Foreign Relations, November 21, 2017, https://www.cfr.org/report /countering-russian-information-operations-age-social-media.

10   So named after *Federalist Paper* No. 68, authored by Alexander Hamilton. "These most deadly adversaries of republican government might naturally have been expected to make their approaches from more than one quarter, but chiefly from the desire in foreign powers to gain an improper ascendant in our councils . . . by raising a creature of their own to the chief magistracy of the Union."

11   Ioffe, "What Putin Really Wants."

12   Amy Moreno, "Top White House Aide Says Russia Looks to Influence Mexico Vote," Radio Free Europe/Radio Liberty, January 8, 2018, https://www.rferl.org/a/russia -mexico-election-meddling-mcmaster-united-states-kremlin/28962224.html.

13   "Well, Well, Well, Steelers Coach Hosted LAVISH 2016 Hillary Fundraiser," Truth- feed, September 26, 2017, http://truthfeednews.com/well-well-well-steelers-coach -hosted-lavish-2016-hillary-fundraiser/.

14   Dylan Gwinn, "Steelers Coach Rips Afghan War Vet Villanueva for Standing for the Anthem," Breitbart, September 25, 2017, http://www.breitbart.com/sports /2017/09/25/steelers-coach-rips-afghan-war-vet-coming-locker-room-anthem/.

15   Joshua Kaplan, "NFL Hell: Several Stadiums Nearly Empty as Anthem Protest Backlash Rolls into Week 7 (PHOTOS)," Gateway Pundit, October 22, 2017, http://thegatewaypundit.com/2017/10/nfl-hell-several-stadiums-nearly-empty-anthem-protest-backlash-rolls-week-7-photos/.

16   Jessica Taylor, "Majority of Americans Believe Trump Acted Either Illegally or Unethically with Russia," NPR, July 6, 2017, https://www.npr.org/2017/07/06/535626356/on-russia-republican-and-democratic-lenses-have-a-very-different-tint.

17   McNamee, "How to Fix Facebook—Before It Fixes Us."

18   Mark M. Lowenthal, *Intelligence: From Secrets to Policy*, 6th ed. (Thousand Oaks, CA: CQ Press, 2014), 253.

19   Which is a charge I know has been leveled against the IC in the Bush administration because of the National Intelligence Estimate on Iraqi weapons of mass destruction. But that was intelligence being wrong, rather than accommodating, and before the administration was out the IC had rejected theories that there was a relationship between Iraq and al-Qaeda and had found that Iran had stopped work on building an actual nuclear weapon—neither of which were especially welcome in the West Wing.

20   Eli Watkins, "Trump Jr. Suggests Conspiracy of People Who Don't Want To Let 'America Be America,'" CNN, December 20, 2017, http://edition.cnn.com/2017/12/19/politics/donald-trump-jr-russia/index.html.

21   Glenn Kessler, Meg Kelly, and Nicole Lewis, "President Trump Has Made 1,950 False or Misleading Claims over 347 Days," *Washington Post*, January 2, 2018, https://www.washingtonpost.com/news/fact-checker/wp/2018/01/02/president-trump-has-made-1949-false-or-misleading-claims-over-347-days/.

22   Greg Miller, "CIA Director Distorts Intelligence Community's Findings on Russian Interference," *Washington Post*, October 19, 2017, https://www.washingtonpost.com/world/national-security/cia-director-distorts-intelligence-communitys-findings-on-russian-interference/2017/10/19/d7f8e05e-b4ed-11e7-9e58-e6288544af98_story.html.

23   Greg Miller, "Ex-Spy Chief: Russia's Election Hacking Was an 'Intelligence Failure,'" *Politico*, October 19, 2017, https://www.politico.com/magazine/story/2017/12/11/the-full-transcript-michael-morell-216061.

24   "Excerpt from Trump's Interview with the Times," *New York Times*, December 28, 2017, https://www.nytimes.com/2017/12/28/us/politics/trump-interview-excerpts.html.

25   Timothy Snyder, *On Tyranny: Twenty Lessons from the Twentieth Century* (New York: Tim Duggan Books, 2017), 65 and 71.

Afterword

1   Rachel Wolfe, "Read Deputy Attorney General Rod Rosenstein's Remarks on the Russia Indictments," *Vox*, February 16, 2018, https://www.vox.com/2018/2/16/17020872/rosenstein-russia-indictments-transcript; and *United States of America v. Internet Research Agency LLC a/k/a/ Mediasintez LLC et al.*, Criminal No. (18 U.S.C. §§ 2, 371, 1349, 1028A), United States District Court for the District of Columbia, filed 2/26/18, https://www.justice.gov/file/1035477/download.

2   "Worldwide Threats Briefing: Takeaways, from Russia to China," *Wired*, February 13, 2018, https://www.wired.com/story/worldwide-threats-briefing-russia-election-china/.

3   David Welna, "NSA Chief: U.S. Response 'Hasn't Changed the Calculus' of Russian Interference," NPR, February 27, 2018, https://www.npr.org/sections/thetwo-way/2018/02/27/589143771/nsa-chief-u-s-response-hasn-t-changed-the-calculus-of-russian-interference.

INDEX

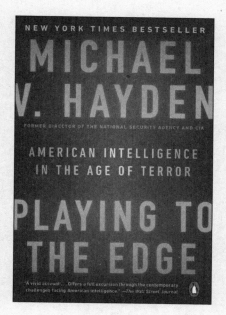